PENGUIN BOOKS

Cosmopolitan Guide to The Big Trip

Suzanne King is a journalist who has worked on a number of magazines, including *Cosmopolitan*, *SHE* and *Radio Times*. Now a freelance writer and commissioning editor, she is also series editor of the *Cosmopolitan* Careers Guides and author of two books in the series: *Cosmopolitan Guide to Working in Journalism and Publishing* and *Cosmopolitan How to Get Ahead in Your Career*, both of which are published by Penguin.

Elaine Robertson is a former assistant features editor of *Cosmopolitan* and previously worked on the British Tourist Authority magazine, *In Britain*. Now a freelance writer and sub-editor for a variety of publications, she is also the author of the *Cosmopolitan Guide to Working in Retail*, which is available in Penguin.

Both Elaine and Suzanne have lived and worked abroad: Elaine in Austria, Germany and the Netherlands; Suzanne in France, Greece and South Africa. Both are former travel editors of *Cosmopolitan* – and both left full-time careers to go freelance, so that they could spend more time travelling. They are seasoned backpackers and between them have travelled on every continent, visiting countries as diverse as Iran and India, Morocco and Mongolia, Norway and Namibia. As this book went to press, they were backpacking around South America.

COSMOPOLITAN
Guide to **The Big Trip**

SUZANNE KING AND
ELAINE ROBERTSON

PENGUIN BOOKS

PENGUIN BOOKS

Published by the Penguin Group
Penguin Books Ltd, 27 Wrights Lane, London w8 5tz, England
Penguin Books USA Inc., 375 Hudson Street, New York, New York 10014, USA
Penguin Books Australia Ltd, Ringwood, Victoria, Australia
Penguin Books Canada Ltd, 10 Alcorn Avenue, Toronto, Ontario, Canada m4v 3b2
Penguin Books (NZ) Ltd, 182–190 Wairau Road, Auckland 10, New Zealand

Penguin Books Ltd, Registered Offices: Harmondsworth, Middlesex, England

First published in Penguin Books 1997
10 9 8 7 6 5 4 3 2 1

Set in 11½/13pt Monotype Baskerville by
Rowland Phototypesetting Ltd, Bury St Edmunds, Suffolk
Printed in England by Clays Ltd, St Ives plc

Contents

Acknowledgements

A huge thank-you to Rachel Shattock, without whom this Big Trip would never have been finished!

Chapter 1 / **Introduction**

'All places, no matter where, no matter what, are worth visiting.'
Paul Theroux, *The Pillars of Hercules*

If you've bought this book, you must be dreaming about taking a big trip – leaving your normal life behind and jetting off for some sun, fun and adventure. And the good news is that it's so easy to do! You don't have to be rich to travel the world. Just take a look at the classified ads in newspapers and magazines and you'll see dozens of companies offering tempting tickets for amazingly low prices. You don't even have to be particularly adventurous – there are some travellers' routes that are so well-worn you'll sometimes hardly believe you're so far from home.

Every year, half a million young Brits head off on the backpacker trail. Before they return home, they'll have been to more places, met more people and done more exciting things than most people do in a lifetime. What you do is up to you. You could find yourself sleeping under the stars in the Namibian desert or watching the sun set behind the Taj Mahal. Maybe you see yourself swimming with the dolphins in Florida or diving the Great Barrier Reef. Do you fancy doing a 4WD trip from the Cape to Cairo or tackling the Inca Trail in South America? What about sailing through the islands of Halong Bay in Vietnam or feasting on champagne and strawberries on the Trans-Siberian? The possibilities are endless.

Dreaming about your big trip is exciting – but trying to organize it all can be daunting, especially if it's the first time. There's so much to plan, so many decisions to make, so much to think about. That's why we've taken some of the legwork out of it for you.

From planning your route to packing your bags, from saving money to staying safe, there's nothing we haven't thought of.

It's true there are some things we *can't* help you with. In Cairns, it will be tough deciding whether to spend the next day diving, white-water rafting or lazing on the beach. On a Caribbean island you may have real trouble deciding which two palm trees offer the ultimate spot for your hammock. And when you're faced with a mouth-watering menu in Thailand it's almost impossible to decide what to go for. But, hey, you'll cope.

Once you've made your mind up to go, you'll find everything falls into place with amazing ease. The most important thing is to go with the right attitude. You can't expect things to be the same as they are at home – after all, that's all part of why you're going away. If you travel in the Third World, don't expect constant hot water, flush toilets or transport that runs on time – but do expect the lights to go out just as you're settling down to read your book. Unpredictability is the name of the game. You may end up sleeping on a bench when your train doesn't turn up, spending a day helping to dig your bus out of the mud or being trapped somewhere for three days because of bad weather.

Believe us, we know. Between us, we've been bitten to death by every bug going, over-indulged in the local brew everywhere from Bangkok to Bantry Bay, fallen prey to dramatic bouts of diarrhoea and more. We've been ripped off occasionally and browned off frequently. We've slept in huts, haylofts and hammocks, on beaches, benches and bunks. We've travelled in boats that are barely afloat, planes that are barely aloft and buses that barely stay on the road – not to mention elephants, camels, rafts and the rest. But it's all part of the experience – in time, even the disasters tend to become something you look back on with nostalgia. And we keep going back for more!

Because there's just nothing we can think of that's more exciting than travelling. It's fun, it's confidence-building, it's fulfilling. It gives you a wealth of rewarding memories, an address book full of new friends around the world, and an improved knowledge of geography that will stand you in good stead in pub quizzes! The feeling of achievement and the thrill of making new discoveries about yourself and the world around you are things that will never leave you. So what are you waiting for – get out there and do it!

Chapter 2 / **Where Should You Go?**

More than 400 million people travel abroad each year. Once you've decided to join them, the first question to ask yourself is, '*Where* am I going?' South-East Asia, followed by Australia, New Zealand and home via the States? Circle round South America then across the Pacific? Fly to Moscow, take the Trans-Siberian to Beijing, then travel round China? And what about Africa? The Middle East? India?

Unless you're planning to travel for the rest of your life, you obviously won't be able to visit every country in the world. First, grab a good atlas and start dreaming up routes. Once you have an idea of the destinations that appeal to you most, talk to any friends who've been there, and read books set in the country or continent to get a feel for the place (see chapter 16). If you're on a tight budget, bear in mind that it's cheaper to travel in destinations such as South-East Asia than in the USA or Australia, and save ludicrously expensive countries like Japan for when you're rich!

If it's your first trip away, avoid landing yourself in a 'difficult' country on your first stop. India, for example, can come as a hell of a shock if you go straight from the UK. Although most RTW travellers tend to start off in Asia, why not consider flying the other way round and beginning your trip in the US, where the language, culture and customs are familiar, then move on to the more exotic countries? Another advantage of this is that Asia is a cheaper place to be if you're nearing the end of the trip and funds are running low!

Once you have a rough idea of where you'd like to go, visit a travel agent for advice and a sample of routes and fares. Don't rush it – you can easily spend an hour or more talking through all the possibilities. In chapter 3, you'll find a list of agencies that specialize in independent travel. Most are staffed by people who have travelled extensively themselves, so they can make recommendations based on personal experience or suggest a route you hadn't thought of or didn't know existed. Some also have a bookshop or reference library on site, as well as vaccination and visa services.

If you have time, go to two or three different agents. They'll be able to give you the most up-to-date information on every aspect of your trip – suggested routes and fares, the cost of living, and advice on any visas or vaccinations required. Take everything home and spend an evening or a weekend considering your options and comparing prices before making a booking. You don't literally have to go all around the world – some people choose to spend most of their time exploring a particular area, say, Asia or Africa, in depth.

Wherever you're thinking of going, get up-to-date advice from the Foreign and Commonwealth Office Travel Advice Unit on 0171 238 4503/4; on BBC2 Ceefax, page 564 onwards; or on the Internet at http://www.fco.gov.uk/. This provides the latest information on the political situation in most foreign countries, as well as advising on threats to personal safety arising from internal strife, natural disasters and epidemics. For information on the countries on which advice is most frequently sought (as we went to press these were Egypt, The Gambia, India, Israel, Jamaica, Kenya, Nigeria, Pakistan, Russia, Sri Lanka, South Africa, Turkey and the US), call 0374 500900. If the Foreign and Commonwealth Office say don't go, then don't go – if you decide to travel against their advice, your insurance will automatically be invalid.

When's the Best Time to Go?

When you go depends on (a) your route and (b) how much money you want to spend on your ticket. As far as airlines are concerned, there are generally three seasons to most destinations: low, high and mid-season. For flights within the northern hemisphere, for example, low season is November to March; high season is July and August and mid-season is any other time.

However, if you're travelling to the southern hemisphere, the seasons are different. So for destinations such as South Africa, Australia or New Zealand, December is high season – which means chock-full flights and the highest fares. If you desperately want to be there in December, to spend Christmas with relatives, say, you should book well in advance and accept that there will be no cheap deals on your ticket.

Sometimes you can save money by altering your travel plans by just one day. For example, a flight to New York on 1st July 1996 cost £195; but on 30th June it would have cost just £155.

Local events also play a part in determining air fares and availability. For example, if you want to go to Hong Kong in February, you'll be arriving just in time for Chinese New Year. Not only do air fares go up, but there will be very little accommodation available. And the same will apply to neighbouring countries such as China and Vietnam. So while fares remain roughly the same year-round to a destination such as Bangkok, they could increase (and will certainly be full) at this time of year, because of Thailand's proximity to these countries.

It can be fun timing your visit to coincide with local festivals – but it can also be inconvenient. As well as higher fares and little or no available accommodation, you may find that shops, banks and restaurants are closed. Or if you're in a Muslim country for Ramadan you might find it hard to get food and drink during the day, when everyone's fasting.

If you're travelling in or via Europe, July and August are good months to avoid. This is school holiday time, meaning jam-packed flights, no cheap deals and hordes of tourists wherever you go.

Does your itinerary take in cold climates as well as hot ones? If so, you'll need to carry heavy clothing, so you might prefer to plan an itinerary that – as far as possible – follows summer round the globe. Find out what the weather will be like when you're at each of your destinations. It's not the be-all and end-all of a trip, but if you're planning special activities such as trekking, you should obviously avoid the rainy season. Anyone planning an African safari should aim to be there when there's the greatest chance of animal-spotting (in Kenya and Tanzania, for example, it's July and August). However, on a RTW trip, it's practically impossible to ensure you arrive everywhere at the best time, so don't worry *too* much about it. Also, some places are cheaper off-season, and you're more likely to get discounts in hotels and restaurants when they're competing for your custom.

If you have second cousins in Vancouver, or your sister's best friend is living in Australia, your trip is the perfect opportunity to look them up. Most people are pleased to get visitors, but drop them a postcard or letter first to ask if it's okay to turn up when you're in their part of the world. After being on the road for a while, it's a great treat to stay in a proper house with a proper bed, and get your clothes washed and ironed. You may miss out on the travellers' grapevine, but having a local person show you round their home town or city adds an extra dimension to the place. Be considerate – don't turn up on someone's doorstep penniless, don't bring extra guests without your hosts' permission and don't outstay your welcome. Bear in mind that staying with friends and relatives won't *necessarily* save you money. It's true that you'll be saving on accommodation and food, but these things are often really cheap anyway – and you'll probably end up buying bottles of wine and thank-you presents, instead.

Booking in Advance vs Buying as You Go

Should you buy all your tickets in advance, or just book as far as your first destination and play it by ear from then on? There are advantages and disadvantages to both methods. We've listed some of the main ones below but if you know anyone who's been on a trip, ask them what kind of ticket they had and what option they would recommend. You can also discuss the pros and cons of both options with your travel agent.

Buying in Advance

Advantages

The big advantage of having a return air ticket is security. You don't have to carry extra money around to pay for flights and, if you start running short of money, at least you know you can get home. It can often (though not always) work out cheaper than buying individual flights as you go along. Pre-booking also means you avoid the hassle of trying to buy a plane ticket without speaking a word of Mandarin/Urdu/Swahili. Finding the airline office in a strange city, queuing up, explaining what you want, being told to come back the next day, finding it closed, etc., can eat into your precious time and send your blood pressure soaring!

Most airlines allow you to change the dates of your flights (though some will charge for this), so you can still be flexible to some extent. Knowing where you're going to be on a certain date means you can leave an itinerary behind so that friends and family can write to you – parents will probably be happier with this kind of arrangement.

Disadvantages

The major drawback of booking your ticket in advance is the lack of flexibility and ability to be spontaneous. Before you leave the UK, you might think that a month in Thailand or Malaysia will be more than enough. But what if you fall in love with the country and want to stay for longer? What if your next scheduled stop is Harare but you make friends with a great crowd of travellers who are heading to Cape Town and ask you to go with them? Also, if you fly with an airline that charges you for date changes, it could become expensive if you alter your plans a lot.

Buying Tickets as You Go

Advantages
This is the most flexible option, allowing you just to go with the flow. If you arrive in a city you don't like, you can leave the next day. If you're captivated by Ho Chi Minh City, you can stay an extra week. If you meet someone you really like and want to continue travelling with them a bit longer, you can adapt your travel plans to fit. It turns your trip into more of an adventure. However, some countries don't like letting you in unless you have proof (in the form of a ticket) that you'll be leaving again. This can be especially so if you're flying in. Credit cards help (as evidence of funds), as does dressing as smartly as you can.

Disadvantages
It may be a more expensive way to travel and you will need to carry around more money (and avoid the temptation to spend it on other things) or a credit card to buy tickets as you go along. You might not always be able to get tickets when you want them and might have to hang around waiting for days or find alternative forms of transport. If your first-choice airlines are fully booked, you may have to fly on more obscure (and less safe) domestic carriers. No one at home will know your exact whereabouts at any given time, and it's harder for them to contact you if they have to.

Travel Events

An ever-increasing interest in travelling has led to the introduction of travel fairs and exhibitions. These are terrific places to hear experienced travellers talk about their trips, pick up tons of information on all aspects of travelling, enter competitions to win RTW tickets and meet like-minded people. Best of the bunch for backpackers is probably Independent Travellers World, held in Bristol in January, London in February and Edinburgh in March. Further details available from Helen Caldwell on 0117 930 4440. Look out, also, for: Destinations (held at Olympia, London in February); *Daily Telegraph* Adventure Travel and Sports Show (Chelsea Town Hall, London in January); The Holiday Show (G-Mex Centre, Manchester in January); and Female Eye, a women and travel seminar (Commonwealth Institute, London in June).

Travel Talks

Travellers' clubs (see chapter 4) organize regular evenings where members can hear about other people's adventures. Look out, too, for the following chances to meet and hear from other travellers:
• **Cotswold** hold regular lectures at their shops in London (0181 743 2976); St Albans (01727 847888); South Cerney (01285 860123); Manchester (0161 236 4123); Betws-y-Coed (01690 710234); Reading (01734 268881) and Southampton (01489 799555). Most are free; some carry a small charge. Call each shop for details.
• **The Commonwealth Institute** in London (0171 603 4535) also holds relevant talks.
• Many **overland travel companies** (e.g. Encounter Overland, Exodus, Guerba) give video presentations of their destinations. Write to them (addresses in chapter 4) and ask to be put on their mailing list.
• **Bookshops** such as Waterstone's, Dillons and Stanfords host evenings where writers, including travel writers, read extracts from their books and answer questions afterwards. Ring your local branch for details.
• **The Royal Geographical Society** invites speakers to lecture on various aspects of travelling. Ring 0171 589 5466 for details. Call 0141 552 3330 for the Royal Scottish Geographical Society.

Travellers' Tales

I did a 10-month trip that took in South-East Asia, Australia, Canada, the States and Scandinavia. I don't know how I managed it but, with uncanny ability, I seemed to end up having rain almost everywhere, even when it wasn't the rainy season. Some of my most vivid memories are weather-related – wading knee-high through the flooded streets of Kuta in Bali; getting drenched in the Daintree rainforest in Queensland; sitting out a typhoon in Hue in Vietnam; paddling around the pavements of Beijing; getting so wet in Hong Kong that the dye from my T-shirt ran into my sweatshirt and ruined it (that's those cheap traveller's clothes for you!); and causing great hilarity in Indonesia when I slipped on a muddy path Laurel-and-Hardy style and ended up covered in mud from head to toe. The strange thing is, I loved every minute of it and laughed all the way! The weather was always warm, so it's not like miserable British rain – and somehow it seems more of an experience than having good weather all the way.

Before I went away I bought my parents a map of the world and a set of map pins, so they could chart my progress around the world. It's become a permanent fixture on the kitchen wall now – each member of the family has different coloured pins.

Richard Dawson, 29

Travellers' Tales

I took eight months off a couple of years ago and intended to go to New Zealand via Hong Kong, China, Vietnam, Thailand, Malaysia, Indonesia and Australia. I didn't make it to New Zealand in the end – mainly because we hadn't thought through what the weather would be like in each country. We went to

China in winter, which was fine as we'd taken warm clothing. After leaving China, though, we sent it all back home and then had to buy more when we landed in Australia, where it was also winter! By the time we were ready to go to New Zealand it was July, which would have been their winter, so we decided to head for home. I have to admit, I was tired after eight months' travelling.

I originally left with a girlfriend, but in Thailand we split up for a while and agreed to meet up again later on. Then she broke a bone in her foot in Australia and went to stay with some relatives until it healed, which meant I did a fair bit of travelling around on my own. That did wonders for my confidence – I feel I could go anywhere on my own now.

I saved madly for a year to do the trip and spent about £10,000. I know that sounds a lot, but I'm a shopaholic and was determined to buy anything I wanted to. I bought tons of things and shipped them all home – everything arrived safely. I didn't mind spending the money because the trip was the treat I'd always promised myself when I turned 30. Also, my company had agreed to hold my job open for me, so I knew I'd be financially secure when I got home.

That trip was the best thing I've ever done in my life. I had a brilliant time and adored the sense of freedom it gave me. I'd love to do it again.

Vivienne Ayers, 33

Travellers' Tales

I travelled round the world a few years ago and went to America, Canada, Hawaii, Japan, Thailand and India. I'd recommend thinking carefully about the seasons before you book. I left for the USA and Canada in November and it snowed in Boston and Quebec, although the weather was fine and sunny in California and the Southern states. It was also winter in Asia in January and February – the days were warm but the nights were very cold.

It's worth bearing in mind, too, how enormous some countries are. If you're going to India, for example, and you only have a few weeks rather than a few months to explore it, it's better to concentrate on one specific area and see it properly rather than spend all your time on trains or buses. I only had four weeks to spend there, so I decided to concentrate on exploring Rajasthan.

Travel and accommodation are exceptionally expensive in Japan, but you can save money by hitchhiking. It's very safe and easy, provided you have a board with your chosen destination written in English and Japanese. Ask someone where you're staying to write it for you with a marker pen. If you're travelling long distances, make sure you have one board for each major town or city along the way, as drivers won't stop for you if they're not travelling as far as your final destination. If you're planning to travel round by train, buy a rail pass before you leave the UK – much cheaper than buying it in Japan. And never blow your nose in public – it's considered the height of rudeness.

Andrew Morrison, 27

Travellers' Tales

I've spent some time travelling in Australia, South-East Asia and South America, and I was struck by the different types of travellers to be found exploring there. In Australia, for example, the majority of travellers were young, free and single 18 to 25-year-olds, away from home for the first time. In South America, the age group was older, there were more of the seasoned bearded travellers and more couples. The age span in India seemed much wider, encompassing the year-off-before-university traveller, the five-temples-before-breakfast traveller, and the elderly hippy who has never quite got it together enough to leave. Whilst these are huge generalizations, I think they can be important factors to bear in mind: I recently had a friend cut short her year's travel to Australia and South-East Asia because the people and the travel culture there were so young she felt like a grandmother.

When I was in South America it was common practice to change money on the black market, which was done quite openly on most street corners. In some cases you could double the exchange rate offered by banks, making a huge difference to a tight budget. It was also handy to be able to change small-denomination travellers' cheques (or, even better, dollars) as $50 or $100 converted into some local currencies meant a rucksack full of notes.

Finally, my handy hint for South America: never have a pee whilst swimming in the Amazon. There's a nasty little fish that can swim up your urinary tract, whereupon it erects its spines causing quite considerable discomfort. The cure for men, I believe, is quite drastic.

Liz Halsall, 30

Ten Travellers' Hang-Outs

Dali, China
Anjuna & Arambol, Goa
Cuzco, Peru
Kathmandu, Nepal
Koh Phangan, Thailand
Salvador, Brazil
Byron Bay, Australia
Ubud, Bali
Lamu, Kenya
Yogyakarta, Indonesia

Chapter 3 / **How Do You Get There?**

Air fares are currently at an all-time low – and there are particularly good bargains on round-the-world tickets. No one airline can fly you right around the globe but two or three airlines (or more, depending on your itinerary) band together to offer round-the-world tickets (RTWs) that combine their route networks. To get the cheapest deal, you usually have to travel in one direction only (west to east or vice versa). You'll find dozens of sample itineraries advertised in the newspapers (we give some examples later in this chapter), but basically just about any combination of routes and stopovers is possible. The more stopovers you have, though, the more expensive the ticket will be.

The price of your ticket will also be affected by your departure date and the direction you're flying – some months it's cheaper to go east to west, other months you get a better deal flying west to east (see When's the Best Time to Go in chapter 2).

The cheapest flights are from Monday to Wednesday and it's always best to avoid peak times such as Easter and Christmas. If you're planning to fly at peak period, you will need to book at least three or four months ahead.

Remember to build in overland (or surface) sections. Few travellers would want a ticket that included flights from Bangkok to Singapore, for example, because it makes more sense and is more fun to do the trip overland. Also, it means you don't waste time after exploring Thailand and Malaysia by having to double back to Bangkok to catch your next flight. Obviously, the cost of surface travel is not included in your air ticket, so you need to budget for train/bus fares accordingly.

RTW tickets are usually valid for one year and most allow

you to change your flight dates as you go along if you decide you want to spend more (or less) time in a particular country once you get there. Check with the airline whether or not there will be a fee charged for any changes made.

Always look out for any restrictions – what appears to be the best deal may turn out to cost more if, for example, you have to pay each time you change a flight date. Does your ticket entitle you to free or discounted domestic flights within certain countries? Will you be charged extra for making more than a certain number of stopovers? How long is your ticket valid for? Does it entitle you to discount rates on accommodation and activities once you're away? Is the price particularly cheap because the airline has a reputation for bad service, poor safety standards, lack of reliability or roundabout routings?

Some travel agents specialize in RTW itineraries and can advise you on the best route and the cheapest fares. There are standard RTW tickets (London–Delhi–Sydney–Los Angeles–London, for example) or you can tailor-make your own. Any itinerary that incorporates African or South American destinations will bump up the cost. If you want a flight with no stops, you have to specify a 'non-stop' flight, rather than a 'direct' flight. Direct simply means you won't have to change planes *en route*, but there could be any number of stops.

Once you've booked your ticket and provisional flight dates, phone the airline to double-check that they have a record of your booking.

When you receive your ticket, make sure that the 'status' box has OK on it – if it says anything else, it means you may not necessarily have a confirmed seat on the flight. Check all the other details are correct too – destinations, dates, times – and that there's a coupon for each separate flight. Photocopy the ticket twice. Leave a copy at home with a friend and take a copy with you in case the original gets lost. (Keep the copy separate from the original.)

Always reconfirm your onward journey 72 hours (three days) in advance. In some countries, failure to do so will mean your name is taken off the computer and your seat given to someone else. If you don't speak the language, ask hostel staff or a local friend to do it for you.

Where's the Best Place to Buy My Ticket?

There are dozens of travel agents offering RTW tickets – look for them in the travel section of the Sunday newspapers or in the back of magazines such as *Time Out* or *City Limits*. Remember that the cheapest travel agent isn't necessarily the best. Good service and knowledgeable consultants who know about where they're sending you are just as important. Always check that the agent is bonded with ABTA (the Association of British Travel Agents) or ATOL (Air Travel Organizer's Licence); ring 0171 832 5620 for both; or IATA (International Air Travel Association). There should be a sticker on the window or door.

Here are some of the more well-established firms (prices were correct at the time of going to press):

Austravel, 50 Conduit St, London WIR 9FB (0171 734 7755; 0171 838 1011). Also has branches in Bournemouth (01202 311488); Bristol (0117 927 7425); Leeds (0113 244 8880) and Manchester (0161 832 2445).
Sample route: Manchester–Hong Kong–Sydney–Singapore–Amsterdam–Manchester, **from £739**.

Bridge the World, 1–3 Ferdinand St, Camden, London NWI 8ES, is a RTW ticket specialist and a favourite with adventurous travellers (worldwide: 0171 911 0900; USA/Canada: 0171 916 0990). Another branch at 4 Regent Place, Regent St, London WIR 6BH (0171 734 7447) specializes in travel to Australia and New Zealand. Send e-mail to sales@bridge-the-world.co.uk
Sample route: London–LA–Hawaii–Tonga/Western Samoa–Auckland–Wellington–Christchurch–Melbourne surface Sydney–Auckland–Fiji–Cook Islands–Tahiti–London, **from £674**.

Campus Travel, 52 Grosvenor Gardens, London SW1W 0AG, specializes in travel for students and young people. They have 41 branches at universities and YHA shops around the country, including Birmingham, Bradford, Brighton, Bristol, Cambridge, Cardiff, Coventry, Dundee, Edinburgh, Glasgow, Leeds, Liverpool, London, Manchester, Newcastle, Nottingham, Oxford, Reading, Sheffield, Southampton and Wolverhampton. Telephone bookings: London 0171 730 2101 (North America); 0171 730 8111 (worldwide); Manchester 0161 273 1721; Edinburgh 0131 668 3303. On the Net at http://www.campustravel.co.uk

Sample route: London–Bangkok–Hong Kong–Bali–Sydney–Christchurch surface Auckland–Tahiti–LA surface New York–London, **from £675**.

Flightbookers, 177–8 Tottenham Court Road, London W1P 0LX (worldwide: 0171 757 2444; Americas & Europe: 0171 757 2000; Australia & New Zealand: 0171 757 2468). E-mail can be sent to flightbookers@dial.pipex.com. On the Net at http://www.flightbookers.co.uk/americas

Sample route: London–Bangkok–Hong Kong–Sydney–Fiji–Los Angeles–London, **from £755**.

Quest Worldwide, 29–31 Castle Street, Kingston-on-Thames, Surrey KT1 1ST (worldwide: 0181 547 3322; transatlantic: 0181 546 6000).

Sample route: London–Dubai–Singapore–Brisbane–Auckland–Fiji–Los Angeles–London, **from £695**.

STA Travel, Priory House, 6 Wrights Lane, London W8 6TA (0171 361 6262) are specialists in young independent travel. Their competitive fares are even cheaper if you are a student or under 26. There are more than 100 offices across Europe, Asia, America and Australasia. In the UK, these include: Bristol (0117 929 4399); Cambridge (01223 366966); Leeds (0113 244 9212); Manchester (0161 834 0668); Oxford (01865 792800), plus branches in many universities – call the London number to find your nearest branch. On the net at http://www.sta-travel-group.com/home/

STA Travel run a unique International Help Desk. Wherever you are in the world, you can call them (reversing the charges if necessary) to ask for advice on any problems that have arisen. Up to 15 calls are received daily, on subjects ranging from lost tickets to lost companions!

Sample route: Glasgow–Bangkok–Hong Kong–Sydney surface Cairns–Auckland–Honolulu–Los Angeles–Glasgow, **from £997**.

Trailfinders, one of the best-known independent travel specialists, has offices at 42–50 Earls Court Road, London w8 6ft (longhaul: 0171 938 3366), 194 Kensington High St, London w8 7rg (longhaul: 0171 938 3939) and 215 Kensington High St, London w8 6bd (Transatlantic and European: 0171 937 5400). Also branches in Birmingham (0121 236 1234); Bristol (0117 929 9000); Glasgow (0141 353 2224); and Manchester (0161 839 6969). Trailfinders do gift vouchers (valid indefinitely), which make a nice gift for travelling friends.

Sample route: London–Cape Town–surface Harare–Sydney–Brisbane–Fiji–Los Angeles–New York–London, **from £973**.

Travelbag, 373–5 The Strand, London wc2r 0jf (Australia, New Zealand and RTW: 0171 497 0515; Far East: 0171 379 3990). There's also a branch at 12 High Street, Alton, Hampshire gu34 1bn (Americas and Canada: 01420 88380; Africa: 01420 80828).

Sample route: London–Johannesburg–Perth–Sydney–Bangkok–Kathmandu surface Delhi–London, **from £951**.

Travel Mood, 246 Edgware Road, London w2 1ds (0171 402 4108).

Sample route: London–Boston–LA–Fiji–New Zealand–Sydney–Manila–Bangkok–London, **from £927**.

Travellers' Tales

I was working in advertising and when the recession hit the industry around 1991 I decided to take a year off to travel – something I'd wanted to do for years. I didn't buy a RTW ticket because I wasn't sure how long I'd want to stay in each place and that turned out to be the right decision for me. I bought a ticket to Bombay and stayed in India for two months, then went to Nepal. I also spent time in Thailand, Malaysia and Indonesia before heading for Australia.

Friends from home had been writing to tell me that nothing much was happening in the advertising world, so I decided to extend my trip. I had started off with about £4,000, which lasted me until I got to Australia, where I decided to look for work to keep me going. I got a job in a bar in Sydney and loved it. It's still quite easy to find employment in Australia as long as you're willing to work. They pay a decent minimum wage, too, so you can live quite well. As well as the bar work, I waitressed in a Tunisian restaurant and cooked breakfast in a backpackers' hostel.

Australia was wonderful – it's very easy to get around and the country is really geared up for backpackers. I travelled around on my own a lot and met all sorts of people. Everyone adopts you if you're a solo traveller. Every time I sat down to read a book, someone would invite me for a beer. I gained a lot from my travels – I've got more confidence and feel I can tackle anything. Some of my colleagues say they would like to do it but they're worried about their careers, but taking time out didn't affect my career at all – in fact, one employer said, 'At least you've got it out of your system now,' and gave me a job!

Jane Ogden, 29

Travellers' Tales

My boyfriend Derek and I left London for India two years ago. I don't like flying so we went overland, travelling by train and bus. We spent six weeks going through Europe to Turkey, then across Turkey, through Iran to Pakistan and spent a while travelling around India. I had to buy a chador at the Turkey/Iran border and wear it all the time I was in Iran. Travelling in Iran wasn't as difficult as I thought it would be. We found places to stay by following our Lonely Planet guide and we also got recommendations from the locals, who were very friendly. After travelling around India, we went to South-East Asia and Vietnam, which I loved.

We saved up for two years until we each had £4,000. I gave up my job in sales, but had no problem finding another job when we returned. I don't regret it at all. We had a fantastic time and I'd do it again tomorrow if I could.

Philippa Dickinson, 29

Travellers' Tales

When I went travelling, a RTW ticket seemed the best value. I liked it because you could go overland – you didn't have to fly the whole way – and it gave flexibility of routes – we could go out through Asia and back through Canada and America. We flew into Thailand and went overland through Thailand, Malaysia, Singapore and Indonesia, then took a flight from Bali to Australia. With hindsight, I don't think a RTW ticket is necessarily cheaper. But our ticket was brilliant – we didn't have to pay cancellation charges and it was really easy to change it, which we did several times. Because we wanted to travel in Australia, we flew with an airline that had good deals on internal flights there (Qantas). In fact, we should probably have booked more internal flights – we did most of it by coach but we didn't really need to.

We intended to work in Australia but didn't in the end – we were having too much fun! I didn't want the trip to end. We went away thinking about six months, and extended it to nine months – but it still wasn't enough. When you're planning it, six months seems a long time, but what impressed me was that once you start a trip like that it's so easy. A year is nothing.

Amanda Stone, 37

Ten Travellers' Must-Dos

Swimming with dolphins
White-water rafting
Bungee jumping
Scuba diving
Dune boarding
Whale watching
Elephant trekking
Boogie boarding
Camel safaris
Alligator spotting

Chapter 4 / **Who Do You Go With?**

Now that you know where and when you're going, who will you share your adventure with? There are several options. If you're lucky, you'll have a like-minded friend and you can set off with someone you know well. If you don't know anyone who has the time, money or inclination to travel, there are organizations (see p. 27) that will match you up with a travelling companion who's departing at the same time and has roughly the same itinerary. You could join an organized trip, or, if you don't want to travel with strangers, you can be bold and strike out on your own. There's something to be said for all these options.

Going with a Friend

Travelling with a friend on a budget means, inevitably, that you have little privacy once you're on the road. It's a 24-hour-a-day commitment, during which you'll find yourself eating with, sleeping with, travelling on interminable train journeys with, getting ill with, getting ripped off with and getting lost with the same person for months.

You'll have to get used to them being grumpy in the morning; they'll have to get used to you leaping out of bed at 5 a.m. and singing in the shower. You need to know that you can snap their head off when you've missed the last train out of Istanbul or been ripped off by a ticket tout at a temple in Thailand and that they'll forgive you. And, no matter how good friends you are, there will be times when you each need a bit of space. So if you want to go exploring caves while your friend would rather laze on the beach, just get on with it.

The best part about travelling with someone else is that you'll share some truly unforgettable moments together: having a picnic with cold champagne in a Moscow park, watching the sun set behind Mount Kilimanjaro, strolling through the ruins of Machu Picchu, being adopted by scores of Vietnamese children, playing charades on the Trans-Siberian as it rattles through the darkness of Siberia . . . And while your friends at home will love hearing your stories and looking at your photos, only the person you were with will understand what it was *really* like.

A friend will really come into their own if you don't feel well. Who else will bring you a comforting drink or fetch you some food or cheer you up if you feel homesick?

That said, think everything through carefully before you commit yourself to travelling with a friend. Travelling with the right person can be great fun; travelling with the wrong one can be hell. Ask yourself the following questions:

• Do you have similar interests? (You don't have to like the same things all the time, but if one of you wants to go clubbing till 3 a.m. every night and the other wants to get up at 6 a.m. for an all-day hike, you won't get very far.)

• What's their budget? (It's important to have roughly the same amount of money to spend, otherwise you're bound to run into money arguments.)

• Do you have the same amount of time to spend travelling? (If you're prepared to take up to a year, while your companion wants to be back home in six months, you may end up being rushed along faster than you'd like.)

• Are you as tidy (or as messy) as each other? (You'll be sharing rooms/tents/huts, and wildly differing standards of tidiness and cleanliness can cause trouble.)

• Is your friend normally cheerful and optimistic? (There are times on the road when you'll need to buoy each other's spirits up – if you're travelling with someone who's moody or easily depressed, it can ruin the trip for you.)

• How flexible are you? (If you like to go wherever the wind blows you, it's no good travelling with a friend who needs the security of a fixed route.)

Going Solo

'The man who goes alone can start today; but he who travels with another must wait till that other is ready,' said American writer Henry David Thoreau. If you don't have a friend who can go with you, don't be put off starting out on your own. Travelling alone is less intimidating than it sounds. Budget travellers have a well-worn circuit – favourite bars and restaurants, hotels they use, places they visit – and you'll always meet a crowd you can travel with for part of the time. On a trip round China, we met the same brother and sister in at least eight different cities. They were always a day or two ahead of us and by the time we got to Xian or Shanghai or Beijing, they'd already found the best way to the Bamboo Temple, the cheapest noodle house, the most picturesque (and cheapest) boat trip.

There are advantages and disadvantages to travelling alone. Most people worry about being lonely, but that's unlikely. Single travellers are quickly befriended in hostels and restaurants. All you have to do is join a table of friendly looking fellow travellers and you could end up hanging out with them for a couple of days or even weeks. Your plans can be more spontaneous and flexible when there's no one else to consider, and you'll probably meet more people. When close friends travel together, they often present a united front that stops other people from approaching them – and stops them making the effort to talk to others.

If you're worried about being lonely, try taking a short trip nearer home first to see how you get on. It also helps to stick to well-trodden backpacker routes (overland through Asia to Australia, for example), where you'll meet lots of other travellers.

You'll gain a tremendous sense of achievement from exploring far-flung places alone. Each country conquered will increase your self-confidence, self-esteem and independence. You *knew* you could do it!

The drawbacks of travelling alone are that there's no one else to keep an eye on your belongings if you're nipping off to the toilet or to buy a bottle of water. It can be more expensive if you don't have anyone to share the cost of a room with. Sharing a dormitory is cheaper (and a good place to meet people), but it's less secure and there's only you to watch your possessions. And there's nothing worse than falling ill when you're on your own with no one to bring you an aspirin or a drink.

If you're planning to travel alone, but feel nervous about it, you could join an organized overland trip (see p. 29). At the end of the tour, you'll probably have built up enough confidence to strike out on your own if you want to travel further. There may even be fellow passengers who are going your way with whom you can link up. This is a particularly good idea if you want to travel in countries which might be politically unstable or considered 'difficult' to travel in.

Solo women travellers obviously face different problems to men – but there are masses of them out there and we've yet to meet a solo woman traveller who didn't have a wonderful time. You may be concerned about safety, but a few simple precautions will reduce the dangers (see chapter 11).

Finding a Travel Companion

If travelling alone still doesn't appeal, you could consider joining one of the following travellers' societies that aim to match you up with possible companions. It's obviously more of a gamble going with a stranger than it is with someone you know, so you should devote even more time and thought to making sure you and your prospective companion are compatible. Meet up several times and discuss every aspect of your trip to make sure you agree on the route, how long you want to spend in each place, how much spending money you're taking and any other points that need clarifying.

• **Travel Mate**, 52 York Place, Bournemouth, Dorset BH7 6JN (01202 431520). Membership is £35. Send details of your intended trip and they'll provide a list of people whose travel plans match yours.

• **Odyssey International**, 21 Cambridge Road, Waterbeach, Cambridge CB5 9NJ (01223 861079). Membership fee is £25 (£20 if you're unwaged). Will put you in touch with prospective travellers and provide an information and advisory service. They usually match clients up on a same-sex basis and are specifically targeted at people in their twenties planning a long-haul trip.

• **Travel Companions**, 110 High Mount, Station Road, London NW4 3ST (0181 202 8478). Costs £40. Caters mainly for short-haul trips for travellers in their thirties and older.

• **Women Welcome Women**, 88 Easton Street, High Wycombe, Bucks HP11 1LT (01494 465 4413). Aims to foster international friendship by putting women in touch with women in different countries who will provide accommodation. There are over 2,000 members in more than 70 countries. Suggested subscription of £20, which covers the cost of the membership list and three newsletters.

There is also an increasing number of travellers' clubs you could join. While these don't aim to fix you up with a travelling companion, they're good places to meet like-minded people, who might well be interested in a bit of globetrotting with you:

• **The Amazonians.** Founded by travel writers Dea Birkett and Sara Wheeler, this is a club for professional women travel writers. They meet on the last Friday of each month in a central London venue where they network and exchange travel ideas and information. For further information, contact Dea Birkett on 0171 608 3953.

• **Birmingham & Midlands Travellers Club.** Meets once a month to present slide shows and talks. They also have question and answer sessions from recently returned travellers. Contact

Mike Brander on 0121 356 5086 or Jon Broome on 0121 449 1979.

- **Bristol Travellers Club.** Meets every month at the YHA International Centre, 64 Prince Street, Bristol BS1 4HU. Run by the Marco Polo Travel Advisory Service, which also organizes seminars for women travellers. Ring 0117 929 4123 for further information.
- **Globetrotters Club**, BCM/Roving, London WC1N 3XX (no telephone number). Holds monthly meetings with slide talks in central London, provides a travel query service and publishes a bi-monthly travel magazine, *Globe*.
- **Royal Geographical Society**, 1 Kensington Gore, London SW7 2AR (0171 589 5466). The RGS has a splendid map room (the world's largest private map collection, with 900,000) that members of the public can use. Also houses a unique collection of expedition reports.
- **Royal Scottish Geographical Society**, 40 George Street, Glasgow G1 1QE. Will grant access to their library for some research purposes. For information on becoming a Fellow, ring 0141 552 3330.
- **STEP** (Scottish Travellers Exploring the Planet). Organization of travellers based in Scotland. Meetings are held once a year and guest speakers invited to talk about their travels. Membership is £10 per annum. Further information from Anna Campbell, 20A Suffolk Road, Edinburgh EH16 5NJ (0131 662 4737).
- **Trippers**, Trips Worldwide, 9 Byron Place, Triangle, Clifton, Bristol BS8 1JT (0117 987 2626). Meets once a month. Travel companies such as Top Deck and Dragoman give free lectures and slide shows.
- **Wexas Travel Club**, 45–9 Brompton Road, London SW3 1DE (0171 589 3315). E-mail: mship@wexas.com. Originally founded as a travel club for student and expeditionary travel, Wexas is now a travel association with 35,000 members. Members get discounts on air fares, insurance and car rental among other things, a free subscription to *Traveller* magazine and a reduction

on the price of their *Traveller's Handbook*. Membership is currently £39.58, but you can join on a one-month 'free trial offer' basis.

You can also advertise free for a travelling companion in the Connections page in *Wanderlust* magazine (see chapter 16); the Companions ad column in the YHA magazine, *Triangle*, and the Members' Classified column in the Wexas magazine, *Traveller*. *Overseas Jobs Express* (see p. 57 for details) has a Travel Link column, where travellers can contact other travellers.

En route, you'll come across noticeboards in backpackers' hostels, cafés and bars with details of trips you can join, travellers looking for people to share car rides, etc. Nairobi's famous Thorn Tree Café is a classic example. It has been a backpackers' meeting place for many years, and around the massive thorn tree it was named after are pinned lots of travel tips, details of items for sale, safari offers and so on.

Taking an Organized Tour

If you decide you *will* travel on your own, but still feel apprehensive about it, why not join an organized tour with an overland adventure tour group such as those listed below? Most of these companies attract travellers in their twenties and thirties and tour for anything up to six months in small groups (usually between 12 and 20 people). Many travellers go with a partner or friend, but around half are people travelling on their own. It's a good way to travel in 'difficult' destinations such as some African countries, or, for single women, those countries where it can be hard work for females on their own – such as Muslim countries like Iran.

Collect all the different brochures and check them out carefully to see which company sounds best for you. Compare routes, activities and prices – but also look at the type of clients the company attracts, what ages they are and how many passengers are on each trip. Most companies give slide shows (where you can also meet some of the staff and get a look at potential fellow passengers) or have videos you can borrow; they usually provide project dossiers containing detailed information on individual trips that you can check out.

- **Adventure South America**, Adventure Travel Centre, 131–5 Earls Court Road, London SW5 9RH (0171 370 4555).
- **Discover the World**, 29 Nork Way, Banstead, Surrey SM7 1PB (01737 218801).
- **Dragoman**, 96 Camp Green, Debenham, Stowmarket, IP14 6LA (0171 370 1930 or 01728 861133).
- **Encounter Overland**, 267 Old Brompton Road, London SW5 9JA (0171 370 6845).
- **Exodus**, 9 Weir Rd, London SW12 0LT (0181 673 0859).
- **Guerba**, Wessex Road, 40 Station Road, Westbury, Wiltshire BA13 3JN (01373 826611/858956).
- **Top Deck Travel**, 131–5 Earl's Court Road, London SW5 9RH (0171 244 8641).

Travellers' Tales

I went to South America on my own because none of my friends wanted to go – they all had jobs they wanted to keep. I preferred going on my own anyway – that way I could plan my own itinerary and go where I wanted when I wanted. I saw lots of people arguing in the middle of their trip about where to go because they hadn't thought it out beforehand. I travelled round by coach, bus and minibus (or plane when the roads were washed out). They're quite good, especially between cities, but buses in small towns are small and cramped. The roads were safe – apart from a horrible mountain road to La Paz which had an incredibly steep drop and little crosses by the side of the road where cars have gone over the edge!

There were lots of other travellers around and I joined up with a New Zealander and a German guy and did a bit of travelling with them. I felt lonely occasionally, but I'd listen to my Walkman and drink a few beers and drive those blues away! Going to a bar on your own is a good way to meet people – most of the locals were friendly and would come and chat, so it helps if you speak Spanish or Portuguese. I knew some basics but found it frustrating because I didn't speak enough – if I was going back, I'd make an effort to learn more.

One tip for anyone going to South America: if you're staying somewhere that's at a high altitude, always leave yourself plenty of time to get wherever you're going. In La Paz, it was a 15-minute walk to the bus station but I only left myself five minutes. I had to run uphill with my rucksack, and when I reached the bus station I passed out! While I was unconscious, someone loaded my rucksack on and my ticket was stamped, so when I came round I was all ready to board – quite efficient really. I just stood up, dusted myself down and got on the coach!

Jonathan Konig, 25

Travellers' Tales

I'm just about to leave on a trip round the world. I've bought a RTW ticket and I'm planning to stop off in Singapore, Thailand, Bali, Australia, New Zealand, Fiji and Tonga. From Tonga I'll fly to Los Angeles, travel overland to New York and then fly home from there. I've also bought a Greyhound bus pass to use in the States – it was cheaper to buy it in London.

I've been planning my trip for almost a year and I've saved £3,000, which I hope will be enough. I'd rather have a non-working trip, but if I think I'm running short, I'll do a bit of bar work or waitressing in Australia. I'm meeting my boyfriend in Thailand. He went out three months ahead of me because he wanted to be away for longer and also wanted to go to some places I wasn't particularly interested in. We'll do most of the trip together, but we've already decided that if we want to do very different things, we'll go our own ways for a while. That way, we both get to do exactly what we want.

Rachel Burrows, 23

Chapter 5 / **Handling the Paperwork**

All travellers from the UK must now be in possession of a full ten-year passport (one-year visitor's passports were abolished on 1 January 1996). This costs £18 for a standard passport (32 pages); £27 for a larger one (48 pages).

Passport application forms are available from main post offices in Great Britain and from the Belfast Passport Office and most travel agents in Northern Ireland. Form A is for those applying for their first passport (or who've only had a British visitor's passport before), their first passport in a new name or a replacement for a passport that has been lost or stolen. Form R is for anyone wanting to replace their soon-to-expire existing passport.

Allow plenty of time for your application to be processed – apply at *least* one month before your trip commences. Remember that in peak periods (i.e., the run-up to the summer holidays) passport offices are incredibly busy and you'd be wise to allow even longer. The Passport Office claims to deal with applications between September and December within two weeks; between January and August within four weeks. In emergencies, applications can be delivered in person, but even then they take a week to process. You also have to justify why you need your passport so quickly.

The Post Office has a Passport Application Service – for a charge of £2.75 (on top of the passport fee) they'll check your application through, making sure you've answered all the questions correctly and have included the right payment, then send it by registered post to the relevant Passport Office. Your passport will then be posted to you at home. The aim is to speed up the issuing of passports – at the moment one in five applications is returned because the form hasn't been completed properly or payment hasn't been included.

If you already have a passport, check the expiry date. At the risk of stating the obvious, you need to make sure that it will last until the end of your trip – and probably another six to twelve months beyond that. Many people end up staying away longer than planned, so it makes sense to check that the expiry date allows for you extending your trip. Entry requirements for many countries, including such popular travellers' destinations as Thailand and Australia, insist that your passport has at least six months to run after you plan to leave their country.

If you're planning a big trip, covering lots of different countries, make sure your passport has plenty of blank pages left in it to allow for all the new visa, entry and exit stamps you'll be acquiring. Some border officials are reluctant to use a page with another stamp already on it, which can cause problems as the passport starts to fill up. Memorizing your passport number and date of issue will save time when you're filling out countless forms at borders and signing into hotels. In fact, you'll be writing the information down so often that you probably won't be able to help remembering it!

Bear in mind that some Arab countries, such as Syria, won't let you in if you have an Israeli stamp in your passport. (The Foreign & Commonwealth Office have a list of these countries.) One way round this is to get a second passport, but the UK Passport Agency are reviewing their policy on this (call the Policy Section on 0171 271 8632 for details).

Remember to fill in the next-of-kin details in your passport so that your family can be contacted as soon as possible if anything happens to you and you're not able to call them yourself.

Carry your passport with you at all times, rather than leaving it in your suitcase or a safe. If you lose it or have it stolen while you're away, report it to the police and the nearest British Consulate immediately.

Take two photocopies of the last page of your passport (the first five if you still have the old navy-blue one); leave one at home; take the other with you in case the original gets lost or stolen.

NB, After registering in a hotel in some countries, you must leave your passport with reception until you are checking out. Don't forget to ask for your passport back when you leave!

Passport Offices in the UK

England

Liverpool Passport Office
5th floor, India Buildings, Water Street, Liverpool L2 0QZ (0151 237 3010).

London Passport Office
Clive House, 70 Petty France, London SW1H 9HD (0171 799 2990). Primarily for urgent personal applications.

Peterborough Passport Office
Aragon Court, Northminster Rd, Peterborough PE1 1QG (01733 895555).

Northern Ireland

Belfast Passport Office
Hampton House, 47–53 High Street, Belfast BT1 2QS (01232 232371).

Scotland

Glasgow Passport Office
3 Northgate, 96 Milton St, Cowcaddens, Glasgow G4 0BT (0141 332 0271).

Wales

Newport Passport Office
Olympia House, Upper Dock Street, Newport, Gwent NP9 1XA (01633 244500).

Passport offices are open Monday to Friday 9 a.m. to 4.30 p.m. (4 p.m. in London).

Visas

Most visas are stamped into your passport, although some politically sensitive countries still provide a separate document. Visas are normally obtained from a country's embassy, high commission or consulate (see chapter 17 for a list of addresses), though in some cases travel agents may be authorized to issue them. It can sometimes be less expensive and easier to pick up visas as you travel. In Bangkok, for example, there's no problem picking up visas for travel to surrounding countries such as Vietnam, Cambodia, Laos and Myanmar (Burma). In some cases, it simply isn't practical to get your visas before you travel as they may expire before you even reach a particular country. If you're planning to pick up visas *en route*, don't forget to take plenty of passport photos with you.

Most countries charge a fee for issuing visas and in some cases it can be quite a lot (around £40 for Vietnam, for example), so take this into account when working out how much the trip is going to cost. If time is short, you may have to pay extra for a visa to be issued faster than normal – some countries even have a grading system, with different fees depending on how quickly you need the visa.

Allow plenty of time to get your visa. Some places will issue them immediately or within a couple of days, and most will do it within a week, but other countries (notably the Russian Federation) can take a couple of weeks to process your application. Always take great care filling in the application – any errors or omissions can mean it takes longer to process. If you're going to get your visa in person, be patient – you usually have to queue for ages. If you're applying through the post, always send your passport by recorded delivery.

Check whether your visa is valid for single or multiple entry. If you're going to Thailand, for example, and plan a side trip to Myanmar or Cambodia, you'll need a multiple-entry visa to get back into the country.

Visa information is particularly vulnerable to change. Always check requirements with the relevant embassy or consulate (see addresses in chapter 17) prior to travel.

Visa Services

If you can't face the hassle of getting your own visas, there are agencies who will do the legwork for you – for a fee. The amount charged varies from around £14 to £25 per visa, on top of the visa fee charged by each country. Look in Yellow Pages to find local services or try the following organizations:

- **The Visa Service**, 2 Northdown St, King's Cross, London N1 9BG (0171 833 2709).
- **Hogg Robinson Travel**, Alliance House, 12 Caxton St, London SW1H 0QS (0171 233 2477).
- **Trailfinders Visa Service**, 194 Kensington High St, London W8 7RG (0171 938 3848).
- **The Visa and Passport Service**, 1 St Stephen's Mews, London W2 5QZ (0171 229 1262).
- **Thames Consular**, 363 Chiswick High Rd, London W4 4HS (0181 995 2492).

Travellers' Tales

Arriving in Guatemala involved the worst border crossing of my life. Our bus was stopped by the Guatemalan army and all the men had to get off – I was stuck on the bus with a load of farmers who didn't speak English. The two guys I was with were made to walk up the road away from the bus and, when I tried to go with them, this 15-year-old with a machine gun stood by the bus and wouldn't let me get off. It was four in the morning and very scary. Some of the soldiers got on the bus. When they found out I was English, they made me get my rucksack out and went through everything, looking for political literature. They went through all my books, asking what they were about, and I was desperately trying to explain the finer points of Jane Austen! Eventually they got bored and let us carry on, but it was an unpleasant couple of hours.

Rashna Owtad, 27

Chapter 6 / **Money Matters**

How Much Money Should I Take?

It depends on your route, how you're planning to travel, what kind of accommodation you stay in, etc. Obviously, a week spent living in a straw hut and lazing on a beach will cost next to nothing, while a week in a city or doing lots of travelling will be much more expensive. As a general guide, you should probably allow a minimum of £10 a day, but £15–20 a day will be more comfortable and allow you more leeway.

If you're on a tight budget, aim for countries that you know are going to be cheaper than the UK. India and most of South-East Asia, for example, are still cheap destinations (you can find yourself a Goan bungalow or a beach hut on a Thai island for as little as £1 or £2 per night). North America or Australia will obviously be more expensive – and Japan will probably blow your budget completely. Much of South America is fairly cheap once you get there, but air fares are more expensive. Reading the most up-to-date guidebooks will give you some indication of the cost of accommodation, meals, transport, etc. (though you can assume that they've all risen slightly since the writer was there).

Allow some extra money or take a credit card for the times (and there will be some) when you've had enough of dormitories and dubious hotel rooms and feel like treating yourself to somewhere more luxurious. There will also be activities and events along the way that you won't want to miss out on – like whitewater rafting, or scuba diving on the Great Barrier Reef. This sort of thing doesn't come cheap (though you may get discounts with one of the cards mentioned later in this chapter), but it seems mad to miss out on what would certainly be a highlight of your trip – and possibly a once-in-a-lifetime experience.

You can really cut costs and get by on a minimal budget if you turn teetotal for the trip. Alcohol can be expensive in some places and you may sometimes find that your drinks are costing you more than your accommodation and food put together! If, like most travellers, you fancy a few drinks in the evening, remember that local beers and spirits are always cheaper than imported varieties; and as a general rule local spirits are cheaper (and more lethal) than beer.

A Traveller's Budget

These costs are only very approximate, but will give you a rough idea of the sort of money you'll need for a year away. If you plan to work, or will only be away for six or nine months, you can reduce the cost substantially. If you want to try every activity going and treat yourself to nice meals and hotels now and then, it will bump it up.

Plane ticket	£800
Overland travel	£300
Spending money (365 days @ £10 per day)	£3,650
Insurance	£250
Rucksack and other equipment	£250
Pre-trip vaccinations & visas	£150
Books, toiletries, miscellaneous	£100
Total	**£5,500**

How Do I Take It?

There are three main ways to carry your money – travellers' cheques, cash, and credit/charge cards. Each has its uses, so the best advice is usually to take a combination of all three.

Travellers' Cheques

Travellers' cheques are safer than carrying large amounts of cash and are (usually) quickly replaced if lost or stolen. You may find they make it easier to keep track of your spending. In much of the world, both dollar and sterling cheques are widely accepted, and taking a mix of both means you can change whichever gives the best rate of exchange on the day. However, in some areas (e.g. the US and South America), sterling travellers' cheques are very difficult to cash and dollar cheques are pretty much the only option. In the US itself, dollar cheques can be used just like cash in shops and restaurants.

The downside of travellers' cheques is that you can be stung for commission both when you buy them and when you change them (though any unused sterling cheques can be cashed without charge in the UK). It's always best to buy a well-known name (AmEx, Thomas Cook, Visa, etc.), especially if you're going somewhere unused to mass tourism. Take them in a mixture of small and large denominations. Keep a note of the numbers somewhere separate from the cheques themselves (and leave a copy at home too). If you're travelling with a partner, AmEx and Thomas Cook do two-signature cheques that can be signed by either one of you.

Cash

In some countries (e.g. Russia), and in very remote regions, travellers' cheques are not widely recognized, in which case cash is a better bet. However, it is obviously riskier to carry, and most insurance policies have a limit on how much they will compensate you for stolen cash. Check the cash limit on your insurance policy and try not to carry more than the maximum amount they'll refund in the case of theft.

Take enough local currency (if you can) to pay for a taxi from the airport, drinks when you arrive, etc., but don't change too much here – you usually get a better rate when you're away. Check if you'll be arriving at your destination on a holiday or at a time when banks will be closed and, if so, allow extra. Don't let the bank palm you off with all large notes: get small denominations as well, as large ones can be hard to change. When buying your currency, ask for new, or newish, notes from your bank. Some countries won't change banknotes which have penmarks on them or which have been Sellotaped together.

Always hold some cash back for emergencies.

Credit Cards and Charge Cards

Take at least one credit card. Not everywhere accepts all cards but if you have Visa and MasterCard you should be well covered. As well as being invaluable in emergencies, they can be a cheaper way to pay when abroad as they tend to offer competitive exchange rates. They also help to raise your status in the eyes of otherwise dubious foreign officials who look askance at penniless backpackers. Don't bank on bills taking months to come through, though – they usually turn up on your statement pretty quickly.

Statements will keep coming through every month while you're away, of course, so you need to arrange how you're going to pay.

One way is to pay money into your credit-card account in advance, which avoids interest piling up on your debts. Alternatively, you could ask your bank to arrange for a standing order to pay off a certain amount each month (remember to leave enough money in the bank to pay the bills as they come in). Or you could pay some money into a high-interest account, set up a standing order from that to pay your bills each month and gain interest on the money at the same time.

Remember to make a note every time you charge something to your card so that you don't overspend.

Before you go, check the expiry date on your card to make sure it won't run out while you're away; if necessary, apply for a new one in advance. Check your limit too. If you don't think it's enough, ask for it to be raised so you have the security of knowing it's there to fall back on in emergencies – but don't feel you *have* to use it! You can also use your card to get cash abroad, either as a cash advance over the counter or, if you know your pin number, from cash-point machines abroad.

American Express cards are useful, too, and fairly widely accepted. As well as being able to use AmEx offices as a Poste Restante service, card holders can also cash cheques against their personal bank accounts, up to £500 every 21 days; the money can be taken in cash or travellers' cheques. You'll pay commission on the cheques, just as you would if you bought them at home, but it saves you carrying them around for months before you need them. Remember, however, that the amount charged to your card has to be paid off in full each month when your statement comes in.

Money Tips

• Shop around before you buy travellers' cheques and currency. Fees, rates of commission and minimum charges vary from one bank or building society to another – you may think you're getting a bargain if you find somewhere that doesn't charge commission, but you'll probably find they offer a bad rate of exchange. The Post Office now also sells foreign currency and AmEx travellers' cheques at many branches. If you work for a large organization, ask if they have commission-free arrangements with any banks.

• Don't leave it to the last minute to sort out your travel money – most banks need at least a few days' notice, especially if you're after a more obscure currency. If you need soft currency (e.g., roubles, dong, Kenyan shillings), you can only get it inside that country. Take dollars and change them on arrival.

• Wherever you go, dollar bills are useful for tips.

• Some cash cards can be used abroad just as in the UK. Check with your bank.

• Consider signing up with a credit-card registration service, such as Card Protection Plan (0171 351 4400), so that if your cards are stolen while you're away, you'll only have to make one phone call to sort everything out. Ask your bank for details.

• At the risk of stating the obvious, remember that *Euro*cheques can only be used in *Europe*. Barclays say puzzled tourists try every year to use them on other continents! With Eurocheques, you write cheques out in the foreign currency (either to withdraw cash from a bank, or to pay for goods in shops, restaurants and hotels) and the sum is then debited to your bank account at home, just as with a normal cheque. You have to pay an annual fee for your card, a fee for the cheques, plus commission on each one.

• The costs of treatment and repatriation if you fall ill or have an accident while you're away can be huge, especially in the USA, so don't even *think* about travelling without insurance (see chapter 8).

• If you're planning to buy perfume, alcohol, etc. in duty-free, check out the high-street prices before you go – duty-free isn't always a bargain.

• Look out in newspapers or magazines for travel bursaries or competitions that could help fund your trip.

• Don't leave home without:
  • the number to call if your credit cards or travellers' cheques go missing;

- a separate note of your cheque numbers;
- enough sterling to see you through any transport delays when you leave (and keep some back to pay for a taxi home, a pint of milk, etc. when you come back).

Transferring Money Abroad

If you run out of money while you're away, it is possible to have funds transferred to you quickly and fairly painlessly – for a fee, of course.

Western Union offer an International Money Transfer Service, which they claim is the fastest way to send money worldwide. The person sending you the money from this end can either go into a Western Union agent with cash (sterling), or call them with a credit card number (Visa or MasterCard), and the money should be available at the other end within about one hour. They cover most countries in the world. The charge varies according to how much is sent – sending £500 would cost £42. For information, call 0800 833833.

American Express cardholders can make use of MoneyGram, the company's international money transfer service that claims to transfer funds (up to a maximum of US$7,150) in less than ten minutes and covers 61 countries world-wide. Again, charges are on a sliding scale – to send between $800 and $1,200 costs $60.

Thomas Cook also operate a telegraphic transfer service which allows you to send funds to almost anywhere in the world, usually within 24 hours. The money can be paid into a bank account abroad or sent to a Thomas Cook branch or agent. Contact your local branch for details.

Another way to get access to funds abroad is for someone to deposit money in your credit-card account at home. This avoids the bank charges incurred by transferring money abroad and the hassle of trying to arrange it.

Bank Accounts

Before you go away, let your bank know what you're doing and how you're arranging for your money to be handled. They may be able to offer you help and advice. You could arrange for a relative (a trustworthy one!) to become a signatory on your bank account, which will enable them to pay bills for you.

If you know you're going to be spending any length of time in a particular country, find out about opening a bank account there. In Australia and New Zealand, for example, this is easy, and popular with travellers, because it means you don't have to worry about carrying round too much cash or too many travellers' cheques. Once you get there you can open an account, deposit a nominal sum, then get someone back in the UK to transfer funds to you.

Discount Cards

There are a number of different cards available that can save you money while you're away, entitling you to good discounts (anything from 10 to 30 per cent) on all sorts of things from coach travel to car hire, skydiving to snorkelling, museum entrance to hostel accommodation. Some of the main ones, which you can get before you go, are listed below. In addition, look out for discount cards available once you arrive in different countries, particularly Australia and New Zealand, which are so well geared-up to backpacker travel.

• **International Student Identity Card** (ISIC). Available to students currently in full-time education. As well as qualifying for discounts on a variety of things, holders also get commission-free currency and have access to a free 24-hour emergency helpline from anywhere in the world. The card (issued annually) costs £5 from student travel offices or £5.50 by post. For an application form write to ISIC Mail Order, Bleaklow House, Howard Town Mills, Mill Street, Glossop, Derbyshire SK13 8HT.

- **Under 26 Card** (called Young Scot Card in Scotland). Part of the Euro <26 Youth Card network, and supported by the British Council. Holders are entitled to discounts on fares, goods and services throughout Europe, including the UK; they also receive a regular magazine and have access to a free 24-hour travellers' advice line. Cost is £6. For information, write to Under 26, 52 Grosvenor Gardens, Victoria, London SW1W 0AG, or call 0171 823 5363. In Scotland, call 0131 313 2488.

- **Youth Hostel Association Card.** Open to people of any age, a YHA card entitles the holder to use the YHA's world-wide budget accommodation network and gives discounts on a wide range of other goods and services, especially in Australia. In the UK, YHA members get a 10 per cent discount on all purchases at YHA Adventure Shops. Costs £9.30 (18 and over); £3.20 (under 18).

- **VIP Backpackers Resorts International Pass.** Membership (£12) gives you discounts on hostels, travel passes, etc. in Australia, New Zealand and a few other countries. Ask your travel agent for details.

National Insurance

If you're out of the country for a long period of time your National Insurance contributions will be affected, reducing your pension rights and other benefits. If you go away part way through a tax year, during which you've already been paying contributions, eighteen months after the end of that tax year the computer will check your account. If your contributions for that year are below the required level, and if they have a note of your current address, you will be sent a deficiency notice, notifying you of the amount you need to pay to make the year count towards your pension. If, however, you are away for a full tax year (from April to April) you won't be contacted automatically – you will need to contact the Department of Social Security and ask to pay voluntary contributions if you wish to. You are allowed up to six years in which to pay (though you will pay more after the first two years); after that, you can't pay for the missing year at all.

It's a confusing system, so if you know that you're going to be out of the country for a full tax year or more, it's probably best to contact the DSS and ask for advice. Write to them with your date of departure, a rough idea of where you're going, your contact address in the UK, how long you plan to be away for and what you'll be doing, your expected date of return to the UK, and your National Insurance number. They'll forward it to the relevant section to deal with. The address is DSS, Contributions Agency, International Services, Newcastle Central Office, Newcastle upon Tyne NE98 1YX (0191 213 5000).

While You're Away

• If you're staying somewhere for longer than a few days, try to negotiate a discounted rate on your accommodation – most places will let you have a room cheaper if you're going to be there for a few weeks or months.

• Banks almost always give a better rate of exchange than hotels. Try to avoid changing money at airports, border posts, tourist traps, etc., where a captive market means the exchange rate is often worse.

• Don't call home from hotels – they charge hugely inflated rates. Use the local post office or pay-phone instead.

• Remember that you pay over the odds for a drink with a view – side-street and off-beach prices are lower. In some countries, drinking at the bar is cheaper than sitting down.

• Don't forget to haggle for goods and services – nearly everything is negotiable. Be patient (haggling takes time), stay calm and be prepared to compromise – the aim is for both of you to come away happy, not for you to beat the seller down completely. It's very easy to get carried away and then feel slightly shamefaced later that day when you realize you were arguing furiously for the sake of two pence.

• If you're treating yourself to a night in a good hotel as a change from huts and dives, remember that you'll pay through the nose for any food or drink in a mini-bar – cheaper to sneak in your own supplies (and sneak the empty bottles out again).

• Keep all receipts when changing money in case you need them to change money back or take money out when you leave. You should also keep receipts for any major purchases (if you buy a camera in Singapore, for example), in case Customs ask for them.

• Don't carry all your money in one place – spread it between body and bag. Leave any valuables in the hotel safe – or, better still, leave them at home. As a rule, if you couldn't bear to lose it, don't take it. See chapter 11 for more advice on money and safety.

• Always keep a note of all purchases made with your credit card so you can check the statements when you get home.

• Don't change too much money if you're leaving a country in a few days – you may find you can't spend it and lose out when changing it into the next currency. Have some travellers' cheques in small denominations.

• Each time you arrive in a new country, don't do too much spending (especially on souvenirs) until you've got a feel for prices. It's easy to get ripped off in the first few days, before you've had a chance to learn what things should cost.

• Don't make the mistake of thinking that if everything goes wrong and you run out of funds, you can simply go to the nearest British Consulate and be popped on a flight home. The Consulate is there to help in emergencies, but won't dole out money or free flights at the taxpayer's expense. In an emergency they may be able to cash a personal cheque drawn on a British bank for up to £50 (with a guarantee card), or help you get money on your credit card. They can also help you contact relatives, friends or banks at home to transfer funds to you. Only in the very rarest and most extreme of cases will they advance money to get you home – but it's a loan, not a gift, and once you return to the UK you will not be able to use your passport again until you have repaid it. There will probably also be a charge for any consular service.

• When you leave a country, remember to check *before* you arrive at the airport what departure tax, if any, is payable – otherwise you can find yourself without the right amount (which nearly caused us to miss a flight from Bangkok to Ho Chi Minh on one occasion) or having to change far more than you really need just to pay it.

Black Market

Changing money on the black market is widely practised in many countries and can help your cash go a lot further. Most travellers will change money this way at some point – but you should remember that it's not without risk. Dealing in currency seems to thrive in countries that are dirt cheap anyway, so even the official rate is good value. Using unofficial money changers leaves you open to scams – you could be given old, devalued currency (well, do *you* know what a 20,000-dong note is supposed to look like?), forged notes or wads that are bulked up with cut-up newspaper. You might be cheated on the exchange rate by some nifty calculator work. In extreme cases, you could be mugged, or even arrested. Don't say we didn't warn you.

However, if you do decide to risk it (and most travellers do, attracted by the prospect of up to double the exchange rate offered by banks), always keep your wits about you. Listen to other travellers' recommendations as to the best money changers. Usually, the more money you change, the better the exchange rate. Try to change money in shops and restaurants rather than with dodgy-looking men on street corners. Never allow yourself to be led into a deserted side street. Don't flash too much cash around, and be discreet. Change some money officially first, so that you know how genuine notes look and feel. Always make sure that you are the last person to count the foreign currency before you hand over your money: often the changer will hand it to you to count and it will all be there, but he'll then ask for it back to check once more and will pocket some of the notes so skilfully that you won't even notice until it's too late (if he gets nasty when you don't give it back to him, it's a sure sign that he's trying to pull a fast one).

Travellers' Tales

I took eight months off after finishing university and bought a RTW ticket from Trailfinders. I visited India, Nepal, Thailand, Malaysia, Indonesia, Australia, New Zealand, Hawaii and finally Los Angeles. I didn't follow a rigid schedule – I followed other backpackers' recommendations as I went along and went where the fancy took me. I was with another guy, but we ended up travelling with some other people we met along the way, which was fun. My favourite country was Nepal. It's so different to anywhere else and the people were exceptionally friendly.

I worked for five months before the trip to get some money, then borrowed the rest from my parents. My flight and travel insurance came to about £1,300 and I guess I spent about £4,000 on top of that. It was hard to stick to a budget as the prices were so different from country to country. We could live quite happily on £35 a week in India, but spent a lot more in Australia. That was because we wanted to do so much while we were there, such as diving, bungee jumping, white-water rafting. It seemed a shame to miss out on anything.

Matt Salmon, 24

Travellers' Tales

While travelling round Australia, I decided to do a diving course in Byron Bay. It was the first time I'd been diving, and it was awe-inspiring. After qualifying, I did some pleasure dives in the Whitsundays and on the Great Barrier Reef, then I went to Cairns and did an advanced course there, spending three days on the outer Reef. This made me decide I wanted a complete change of career (helped by the fact that I didn't have a job to go back to). When I got home, I applied for a Career Development Loan and trained as a scuba-diving instructor, which is what I do now.

The trip was too short – only five months – but I hadn't really planned it properly and ran out of money. If you're travelling round Australia, you need to budget for fun things. Everyone plans how much they'll spend on food and accommodation, but there's more to it than that. You need to allow for things like white-water rafting, parachute jumps, scuba diving – in Australia there's so much to do.

Robert King, 33

Chapter 7 / **Working Abroad**

If you need to make your money go further while you're travelling, the best way is to pick up work on the way. It's also a great way to meet other people.

While permanent jobs can be hard to find and require cutting through masses of red tape, casual work, such as fruit picking, bar work, dishwashing and cleaning, is usually easy to find (with or without a work permit). If you're a qualified nurse, secretary, chef or hairdresser, you'll always be in demand. If you are working illegally (and many travellers do), be discreet about it. Telling everybody could get both you and your employer in trouble.

One of the best countries for finding work is Australia, especially if you're under 26 and can get a working-holiday visa (although the Australian government has now started to limit the numbers issued, as they have been deluged with young Brits). As of January 1996, New Zealand also has a working-holiday visa scheme, open to UK citizens aged between 18 and 30.

Europe, too, is more open than ever and UK nationals can work freely anywhere within the European Economic Area, which consists of the fifteen member countries of the EU (Austria, Belgium, Denmark, Finland, France, Germany, Greece, Ireland, Italy, Luxembourg, the Netherlands, Portugal, Spain, Sweden and the UK) plus Norway, Liechtenstein and Iceland. The Overseas Placing Unit (OPU), a department of the UK Employment Service, publishes factsheets on 'Working in . . .', available free from Jobcentres or from the OPU, Rockingham House, 123 West Street, Sheffield s1 4er (0114 259 6051/2).

As far as working visas for America go, forget it – unless you start off going through an official working programme (see Summer Camps in America, below).

If you're thinking of looking for work for which you'll be expected to dress fairly smartly (office work or teaching English, for example), remember to pack suitable clothes. You'll need to be reasonably neat, too, for approaching potential employers. Take a copy of your CV with you and any references or qualification certificates to show to potential employers.

Teaching English

English is used as an official or semi-official language in more than seventy countries, so teaching English offers more job opportunities than almost anything else. Those with TEFL (Teaching English as a Foreign Language) qualifications are greeted with open arms around the world, but are particularly sought after in Japan and other Asian countries, especially China. In addition to an official TEFL certificate, many employers look for two years' teaching experience.

However, there are also plenty of others willing to take on those without experience (and sometimes even without qualifications). Eastern Europe and the Baltic States are crying out for English teachers and it's not difficult to pick up work, even without a TEFL certificate. Generally, the further you are from the UK, the less you need an official qualification. Bear in mind, though, that you'll earn less than someone who's qualified and you'll probably have more pupils, but fewer teaching materials!

A comprehensive guide to the huge array of TEFL courses on offer, both in Britain and abroad, is contained in the *ELT Guide*, which gives details of costs, starting dates, venues and duration of courses. It costs £9.95 from good bookshops or can be obtained from EFL Ltd, 10 Wrights Lane, London w8 6ta (add £3 to cover postage).

Summer Camps in America

American summer camps employ student counsellors to look after
children and teach them new skills. Counsellors usually spend
8–9 weeks at a camp, from June to mid-August. There are also
positions available as camp support and maintenance staff, but
these are usually open only to students. The bonus of going
through an organized programme is that as well as receiving a
(small) salary and free food and accommodation, your return
flight is paid for and you get the chance to travel after camp
has finished. The following organizations all operate working
programmes:

• **BUNAC**, 16 Bowling Green Lane, London EC1R OBD (0171
251 3472). The BUNACAMP counsellor programme is open to
students and non-students; interviews start in November and early
application is advised. In addition, BUNAC also operates other
work/travel programmes in America, Canada, Australia and
Jamaica, though they are either open only to students (or those
taking a gap year) or carry age restrictions.

• **Camp America**, 37A Queen's Gate, London SW7 5HR (0171
581 7373). As well as a counsellor programme, offers a family
companion programme, assigning people to work in American
homes looking after children during the summer break (open to
full-time students aged 18–24 only).

• **Camp Counselors USA**, England: 6 Richmond Hill, Richmond upon Thames, TW10 6QX (0181 332 2952); Scotland and
Ireland: 27 Woodside Gardens, Musselburgh, EH21 7LJ (0131 665
5843); Northern Ireland: 15 Grange Avenue, Magherafelt, BT45
5RP (01648 34381).

• **Au Pair America**, 37 Queen's Gate, London SW7 5HR (0171
581 7311). Open to 18–26-year-olds who are willing to commit to
working a full year and have a valid driving licence.

Kibbutzim and Moshavim

You could also work on a kibbutz or moshav in Israel. Volunteers on a kibbutz are given free accommodation, board and pocket money in return for their work. You must commit yourself to working for at least five weeks. On a moshav (a kind of capitalist version of a kibbutz), you'll be paid more. Neither will make you rich (though on a moshav you may be able to accumulate some savings), but both are good ways to make friends who might then want to travel on with you (but see note about Israeli passport stamps in chapter 5). For more information, contact the following organizations:

- **Kibbutz Representatives**, 1A Accommodation Road, London NW11 8ED (0181 458 9235). Open to those aged 18–32.
- **Project 67**, 10 Hatton Garden, London EC1N 8AH (0171 831 7626).
- **Transonic Travel**, 3 Phoenix Street (off Charing Cross Road), London WC2H 8PW (0171 240 9909).

Tour Operators

Another way to earn money while travelling is by working as a representative for a tour operator abroad – travel and tourism is set to become the world's single largest industry by the year 2000, so there are plenty of opportunities. You'll usually be expected to be aged between 18 and 35, have a knowledge of the relevant country and preferably a second language, though this isn't always necessary. Depending on the organization, your duties can include anything from appearing in cabaret to lecturing on historical sites in Europe, from erecting tents on campsites to babysitting for clients. Look out for adverts in national newspapers two or three months before the season starts (January/February for summer jobs in Europe; August/September for ski resort work). Below are a few contacts to get you started; you could also try the overland travel companies listed in chapter 4. If you're going out to look for work on spec, it's best to go just before the season starts, when bars and restaurants are gearing up for the tourist invasion.

• **Eurocamp Summer Jobs**, Canute Court, Toft Road, Knutsford, Cheshire WA16 0NL (01565 625522).

• **Mark Warner Ltd**, 61–65 Kensington Church Street, London W8 4BA (0171 393 3178).

• **Canvas Holidays**, 12 Abbey Park Place, Dunfermline, Fife KY12 7PD (01383 644000).

• **Keycamp Holidays**, Courier Recruitment Department, 92–6 Lind Road, Sutton, Surrey SM1 4PL (0181 395 8909).

Other Useful Addresses

• **Gap Activity Projects**, Gap House, 44 Queens Road, Reading, Berkshire RG1 4BB (01734 594914). Offers school-leavers the chance to spend six to nine months overseas in the gap year before university. Most volunteers teach English as a foreign language, help with the disabled and underprivileged, assist in schools and activity camps or participate in farming and conservation work. You pay a fee of around £500 plus air fare, in return for free board and lodging and usually some pocket money.

• **Raleigh International**, Raleigh House, 27 Parsons Green Lane, London SW6 4HZ (0171 371 8585). Sends 17–25-year-olds on ten-week expeditions in many parts of the world. Those over 25 can also join expeditions as volunteer members of staff.

Further Information

We only have space to give a brief idea of the type of work available. For more details, read the following books, all published by Vacation Work and readily available in good bookshops: *Work Your Way Around the World*; *Kibbutz Volunteer*; *Working in Ski Resorts*;

Working on Cruise Ships; *Summer Jobs Abroad*; *Summer Jobs USA*; *Emplois d'Eté en France*; *Teaching English Abroad*; *Teaching English in Asia*.

Other Publications

How to Find Temporary Work Abroad (How To Books Ltd; 01752 202300).

The Gap Year Book (Cavendish Educational Consultants; 01223 69483).

Working Holidays 1997 (Central Bureau for Educational Visits and Exchanges; 0171 486 5101).

The Year Off Handbook (Sabre Publishing; freephone 0800 393585).

Newspapers

Overseas Jobs Express is a newspaper for international job-hunters and carries ads for permanent and temporary jobs, as well as articles of interest to anyone planning to work abroad. A three-month subscription (6 issues) costs £18.95. For details, call 01273 440220 or write to Premier House, Shoreham Airport, Sussex BN43 5FF. New subscribers will be sent a free copy of their excellent booklet, *Working Abroad*. *Overseas Jobs Express* can be contacted, and the subscription paid by credit card, on the Web at the Internet Employment Service URL listed overleaf.

Job-Search Overseas is a similar publication; it costs £20 for a six-month subscription. For information, call 01872 870070.

Networking

The Internet Employment Service can be contacted on http://www.netjobs.com/ or e-mail them on info@netjobs.com

---

Travellers' Tales

My girlfriend bought me a yachting magazine one day and when I read it I saw an ad from someone looking for people to help crew a yacht across the Atlantic. Although I didn't have much sailing experience I'd always fancied doing something like that, so I applied – and got taken on. I flew to Florida, where I met up with the owner of the yacht, his girlfriend and two other guys who were helping crew. We didn't get paid for it – in fact, we had to contribute money towards the cost of provisions. We spent a week in Florida getting everything ready, then sailed across the Atlantic, stopping off in Bermuda and the Azores and spending some time in each, before ending the trip in southern Portugal. It took about two months and was brilliant fun.

Once we got to Europe the two guys and I travelled round Portugal and Spain, then I headed down through Italy and Greece to meet up with my girlfriend, who was working on one of the Greek islands. I ended up getting work there too, then took off to Egypt and travelled down the Nile. I ended the trip with some snorkelling on the Red Sea, then flew back to England. It wasn't a problem with work because I've always worked freelance anyway, so I just slipped back into it when I returned.

Pete Wright, 38

Travellers' Tales

I very much wanted to travel in America, but couldn't afford to do it on my own so I took a job on the BUNAC scheme and worked in a children's camp in Maine. I worked there for ten weeks – most of the English staff were employed on the kitchen and maintenance programme. They prepared meals, washed up, etc. and worked an eight-hour day. I was a cleaner, which wasn't the most desirable job in the camp, but I only had to work a two-hour day, which left me lots of spare time. The camp was in the middle of nowhere, but there were lots of sports facilities I could use, such as swimming, tennis and archery. At the end of my contract, I joined up with some other girls and spent six weeks travelling around America by train – from New York to San Francisco, then down to San Diego, along the bottom of the States and back to New York. I'd highly recommend the BUNAC scheme. I enjoyed working in the camp, and it's a very cost-effective way of seeing the country.

Fiona Wright, 25

Travellers' Tales

I spent four months working in Greece one summer. After coming home, I fancied doing some more travelling so my girlfriend and I jumped on a plane to Tenerife where a friend of ours was already working. We found a cheap apartment in Playa de las Americas and our friend fixed us up with jobs selling timeshares. We became the sort of people I hate when I'm on holiday, harassing people and persuading them to visit timeshare resorts. We worked from nine to five, walking up and down the streets and beach, seeking tourists out everywhere (there was no escape!) and giving them the spiel. I didn't like doing it but I wanted to stay in Tenerife. The work was commission-based and paid well if you were good at it – the best ones approach everyone, but I only went to people who looked quite kind and wouldn't shout at me, so I didn't do very well!

After three months, I got a job driving the minibus taking people back from the timeshares. I was on an hourly wage and worked long hours so I was earning quite well. Then I got more involved with the administrative side and ended up as the supplies person – picking up stationery, catering, equipment for the villas. I had an excellent time – Playa de las Americas is definitely for young people and the evenings were wild. It was just party, party until I ran out of steam and came home – it took me two years though, so that's not bad!

Peter Day, 25

Travellers' Tales

I wanted to go travelling but didn't have much money, so working my way round seemed the only option. I went to France and met up with a friend in Paris. She had a childminding job which came with free accommodation in the form of a garret room, so I slept on her floor. I found work pretty quickly and ended up with one cleaning job and two jobs that were a mix of childminding and English teaching. The pay wasn't great, but it was enough to live on (especially as I wasn't paying for accommodation). We became experts at finding the cheapest places to eat, the days museums were free, the best places for cheap clothes and second-hand books. We spent four months in Paris, then moved to Greece, and ended up in Paros, where we stayed for six months, working in a little sea-front bar. At first they paid us just to sit in the bar so that it wouldn't look empty and other customers would come in. We'd chat and play backgammon and the drinks were free – it's a tough job but someone's got to do it! We were living on the camp-site so we got to know lots of other travellers, who started coming down to our bar in the evenings to see us and that, in turn, attracted more people so the bar ended up really lively. As the season hotted up we started working behind the bar too. It was great fun though very exhausting, working all night – we spent the days just lying out on the beach, recovering.

Eileen Victor, 23

Chapter 8 / **Insurance**

Although almost £400 million is spent on travel insurance every year, it's one item that some backpackers think they can skimp on. Our advice is, wherever you're going, and however long you're going for, don't even *think* about saving a couple of hundred pounds by not taking out medical or personal insurance. It's the biggest false economy there is, and you won't be able to relax all the time you're away. If you have an accident, the cost of evacuation and repatriation can be astronomical. An injured person might need four airline seats, plus two more for medical staff, as well as ambulances at each end. One patient who was evacuated from the Himalayas to Singapore was faced with a bill for more than £30,000. If you're including America in your itinerary, medical insurance is essential – you should be covered for up to £5 million.

Take out insurance cover as soon as you book your ticket. This means you're covered if you have to change or cancel your travel plans for any reason. It's important to check exactly what your insurance covers (and what it *doesn't* cover). If you're planning an Indiana Jones-type of trip with lots of paragliding, white-water rafting, scuba diving, off-piste skiing or bungee jumping, you must mention this at the time, as some insurance policies don't cover 'dangerous' sports.

Check, too, that you're covered for unexpected losses or expenses incurred due to missing a flight, having cash and credit cards stolen or losing your passport. And is there a 24-hour emergency back-up service or number that you can contact if necessary?

Once you're on the road, you may decide to extend your trip. Find out how easy it would be to extend your period of insurance cover while you're away and ask if someone else, such as a parent, can arrange to do this for you.

If you are travelling within the EC, you can get some medical cover by filling in form E111 (see p. 87 for details). Some insurers waive their excess charge if you've used an E111.

What to Look For in an Insurance Policy

Cancellation or curtailment

This insures you in case you have to change your travel plans. It should cover the following:
- being called for jury service or as a witness;
- you or a close family member becoming ill;
- being made redundant;
- your home being severely damaged by fire, flood or storm.

Delay

- Compensation is paid if your departure is delayed by a specific number of hours or cancelled altogether. The amount is dependent upon the length of delay.

Personal Accident

- Money will be paid to you if you are permanently disabled, or to your next of kin if you die.

Personal Liability

- This will cover your personal liability for injury or damage to others and their property. The normal maximum payout is around £1 million, though it may be double that in the United States.

Medical and Emergency Expenses

• Your policy should pay for emergency medical treatment, as well as hotel and travel expenses incurred because of sickness or injury.
• Medical insurance should also cover your repatriation costs because of illness, injury or death of a friend, relative or business colleague. In Europe the normal minimum payment is £250,000, maximum payout is up to £2 million. In America, however, it could be as high as £5 million. Check that it also includes the cost of accommodation and travel costs for a friend or relative to stay behind or fly out to help look after you.
• You must disclose full details of any illness of a permanent or recurring nature. Failure to do so will invalidate your policy.
• Most insurers provide 24-hour emergency service and tele-phone-advice lines. Take a copy of the policy and a note of the UK telephone number with you.

Baggage and Personal Belongings

• If you've bought a new, expensive rucksack, it's probably worth insuring it. If it's ten years old, and you're not worried about losing it, going for a policy that doesn't include baggage will save you money.
• Most policies allow up to £100 for the emergency purchase of essentials if your baggage is in Nantucket and you're in Nairobi.
• If you wear contact lenses or glasses, check your policy to see if they are covered.
• Check if your passport comes under personal belongings – you may have to pay a supplement to cover loss of passport.
• Valuable items, such as cameras, are usually subject to a limit.

• If you have a personal-possessions or all-risks extension for certain belongings on your house-contents insurance (such as a camera), these will be covered if you take them out of your home, as will any money you're carrying. Check the cash limit, however – the limit for all forms of money can be between £200 and £500. The limit for cash itself can be half this. Check, too, that the policy covers you for where you are going and for the length of stay away. (Some policies will only cover you for thirty or sixty days outside the UK.)

• If you're leaving your home empty, or renting it out to tenants, check that your insurers are aware of the situation and that you're still covered. If you don't tell them, they could refuse to pay up if you're burgled in your absence. Tenants should make their own separate insurance arrangements.

Sporting Activities

• Planning a bungee jump while you're away? You'll probably have to pay a supplement to be covered for this activity – the cost will depend on how many jumps you plan to do and the level of supervision. Ask your insurer for details.

• Many other adventurous activities such as hiring a motorbike or scuba diving may also be excluded from your policy. Always check the small print to see what's covered. (Trailfinders has an insurance scheme called Adventure Travel Insurance, which covers the most dangerous of outdoor and sporting activities.)

Working Abroad

• Will you be insured if you have an accident while working abroad? Tell your insurer before you go if you're planning to look for work *en route*.

NB, many insurance policies have an excess charge of around £35, which means you have to pay the first £35 of any claim yourself. It's vital you check if this sum is applied *separately* to individual sections of your policy – meaning you could end up paying out more. For example, if you were the victim of a mugging and needed to claim for medical costs as well as loss of money and possessions, you could have to pay three excesses, totalling more than £100. This is clearly unfair, since your claim would arise from a single incident. Read the small print carefully. If you're not sure about excess charges, ask your insurer to explain the policy in detail. It may be possible to pay an excess waiver – an extra £15 or so added to your premium, which means that any claims you make won't be subject to an excess charge.

Flexible Friends

If you pay for a holiday with a credit card you can claim a refund from your credit-card company if your holiday company goes bust. Most credit cards also give you some form of insurance if you use them to pay – but not usually enough to rely on. Check with your credit-card company.

Where Will I Get the Best Deal?

Insurance is a competitive business and mainstream insurance companies, banks, building societies and the Post Office all offer insurance services, as do most of the travel agents featured in this book. The price of policies can vary from £150 to £500, according to your age, destinations, length of time away, whether or not you'll be working or indulging in 'dangerous' sports, and numerous other variables. It's impossible for us to provide a quote from each company, apart from the most basic cover. Shop around, stating your precise requirements, to get the policy that suits you best on price and cover. You can also get further information from a free fact-sheet, *Holiday Insurance*, if you send a large s.a.e.

to the Association of British Insurers, 51 Gresham St, London EC2V 7HQ (0171 600 3333).

Short Trips

We appreciate that not everyone can take as long as a year off to travel. Companies currently offering travel insurance for trips lasting up to 90 days include:

- **General Accident**, Pitheavlis, Perth, Scotland PH2 0NY (01738 621202). The maximum sum payable for loss of cash is £250. They also provide cover up to £250 for loss/theft of passport, but only if you have reported this to the police within 24 hours and have a police report. Provide medical cover up to £2 million (though you should really be covered for more if you're going to the States).
- **Meridian Insurance**, PO Box 899, Glasgow G64 2QP (0141 772 9005). Quoted £140 for 90 days' world-wide cover, again with medical cover of up to £2 million. Maximum sum payable for loss of cash is just £150; £300 for travellers' cheques.
- **International Private Healthcare Ltd**, PO Box 488, IPH House, Borehamwood, Herts WD6 4AN (0181 905 2888). Offer an annual, multi-trip travel-insurance policy, though any trip must be for a maximum of 90 days. Prices from £95.
- **Lloyds Bank Annual Travel Insurance**, (0171 512 0012) costs £98.95. This covers you for a year but there is a maximum duration of 90 days per trip. Ask at any branch of the bank for details.

Long-Stay Trips

There are hundreds of insurance companies around, but the following are particularly experienced in catering for backpackers' needs:

- **Club Direct**, Freepost PT577, Chichester, West Sussex PO19

1YQ (01243 787838). Offer almost thirty different policies, including a backpacker holiday insurance scheme. Will also insure anyone wishing to work while travelling. Basic premiums start at £200 per year.

• **Campus Travel**, 52 Grosvenor Gardens, London SW1W 0AG (0171 730 3402) plus regional branches. For those aged 34 and under, world-wide cover for 12 months costs £252 (excluding baggage) or £346 (including baggage). European cover for a year is £152 or £210 with baggage. Will also insure against eventualities such as the miserable prospect of having to stay home to do resits!

• **Columbus Travel Insurance**, 17 Devonshire Square, London EC2M 4SQ (0171 375 0011). Columbus offer fully comprehensive policies, standard policies (which don't cover loss of camera, cash or documents) or Globetrotter policies (which are basically just medical cover). Globetrotter rates: 90 days – £53; 185 days – £106; 365 days – £179.

• £106; 365 days – £179.

• **Endsleigh Insurance Services Ltd**, Endsleigh House, Ambrose St, Cheltenham, Gloucs GL50 3NR (01242 258258). Endsleigh have a Standard policy for 12 months for £344 or a Premier policy for £359.50. The Premier policy offers higher levels of cover and also covers money up to £250, delayed flights, missed departure and luggage delay. If you're travelling in the USA, you need a Premier policy.

• **STA Travel** (for contacts see chapter 3). An annual world-wide policy for 12 months costs £351 (Standard) or £484 (Premier). Premier offers higher levels of cover, which are advisable for travel in the US and Canada. STA also runs a 24-hour international helpline which you can call from anywhere in the world if you have problems.

• **Trailfinders** (for addresses see chapter 3). Provide personal travel-insurance cover from 4 days to 12 months. They also have an emergency service, Voyagers Assistance, with staff on call 365 days a year. Premiums start at £236 for 6 months. Further information from individual branches.

• **Wexas International**, 45–9 Brompton Road, London SW3

IDE (0171 589 0500). Wexas offer members one fully comprehensive world-wide policy for £480.90, which gives medical cover up to £5 million. Anyone participating in activities such as bungee jumping or white-water rafting will need to pay an extra premium.
• **Worldwide Travel Insurance Services Ltd**, PO Box 99, Elm Lane Offices, Elm Lane, Tonbridge, Kent TN10 3XS (01732 773366). Their long-stay travel insurance gives cover for up to 18 months and covers anyone who wants to take up work (excluding manual labour). There's a 24-hour emergency service and their medical cover goes up to £5 million. Also, if you pay for 12 months' cover, but return after nine months, they'll refund the difference. Policies from £16.50 per month (medical only) or £27.50 per month (medical and baggage).

While You're Away . . .

• Leave a photocopy of your insurance documents at home with parents or whoever is looking after your affairs. Take another copy with you in case you lose the original.
• However insecure the hotel safe looks, use it rather than leaving belongings in your room. Most insurance companies will refuse to pay up if items are stolen from your room when there was a safe available.
• If you're robbed, you *must* report it to a police station immediately (i.e., within 24 hours) and obtain a police report. Even if you think they'll never catch the culprit, you'll need their report to present to your insurers back home when you make a claim.

When You Come Home . . .

• If you do need to make a claim on your insurance policy, lodge it immediately upon your return to the UK – it's often a condition of the policy that claims be submitted within one calendar month of your return.

- Keep all receipts for any treatment, prescription drugs, services, etc. and submit them with your claim form, together with any back-up documents such as police reports. (Keep photocopies of everything, in case of any dispute.)
- If your claim is rejected, the insurer must tell you why. If you don't agree with their decision, take your complaint to the highest level within the insurance company. If you're still not satisfied, take your claim to the Insurance Ombudsman (0171 928 7600) or Personal Insurance Arbitration Scheme (0171 837 4483).

Think It Couldn't Happen to You?

Here are some of the claims submitted to insurance companies during 1996.

- A couple visiting the Rock of Gibraltar had their camera stolen by one of the apes.
- A couple buying petrol in India were attacked by a tiger.
- A holidaymaker in the US went for a midnight swim and was bitten by a vampire bat.
- An alligator swallowed a tourist's glasses in Jamaica.
- A safari group in Africa lost all their equipment when a hippopotamus capsized their boat.

The insurance companies paid up in every case.

Travellers' Tales

A couple of years ago, I spent three months in South America travelling through Brazil, Bolivia and Argentina. I had a great time everywhere. South America is very exciting. It seems more unexplored than other parts of the world, and I felt very intrepid.

About a month into the trip I had lots of stuff stolen in Salvador, in Brazil. I went out for the evening and, because the hotel 'safe' was just a locked cupboard that everyone knew about, and looked really easy to get into, I left everything in my room. I hid valuables in my rucksack and under my mattress. I locked the windows and door and took the key with me, but when I got back everything was gone. They took my camera, film, Walkman, cash, electric razor – anything they could sell. I think it was an inside job because the room was locked when we got back, but I couldn't prove it. I spent all day getting a police report, but the insurance company in England wouldn't pay out because my belongings weren't in the safe. So no matter how dodgy the safe looks, always use it or you won't get any compensation.

Kenneth McPhee, 33

Travellers' Tales

I hadn't travelled widely, and hadn't travelled on my own, when I decided to go to Australia for a while. I was due to change planes at Hong Kong, but just as we were about to arrive I noticed that the plane on the little map on the video screen showing where you are suddenly switched from heading to Hong Kong to flying back out to sea. We couldn't land in Hong Kong due to a typhoon, so, after flying around in circles for a while, we ended up landing in Taiwan. We were kept waiting at the airport for eight hours. No one told us what was happening and we couldn't understand the language, so it was a bit worrying. Eventually our passports were taken from us and we were informed that we'd be staying the night in a hotel in Taiwan. At the hotel I was told I'd be sharing a room with two elderly women who'd also been on my flight, which was fine until we got to the room and there was only one bed. We were told it was big enough for three! The next day, we were put on a flight to Hong Kong, where I had to wait 11 hours for the next flight to Sydney. When

I arrived I was exhausted and had already missed a day of my holiday. I had pre-booked a hotel from England, fortunately, so went straight there and had a good sleep. I had a great time in Australia and hope to go back. One word of warning though: I had taken out insurance, but it didn't cover me for the delay, or for missing my first night's accommodation at my hotel, because the typhoon was considered an Act of God!

Emma Payne, 22

Travellers' Tales

A friend and I went diving in Honduras, but didn't know that the diving school was a bit of a cowboy outfit. They didn't train us properly, and took us into water that was too deep. My friend's equipment was faulty, and he ran out of air. He surfaced quickly while holding his breath, which is the worst thing you can do. One of the instructors got him back to the beach, but a couple of hours later he started coughing up blood. A doctor told us he should go into a decompression chamber, but the nearest one was in Florida.

They said, 'If he's going to die it will be in the next 20 hours, so you'd better get him to hospital quickly.' We tried to get off the island and eventually managed to get a charter flight on a dodgy old plane, then a bus back to Guatemala and went to the nearest hospital. He was kept in hospital for observation, but it all turned out OK in the end. He was incredibly lucky.

Before leaving the UK we'd taken out medical insurance, and I'd complained at how expensive it was. But once that happened, I was so thankful we were covered. Who knows what would have happened if we hadn't been.

Sian Williams, 29

Chapter 9 / **Health Matters**

An alarming number of travellers leave the country without bothering to take any medical precautions, yet many travel health problems can be avoided with a bit of foresight and sensible planning before you go and by following a few simple rules while you're away.

Vaccinations

The first step towards a healthy trip is booking an appointment with your GP or travel clinic to sort out which vaccinations you need and when. You should do this *at least* a couple of months before you go. Don't leave it to the last minute: some vaccinations take time to become effective; some have to be administered in stages, or can't be given at the same time as other vaccinations. You need to provide the doctor with the following information:

- Which countries you'll be visiting and when;
- How long you'll be there;
- What kind of areas you'll be visiting (rural or cities?);
- What your living conditions are likely to be (tents, straw huts or five-star hotels?);
- What existing allergies or illnesses, if any, you have;
- Whether or not you're pregnant (or soon likely to be);
- What medication (including the Pill) you're already taking.

In exchange, the doctor should tell you which vaccinations you need (both to meet official requirements and for your own health), how much they'll cost, for how long they'll protect you and what possible side-effects there might be.

Keep a record of which vaccinations you receive and when.

Some clinics give you a 'health passport' or form on which details of dates and vaccinations are recorded for easy reference and for showing to officials. Carry the form with your passport.

The cheapest source of jabs is your GP. Some vaccinations (e.g., typhoid, hepatitis A and polio) are available on the NHS, so your GP should provide these free (or just for the cost of the prescription). Other vaccinations (e.g., rabies, diphtheria, Japanese B encephalitis) are not available free on the NHS, and whether or not your GP charges you for them (and how much) seems to be down to the luck of the draw – the rules differ from one clinic to the next. Some GPs may also charge a small fee for entering your vaccine details on your form; others will do it free of charge.

You can also have your jabs at a travel clinic (see the end of this chapter for contact addresses or look in Yellow Pages). Prices vary greatly, so shop around. Having all the required vaccinations can cost a hefty whack, especially if you're going to a Third World country (you can easily end up spending £100 plus), so it really is worth checking out all the options rather than booking into the first travel clinic you find. When you're comparing prices, remember that some vaccines are given in two or three doses, so check whether the price quoted is per dose, or per completed vaccination. Some clinics may charge you a consultation fee if you're asking for advice, though this may be refundable against the cost of your vaccinations if you have them done there.

Potential Health Problems

This is a selective list (in alphabetical order) of some of the more common or widely publicized travel ailments or worries. It's not exhaustive but you may still feel, looking at it, that perhaps the world is too dangerous a place for travelling. However, you should remember that the chances of catching some exotic disease are actually very remote – most travellers return home having experienced nothing more serious than the occasional bout of diarrhoea.

Remember, though, that just because you've had a full course of jabs doesn't mean you're invulnerable. In fact, the illnesses you're most likely to come into contact with are those caused by consuming contaminated food and drink, and for many of these there is no vaccine. It's therefore important to take care of your health while you're away, both by watching what you eat and drink (see p. 92) and by guarding against insect bites (see p. 85).

Altitude sickness can occur above 10,000 feet (3,000 metres) and can be fatal. Symptoms may include dizziness, sickness, headache, lack of coordination, breathlessness, fatigue, sleeplessness, loss of appetite and coughing. If you're affected, there are drugs you can take (available on private prescription before you leave the UK), but it's better to take preventive action. It takes your body a while to acclimatize to high altitude, so you should avoid going straight off on a mountain trek, especially if you've just flown in somewhere that's already at high altitude. Spend a few days getting used to the height and, when you do start to ascend, do it gradually. Any trek should ascend no more than about 1,000 feet a day and should include rest days to allow your body to adapt. Even then you may be affected. Don't let yourself be pushed further or faster than it's safe to go because of peer pressure. The simplest remedy is to descend to a lower level. If you have respiratory or heart problems, you should avoid spending much time at very high altitude. Even if you are in perfect health, allow yourself some time to acclimatize. Remember also that the thin air at high altitude will give you little protection against sunlight. Take plenty of sunblock and apply it frequently.

Bilharzia (also known as schistosomiasis) is caused by tiny larvae found in freshwater lakes, canals and rivers. Water close to human habitation is particularly likely to be infected, but infection is not a problem in salt water so the sea is OK. It's found in most of Africa, but also in parts of the Middle East, South America and South-East Asia. Larvae can penetrate the skin and, once in your body, develop into worms which produce eggs. You can help reduce the risk by frequent application of waterproof insect repellent, and by drying yourself thoroughly and rapidly as soon as you leave the water (the larvae can't survive out of water). No vaccination is available, but the disease can be treated once you have it.

Cholera is spread via contaminated food and water and is a problem in any area where sanitation is poor, especially in Asia, Africa, South America and the Middle East. The best way to avoid it is to take care over what you eat and drink (see p. 92). A vaccination is available but is not very effective. Some G P s won't give it; some may (for a fee) give you a vaccination certificate without actually giving you the jab. This can be useful to have, as although immunization is no longer officially required by any country, the authorities in some countries may still, very occasionally, ask for proof of vaccination. If there is a cholera outbreak, they may also administer compulsory vaccinations – better to have it done in this country where you don't have to worry about how clean the needle is or how often it's been used before. Given as a single injection, the vaccine's effectiveness, such as it is, lasts for three to six months.

Cuts and scratches. Take care with minor injuries in hot climates, as they can become infected more easily than they would at home. Clean well, put antiseptic on them and cover with a plaster or dressing.

Diarrhoea. All the vaccinations in the world can't protect you against the illness you're most likely to come into contact with. Delhi belly, Montezuma's revenge, the Turkey trots – call it what you will, diarrhoea affects most travellers at some time, to a greater or lesser extent. However, you *can* take sensible precautions (see p. 92). If you get diarrhoea: drink lots of water to prevent dehydration; eat only plain foods; stay out of the sun; forget alcohol and milk. It usually clears up on its own after a couple of days, but if necessary (if you have to make a long journey, for example) Imodium is an effective remedy, and a rehydration solution (e.g.

Dioralyte) replaces lost minerals. If the diarrhoea is accompanied by fever and the passing of blood or mucus, seek medical advice. If you're on the Pill, remember that diarrhoea or vomiting can reduce its effectiveness so you should take extra precautions for the rest of your cycle. For more information, call the London School of Hygiene and Tropical Medicine's recorded telephone information line on diarrhoea: 0891 600 272.

Dengue fever, a viral infection carried by day-biting mosquitoes, occurs throughout the tropics, in Asia (it's recently returned to Singapore), the Caribbean and South America (especially Colombia). The disease lasts between a week and ten days but has no long-term effects. Although not fatal, it is extremely painful. There is no vaccine or known treatment so it's important to avoid getting bitten in the first place (see p. 85).

Diphtheria is caught by close contact with an infected person and is found especially in tropical countries with overcrowding and poor sanitation, and also in parts of Eastern Europe. You were probably vaccinated against this as a child, but that doesn't give lasting immunity, so if you're going to an infected area and are planning to spend time with local people, you should consider having a booster, which is effective for ten years. Diphtheria may sometimes be given in a combined vaccine with tetanus.

Dysentery. There are two types of dysentery – amoebic and bacillary – both spread via contaminated food and water and common in the tropics, especially India and Africa. There is no vaccine against either form but they can be treated with antibiotics. The most important thing is to take steps to prevent dysentery by taking care over what you eat and drink (see p. 92).

Giardiasis is caused by the giardia parasite in infected food and water and seems to be on the increase. It is common in North Africa but is also found in other parts of Africa, Iran, India and even Eastern Europe. It may start like diarrhoea but will last much longer if not treated. No vaccine is available but it can be treated with antibiotics. The best ploy is to take great care over food and drink.

Heatstroke or sunstroke is brought on by overheating, so take things easy and don't do anything too active in the hottest part of the day (do as the locals usually do and have a siesta instead). Early warning signs include nausea, headache, hot red skin, and light-headedness. Get into the shade straight away. If possible, lie down in a cool room, with a fan or air conditioning. Loosen any clothing and use water to cool your body. Drink plenty of water.

Hepatitis A (also known as infectious hepatitis) is spread via contaminated food and water or from person to person in areas of poor sanitation. It is more common amongst backpackers and hikers than amongst other tourists – yet it is preventable with a vaccination. A gamma-globulin vaccination (a big jab in the bum) shortly before travelling takes effect immediately and helps protect you for three to six months. However, if you're away for longer or travel frequently, two injections of the Havrix vaccine (a small jab in the arm), four to six weeks apart, will protect you for a year; if followed by another, six to twelve months later, it will give you protection for up to ten years. The Havrix vaccine takes between two and four weeks to become effective, so if you leave vaccination to the last minute you'll have to go for the gamma globulin. Vaccination is recommended anywhere outside Northern and Western Europe, North America, Australia and New Zealand. You should also take great care over what you eat and drink and over personal hygiene (see p. 92).

Hepatitis B is more severe than Hepatitis A and is highly infectious. It is transmitted, like HIV, via infected blood or body fluids. A vaccine is available (given as three injections over a period of six months, and providing protection for five years) but can take six months to become effective. It's recommended only for travellers who will be living for long periods in high-risk areas (which include parts of Asia, South America, Africa and Eastern Europe). You should protect yourself by not engaging in high-risk activities (such as unprotected sex, using infected needles, having a tattoo or acupuncture).

HIV/AIDS. HIV is widespread throughout the world and there is no vaccine or cure for either HIV or AIDS, so it's important to be aware of the risk of contracting it when you're travelling. It's easy to get carried away when you're out in a hot climate, meeting attractive fellow travellers from around the world and drinking the night away together. Excessive alcohol consumption on holiday can blur your normally good judgement, and you're much more likely to make silly mistakes while you're travelling than you would at home. Don't get so carried away by holiday romance that you forget the rules of safe sex – always use a condom. In countries like Australia and America, reliable condoms are readily available, but take a supply with you for countries where the local versions might be suspect. Visiting prostitutes, especially in places like Thailand and East Africa, is highly risky and just asking for trouble.

If you're travelling in developing countries where medical facilities are sparse, carry a sterile medical kit to reduce the risk of HIV contamination through dirty needles, syringes and other medical equipment (see chapter 9). In the unlikely event that you need a blood transfusion, ask for screened blood. Reduce your risk by avoiding unnecessary medical or dental treatment. Remember that tatooists' needles can be infected too – don't have a tattoo or get your ears, nose or anything else pierced unless you're absolutely sure the equipment is sterile.

Japanese B Encephalitis is a viral inflammation of the brain, spread by daytime-biting mosquitoes. It occurs in rural parts of Asia and can be fatal, so you should consider vaccination if you're going to be travelling in rural areas of those countries, especially during the monsoon. Two (sometimes three) jabs, taken one or two weeks apart (and sometimes followed by a booster a year later), provide protection for up to three years and should be given at least a month before you leave to allow time for the full course and for the vaccine to take effect.

Leishmaniasis is transmitted by sandflies and can be fatal. Although rare, it occurs in parts of Asia, Africa, South America and the Middle East. It can cause skin scarring or various internal infections. No vaccination is available but it can be treated. The best thing is to guard against being bitten in the first place (see p. 85).

Malaria is transmitted in tropical areas by mosquito bites. As long-haul travel has boomed, so has the incidence of malaria in the UK. Each year at least 2,000 British travellers return having contracted malaria abroad – and some of them die. It's *essential* to take precautions if visiting an affected area. This includes much of Asia, Africa and South America (and even some places you might not expect, such as parts of Turkey). Having said that, many areas where you might expect to need malaria tablets (e.g., much of Thailand, Malaysia, Indonesia and South Africa) are actually malaria-free, so don't just assume that if you're going somewhere hot and tropical, you *must* take them. As most malarial prophylactics have some side-effects, you don't want to take them unless you have to. Lariam/mefloquine, in particular, has had much criticism, and we know many people who've experienced problems with it.

Which anti-malarial tablets to take will depend on where you're going. Strains of malaria vary in different parts of the world, and mosquitoes in some areas are developing resistance to certain drugs, so always get up-to-the-minute advice from your GP or travel clinic – don't just listen to what your friends say. Some malaria tablets are available over the counter, including chloro-quine (Avloclor/Nivaquine) and proguanil (Paludrine) but meflo-quine (Lariam), now being prescribed for areas where mosquitoes have become resistant to chloroquine, is available on private pre-scription only and costs a bomb (around £3 per tablet plus a £6 fee for your doctor for writing a private prescription).

Start taking the tablets a week or two before you reach the malarial area (taking them after a meal) and follow instructions on how long to continue after you leave (usually a further four weeks).

Always ask your doctor about potential side-effects (which, depending on the tablets, can include hair loss, skin problems, disruption of sleep patterns, panic attacks and nausea) and find out if there are alternatives.

Even anti-malarial drugs aren't 100 per cent infallible – the best protection of all is to avoid being bitten in the first place (see p. 85). You should be particularly vigilant between dusk and dawn, which is when most biting takes place. However careful you are, there are no guarantees that you won't be bitten, so if you fall ill with flu-like symptoms after you've been travelling in a malarial zone (even as long as six months or a year after you left it), contact a doctor and let them know where you've been.

The London School of Hygiene and Tropical Medicine has a recorded telephone information line on malaria medication: 0891 600350.

Meningococcal Meningitis, found in much of Africa and parts of Asia, Central America and the Middle East, is spread by close contact with an infected person and can be fatal, but is treatable with drugs. Vaccination (one injection) takes two weeks to become effective and gives three to five years' protection.

Natural hazards
• Jellyfish. In Europe these are generally not lethal but can give you a painful sting, so check with the locals before you swim. If you are stung, there's little you can do other than to rub the area with dry sand or neutralize the sting by bathing the affected part in vinegar or alcohol. Poisonous jellyfish are found in Australia, parts of Asia and the Pacific; if stung, you need to get medical attention. In Australia during stinger (poisonous jellyfish) season, make sure you swim only on beaches that have nets to protect bathers.
• Corals and anemones can give you a nasty graze, which can become infected, so look out for them. If they are present you may need to wear shoes in the water.
• Sea urchins have sharp spines: if you know they're there, wear shoes when swimming. If you tread on one and get a spine stuck

in your foot, remove it as soon as possible, using ointment or olive oil to soften the skin and spine first.

• Snakes are generally more scared of you than you are of them and won't attack unless they feel under threat. You're highly unlikely ever to come across one, but if you're walking in snake territory, keep your feet and legs covered with thick boots and trousers, and make plenty of noise as you walk so any nearby snakes are warned in advance. Don't stick your nose into under-growth or trees. In the unlikely event that you are bitten, keep the limb as still as possible or you'll increase the blood flow – put a splint or bandage on to help immobilize it – and get to a doctor. Try to give a description of the snake so that they know what anti-venom to give you. Don't take aspirin as that will also increase the blood flow. Remove any rings in case of swelling.

• Spiders can lurk in all kinds of places (under the toilet seat, in your empty shoes, etc.), but again, most will scuttle a mile from you given the chance and very few are dangerous (though you may feel happier always checking the toilet first and shaking out shoes before you put them on). If bitten, get to a doctor as soon as possible, and, as with snakes, try to give a description of the beast.

• Sharks are many people's big fear but hardly anyone dies from a shark attack – only a couple a year even in Australia. Always heed local advice on when and where it's safe to swim.

• Wear flip flops or sandals when you're in the shower or wading in a stream to prevent burrowing thingies getting into your feet.

Polio (Poliomyelitis) is spread via infected food and drink or by contact with an infected person. Most of us are immunized against polio as children, but you should have a booster (taken orally) if you are travelling to areas where the disease is still found (which means anywhere outside Northern and Western Europe, North America, Australia and New Zealand). The vaccine (either the full course of three doses or one booster) is effective for ten years.

Prickly heat is a nasty and maddening rash that occurs when your sweat glands are blocked, and can be a problem in high humidity. Guard against it by wearing loose clothing, preferably in natural fibres. If you get prickly heat don't scratch, however desperately itchy you are. Take a cool shower, soothe the skin with calamine lotion, talcum powder or one per cent hydrocortisone cream, and cover up so that you can't scratch.

Rabies occurs in all continents except Australia and Antarctica, though individual countries on other continents are rabies-free or low-risk. A vaccine is available: given as a course of three jabs over 28 days, it gives you two to three years' protection but does not, however, give you total immunity. If you're bitten by a rabid animal, you'll still have to have another two injections. If you don't have pre-exposure jabs, you'll need a course of seven injections over a period of months. (Either way is a huge improvement on the old treatment, which was a horrendous course of needles in the stomach.) Avoid strange animals, however cute and tame they look – and that applies to *all* mammals, not just dogs. Remember, also, that you don't have to get bitten – even just a lick or a scratch can be enough to infect you. The World Health Organisation claims over 20,000 rabies-related deaths a year in India; it has also been estimated that between four and seven per cent of street dogs in Thailand are infected. If bitten or scratched, wash the wound immediately and put alcohol on it if possible. The most important thing is to get medical help *immediately* if you think you've been at risk – if treatment is given straight away, the disease can usually be prevented from developing, but once the symptoms of hydrophobia start to show, it's too late and the disease is fatal.

Tetanus is a dangerous disease caused by bacterial spores entering the body through a cut, scratch or other wound. The spores are found all over the world so you should make sure your tetanus protection is up to date wherever you're going. It's particularly important if you're likely to be in remote areas with no access to medical facilities. You were probably vaccinated against tetanus at school, but you will still need a booster dose if you haven't had one in the past ten years. The vaccine (either a full course of three injections at one-month intervals, or one booster) is effective for ten years.

Tick-born encephalitis is an inflammation of the brain caused by a bite from an infected tick. It can be a problem in forest areas of Northern and Central Europe, Austria and Scandinavia, especially where there is heavy undergrowth. It's most common in late spring and summer. Make sure you keep well covered up in affected areas and take precautions not to be bitten (see p. 85). A vaccine is available.

Travel/motion sickness. Whatever form of transport you're using (train is favourite), try to get a seat in the area with least movement – in the middle of the middle decks on a boat, for example (and the larger the boat, the better); in between the wings on a plane. If possible, lie down and close your eyes. Alternatively, keep your eyes focused on something fixed, like the horizon. Sit near the front of a bus or in the front seat of a car, look forward rather than out of the side windows and don't read books or maps. Fresh air helps, so keep the window open.

Avoid eating greasy or rich foods before you travel. Indeed, don't eat or drink too much of anything (even water) – the more you have the sicker you'll feel. Steer clear of alcohol altogether. If you take any travel sickness medication, remember that most include drowsiness among their side-effects so you should not drive after taking them. Check the packet to see how far in advance of the journey you need to take them (usually two to four hours) – they're unlikely to be much use if you leave it until you start throwing up. You could also try elasticated wrist bands that work on your acupressure points and have no side-effects. Ginger in various forms is also said to be an effective remedy. See chapter 10 for more travel tips.

Tuberculosis is on the increase world-wide. You were probably immunized against it at school (it's the BCG immunization); if so, you don't need a booster. If not, and if you're planning to spend a month or more in Asia, Africa or Latin America (especially if you're going to be in close contact with the local people), you should consider getting immunized. You should talk to your doctor at least two months before you go because you'll need to have a skin test first to see if you're already immune.

Typhoid is transmitted via contaminated food and water, so is particularly prevalent in countries with poor standards of hygiene. Typhoid jabs used to be particularly unpleasant, with side-effects such as headaches, fever, vomiting and diarrhoea (a brief taste of the disease itself). However, the new vaccines don't have the same side-effects. Available as an oral dose or injection, they provide one year's or three years' protection respectively and need around ten days to take effect. Typhoid vaccination is recommended for most of Africa, Asia, and Central and South America.

Yellow fever is a viral infection transmitted via bites from insects such as mosquitoes, ticks and flies. It can be fatal. Vaccination may be compulsory for visitors to some African and Latin American countries, where the disease is endemic. Other countries may also insist on proof of vaccination from travellers coming *from* an infected region. The vaccination (a single jab) must be given at a designated yellow-fever vaccination centre, who will issue an internationally recognized certificate as proof you've had the jab. To allow time for it to take effect, it must be given at least ten days before you travel – if it isn't, your certificate won't be valid. Immunity lasts for ten years.

Repelling Insects

Diseases such as malaria, dengue fever, yellow fever and Japanese B encephalitis are spread by insects in tropical climates. Even in cold climates, mosquitoes and gnats can be a nuisance and give you a nasty bite. So it makes sense to take all precautions to avoid being bitten.
• Avoid camping by stagnant or slow-moving water as this is where mosquitoes and other insects lay their eggs.

- At peak biting times (from dusk to dawn for mosquitoes), wear thick cotton trousers and long-sleeved tops as a barrier against bites (light colours are better than dark).
- Use a good-quality insect repellent, both indoors and out. Repellents come in a range of forms: lotions, gels, creams, sprays, sticks and soaps. Recommended makes include Autan, Jungle Formula and Ultrathon. The most effective repellents are those containing DEET, but it's powerful stuff so treat it with respect, especially if it's in a high concentration. Use sparingly, keep it away from the eyes, and avoid it if it causes a skin rash. If you have sensitive skin, some swear by Avon's Skin-So-Soft bath oil or a daily vitamin B supplement. You could also use Mosiguard.
- Your repellent will last a shorter time if you are sweating profusely, in which case wrist or ankle bands impregnated with repellents can be useful. Cotton clothing can be impregnated with DEET and should be kept in a plastic bag when not being worn.
- Mosquito coils are usually widely available as you travel, though good repellent can be hard to find, so it's worth taking a stock with you.
- Try to ensure that your accommodation is mozzie-proof. Look for rooms with insect screens on the windows and check that the screens are intact. If there are holes or gaps, plug them with sticking plaster or similar. Clear your room every evening with a knock-down spray containing pyrethrum. Overnight, you can get protection from burning mosquito coils or using small electrical hot-plates fitted with tablets which vaporize slowly over up to ten hours. These work best in sealed rooms; otherwise, place them upwind. Electrical buzzers have been proved to be totally useless in tests.
- Look for rooms with a mosquito net round the bed or carry your own (you can buy them in travel stores and clinics), preferably impregnated with a repellent. An impregnated net will also keep out sandflies, whose bites can cause leishmaniasis. It can sometimes be a problem finding somewhere to fix your own net up – you could carry some sticky hooks to use if there aren't any hooks on the wall already. Take care the net is not torn, fill any gaps

with cotton wool and tuck it in well all round. Try not to touch nets. If there is no net, a fan blowing over the bed can help, as can a heavy cotton sheet. You're also less likely to be bitten in an air-conditioned room.

If you are bitten, don't scratch your bites – they'll just become more swollen and inflamed and may become infected with bacteria. Put tiger balm, tea tree oil or other antiseptic cream on as soon as you're bitten.

The London School of Hygiene and Tropical Medicine has a recorded telephone information line on 0891 600274 with advice on avoiding mosquito bites.

Medical Treatment Abroad

If you're travelling within Europe, get hold of Form E111, a certificate which entitles UK nationals to free or reduced-cost emergency medical treatment in other European Economic Area countries – i.e., EC members, Iceland, Norway and Liechtenstein. You should be aware, though, that it doesn't cover repatriation and is no substitute for a proper insurance policy. You'll find an E111 application form in the Department of Health leaflet T5, *Health Advice for Travellers*, available at health centres, post offices and travel agents or by calling Freefone 0800 555777.

There are forty more countries around the world with which the UK has reciprocal health-care agreements that entitle you to emergency medical care. These include Australia, Hong Kong, New Zealand, Russia, some Caribbean islands and some East European countries. The Department of Health leaflet T5 has full details of what the agreement covers in each one.

For the rest of the world (indeed, most of the world), however, you're on your own – and that includes such popular destinations as the US, India, the Far East, Africa and Latin America, so you must take out full medical insurance if travelling to these areas (see chapter 8). We get so used to free treatment on the NHS in the UK that it's easy to forget that falling ill or having an accident abroad can end up landing you with a bill for thousands of pounds.

Before You Go

Dentist
If you haven't been to the dentist for a while and you plan to be away for a long time, have a check-up a month or so before you leave. You can buy dental emergency kits to take with you, but it's better to get any potential problems sorted out before you go. Dental treatment abroad can be costly and/or risky.

Optician
If you wear glasses or contact lenses, ask your optician to tell you what your prescription is so that you can replace them while you're away if they are lost or damaged. If you can afford it, treat yourself to a pair of prescription sunglasses. Take a spare pair of lenses or glasses with you, or buy yourself a cheap pair somewhere like Bangkok or Hong Kong. Even if you usually wear lenses, take glasses with you as a back-up – there are times (on dusty desert roads or at altitude, for example) when wearing lenses can be uncomfortable. You should also take eye drops in case of minor eye infections (fairly common among travellers in hot countries). The big pain about contact lenses is the weight of the solutions you have to carry. If you're going off the beaten track you'll need to take enough to see you through, but if you'll be visiting plenty of big cities along the way you should be able to pick up solutions as you go. Alternatively, you could consider getting disposable lenses.

GP
If you don't already know your blood group, get your G P to test it before you go; knowing it will save time in the event of accidents.

First aid
Consider taking a basic first-aid course before you go, especially if you're going to be spending much time away from major population centres and medical facilities. Contact the St John Ambulance Brigade or St Andrew's Ambulance in Scotland for details.

Are You Fit to Travel?

Consider how fit you are before you embark on anything too ambitious. Trekking through the Himalayas, walking the Inca Trail or rafting down the Colorado River call for a great deal of physical exertion, and if you're planning anything active, you should start preparing at least a few months before you go. If you don't already have one, establish a regular exercise routine and work your way up to the trip gradually. Swimming, cycling and other aerobic exercise will boost the efficiency of your heart and lungs and increase your stamina, while weights will help build up strength in your legs and arms.

Even if you're not out there conquering the great outdoors, travelling can be exhausting. Sleepless nights, long journeys, soaring temperatures and humidity, extremes of temperature and altitude can all take their toll. Some people cope better than others, but the better your general fitness, the greater your enjoyment will be.

If you have a medical condition such as angina, asthma, diabetes or epilepsy, carry an identity card or wear a tag giving details and names of any medication you're taking.

What to Take with You

If there are any regular medicines you need, take a supply of these with you (pack them in your hand luggage in case your baggage goes astray). Your doctor may only be able to prescribe a limited amount, so check whether or not they will be available in any of the countries you're going to. Keep a note of their generic names (rather than particular brand names), because they may be sold under different brand names abroad. Some medicines available in the UK may be restricted abroad; if in doubt, check with the relevant embassy or high commission or call the Home Office Drugs Branch on 0171 273 3806. (It may also be the case that any medicines you're given abroad are illegal to bring back into the UK, so if you're carrying anything you're not sure about when you come back home, declare it at Customs.)

Make sure that all medicines are clearly labelled and keep them in their original containers rather than decanting them into smaller, unmarked ones which may look suspect to Customs and border officials. You should also carry a doctor's letter explaining that you require these medicines for personal use (your doctor may charge for writing this).

Take a sterile medical kit if you're going to be travelling in countries where hygiene is poor and where needles and other medical equipment are reused. You can get these in travel shops, chemists and from MASTA (Medical Advisory Services for Travellers Abroad: 0171 631 4408). You can buy sterile equipment separately, but ready-made kits will have a selection of the necessary items and will also look less suspicious to Customs officials than a few loose syringes and needles in your washbag. Get a doctor's letter explaining that they are for use in case of emergency. If necessary, they should be handed to a doctor or nurse to use.

If you're on the Pill, ask your doctor for an extended prescription so you'll be covered for the time you're away. Remember to take time differences into account when working out when to take your pill – if you normally take it when you go to bed, you may have to change to breakfast instead. If you do get sick while you're away, remember that it will reduce the effectiveness of the Pill. Take condoms as a back-up.

You should take a mini first-aid kit. Either make up your own or buy a ready-made one and add to it. You should include the following items:

- a broad-spectrum antibiotic (ask your doctor's advice on which to take and when to use it);
- anti-diarrhoea remedies (e.g., Imodium);
- antihistamine cream (for bites and stings);
- antiseptic or antiseptic wipes (for cuts and scrapes);
- aspirin or paracetamol (painkiller);
- bandages and safety pins;
- dressings;
- blister kit (if trekking);
- indigestion tablets;
- malaria tablets;
- multivitamins;
- plasters;
- oral rehydration powders (e.g., Dioralyte); in an emergency you can make your own by dissolving 1 level teaspoon of salt and 8 level tablespoons of sugar in 1 litre of safe water;
- sore-throat lozenges;
- travel-sickness tablets (ginger capsules are a natural alternative);
- eye drops;
- some means of water purification;
- tiger balm, which you can buy *en route*, is good for dealing with insect bites and aches; tea tree oil is good for bites and burns.

If you're prone to cold sores, they can be triggered off by hot climates, so take some Zovirax or another cold-sore cream. You might also like to consider an anti-fungal powder as athlete's foot can be a problem in tropical countries.

When You're Away

Watching What You Eat and Drink

The best health precaution you can take when travelling is to keep a careful eye on what you eat and drink. Many diseases are spread via contaminated food and water, but following these precautions should help safeguard you to some extent.

• Always wash your hands before eating.

• Avoid tap water. Use only bottled water for drinking and even for cleaning teeth. Bottled water is available in most places but check the seal is intact before you buy (if you go for fizzy water you can be absolutely sure it isn't actually tap water). Don't have ice in drinks (you can cool them by packing ice outside the glass).

• Boiling water kills germs so you're usually OK with hot tea and coffee. There should also be no problem with bottled soft and alcoholic drinks.

• Be wary of salads (which may have been washed in tap water).

• Only drink fruit juice if you're sure it isn't diluted with water.

• Water in rivers, lakes, swimming pools and the sea can also be contaminated, so try not to swallow any water when you go swimming.

• If you're vegetarian you should be wary of dishes using pulses or legumes that have been soaked in water and cooked slowly at a low heat – the bacteria may not have been destroyed.

• Off the beaten track, make sure you have some way of purifying water, either in tablet or tincture form or by means of a portable purifier or filter. Tablets are small and light to carry though some (especially the chlorine-based ones) leave an unpleasant taste. They're also convenient if you want to purify water in a café, etc. If you're using water-purifying tablets follow the instructions closely, and bear in mind that you should not take iodine-based tablets for a prolonged period of time. Alternatively, you can take a filter or a purifier which pumps water through a chemical filter to render it instantly drinkable. These are more thorough than tablets but also more expensive and bulkier to carry. Boiling water for two to three minutes (longer at altitude) is the most effective way to make it free from infection; if you cool it in a clean, covered container it will stay safe for several days.

• Yoghurt is generally safe to eat (and eating a little when you first arrive will help accustom your stomach to the local bacteria), but avoid ice creams and other dairy products made from un-pasteurized milk.

• Fish and shellfish can be dodgy, especially if eaten raw (e.g., oysters).

• Steer clear of food that has been reheated or kept warm – buffets in particular are a breeding ground for bacteria – and go for food you *know* has been freshly cooked, such as omelettes, piping-hot fried or deep-fried dishes, or something cooked in boiling water, and eat it while it's still hot.

• It's better to have meat well-cooked, even if you normally prefer it rare.

• Avoid uncooked foods and only eat fruits you can peel yourself.

• Don't assume that food in posh hotels will automatically be safe, and avoid dishes which involve a lot of handling to prepare.

• Look at the place you're thinking of eating in – is the food covered or is it swarming with flies? Does it look fresh or has it obviously been sitting round for a while?

Handling the Heat

It's been said a million times before but we'll say it once again: go easy on the sun. Sunstroke is no joke; neither is skin cancer. And do you really want to have that leathery look later in life? Even in the UK, UV rays can damage your skin – and the nearer the equator you go, the stronger those rays are, so the more careful you need to be. Bear in mind also that sun can be reflected off sand, water and snow.

• Don't set straight out for some serious sunbathing the minute you hit a hot climate – work up gradually. The joy of extensive travel is that there's plenty of time for you to build up a golden suntan – so there's no excuse for succumbing to the kind of suntan panic that hits people when they only have one week to go brown.

• Make sure you always protect your skin with a high-factor sunscreen (SPF15 at least) or sunblock. If you'll be in and out of the water a lot, make sure to get one that's water resistant. You may already have your own favourite suncare product, but after years of trying different ones, our own favourite is Clinique's Oil Free Sun Block. You can also buy sunscreens that contain an insect repellent, which will help cut down on the number of bottles you have to lug around! If you're feeling self-conscious about being glaringly white (which marks you out as a beginner), put some fake tan on before you leave.

• Whichever sunscreen you use, reapply it frequently, paying particular attention to sensitive areas like your neck, nose, ears and, if you're lying on the beach, nipples and the soles of your feet.

• Sun lotions are readily available in most places but the choice may be limited, so if you have sensitive skin or prefer a certain brand, take enough supplies with you.

• If you're sunbathing, set sensible limits and stick to them: don't 'just give it another fifteen minutes' and don't be fooled by hazy or cloudy weather or breezes – you can still burn, and surprisingly quickly. Remember, however bad you think your pasty skin looks, it looks a hell of a lot worse when it's beet red and peeling.

• Always stay out of the sun between 11 a.m. and 3 p.m. when it's at its fiercest.

• Follow the Aussie slogan of 'Slip, Slop, Slap': slip on a shirt, slop on the sun lotion, slap on a hat.

• Buy a decent pair of sunglasses (with a UV filter) to protect your eyes.

• Remember that you can burn even in water, so if you're going snorkelling wear a T-shirt to protect your back and use waterproof lotion on exposed parts of your body.

• Always drink plenty of fluid in hot climates so that you don't get dehydrated (don't wait until you're thirsty). If you notice that your urine is dark in colour, it shows that you need to drink more water. Other early warning signs of dehydration are thirst, lethargy, nausea and weakness.

• Make sure you're eating enough salt to compensate for the amount you're losing in sweat.

Pacing Yourself

Friends can be one of the biggest health hazards on holiday. It may be grossly unfair (OK, it *is* grossly unfair), but just because your mate can lie all day in the sun without burning doesn't mean you should follow her example. And the fact that your boyfriend has a cast-iron constitution that allows him to feast on shellfish and ice-laden drinks from day one, doesn't mean *you* can too. Your friends may have no problem swimming out to that little island, but if you know you're a weak swimmer don't even think about it. Never feel pressurized to keep pace with others: stay safe and healthy by knowing your own limits and sticking to them.

When You Come Home

Remember that some diseases don't produce symptoms immediately. If you feel unwell or notice unusual symptoms after your return, visit your doctor and explain where you've been travelling.

Travel Clinics and Advice Lines

• **British Airways Travel Clinics**. There are about 40 BA Travel Clinics around the UK – call Talking Pages free on 0800 600900 for details of the one nearest you. You can also find the British Airways Travel Clinic Web page on http://www.british-airways.com/bans/lworld/clinic.htm

- **The Health Control Unit** at Heathrow Airport (0181 745 7209) can provide immunization advice.
- **Hospital for Tropical Diseases Travel Clinic Healthline**, 4 St Pancras Way, London NW1 0PE. For advice and information call the Travel Clinic's pre-recorded healthline on 0839 337722 or 337733 (calls charged at 39p per minute cheap rate/49p per minute at all other times). For appointments only, call the clinic on 0171 388 9600.
- **Liverpool School of Tropical Medicine**, Pembroke Place, Liverpool L3 5QA; 0151 708 9393 (pre-travel advice and queries); 0891 172111 (recorded advice line).
- **MASTA** (Medical Advisory Services for Travellers Abroad), London School of Hygiene and Tropical Medicine, Keppel St, London WC1E 7HT (0171 631 4408). For detailed advice on health abroad, call the MASTA Travellers' healthline on 0891 224100. A recorded message talks you through your itinerary, and a health brief tailored to your journey is then drawn up and sent by return first-class post. It includes any Foreign and Commonwealth Office advice as well as information about immunizations and malaria. The line is open 24 hours a day, 7 days a week; calls are charged at 39p per minute cheap rate, 49p per minute at all other times. If you're planning to visit more than six countries, call 01705 553933 first to find out which countries to leave on the answering service.
- **Pro-Choice Traveller** is a service offered by high-street chemists and Tesco in-store pharmacies (look for the traveller-health-information sign in the window). You give them the details of your trip; they give you a personalized advice print-out with current medical recommendations, plus general health tips.
- **Nomad Travellers' Medical Centre**, 3–4 Wellington Terrace, Turnpike Lane, London N8 0PX (0181 889 7014).
- **Thomas Cook Vaccination Centre**, 45 Berkeley St, London W1A 1EB (0171 499 4000).
- **Berkeley Travel Clinic**, 32 Berkeley Street, London W1X 5FA (0171 629 6233).
- **International Medical Centre**, 32 Weymouth Street, London

WI 3FA (0171 486 3063) and 131–5 Earl's Court Road, London SW5 9RH (0171 259 2180).

- **Tropical and Communicable Diseases Department**, Birmingham Hartlands Hospital, 45 Bordesley Green East, Bordesley Green, Birmingham B9 5SS (0121 766 6611).
- **Travel Advice**, Ruchill Hospital, Bilsland Drive, Ruchill, Glasgow G20 9NB (0141 946 7120).
- **Leeds Overseas Travellers' Clinic**, Leafield Clinic, King Lane, Moortown, Leeds LS17 5BP (0113 231 9548).
- **Trailfinders**, 194 Kensington High Street, London W8 7RG (0171 938 3939).
- **Prestel** carries health information (updated daily) on page 50063.

Useful Books

Stay Healthy Abroad, Rob Ryan (Health Education Authority Publishing).
Travellers' Health, ed. Richard Dawood (Oxford University Press).
Health Information for Overseas Travel (Department of Health; available from HMSO, 0171 873 9090).
The Tropical Traveller, John Hatt (Penguin).
Health Travel – Bugs, Bites and Bowels, Dr Jane Wilson Howarth (Cadogan Books).

Ten Foods You Don't Get at Home (Usually)

Roasted guinea pig (South America)
Cold fried ants in chocolate sauce (Brazil)
Monkey brains (China)
Bear's liver liqueur (Hong Kong)
Sheep's eyes (Middle East)
Double-boiled deer's penis (China)

Dried antelope (South Africa)
Kangaroo steak (Australia)
Pig's uterus (Vietnam)
Goat's bone stew (Ethiopia)

Travellers' Tales

I spent six weeks travelling around India and fully expected to lose lots of weight. However, I'm proof that you can travel around India and actually come back fatter! Yes, I got the occasional bout of diarrhoea, but that's inevitable. I'm always very careful about what I eat when I'm travelling, especially at the start of a trip before my body's had a chance to acclimatize. I'm vegetarian, which probably helped in India – some of the meat looked decidedly dodgy and my meat-eating friend certainly got sick more often than I did. Even if you're a meat-eater normally, it might be best to become a vegetarian during your stay in India. I was also very wary of anything cloaked in mysterious sauces and tended to go for the drier curries. I was careful with what I drank too, sticking to bottled water and beer most of the time. We ended up in Goa, where the food was absolutely delicious – fabulous fresh seafood and great vegetable sizzlers. We ate anything we liked there and had no problems at all.

Anne Millen, 22

Chapter 10 / **Transport Tips**

Planes

Planes are undoubtedly the fastest and most convenient way to get from A to B but they take their toll on you physically, with the combination of changing time zones, lack of sleep, tension, dry cabin air, and cramped conditions. Follow our tips to make sure you reach the other end in the best possible shape.

• Set your watch to the time at your destination the minute your flight takes off, and try to adjust to the new times. If you can fall asleep easily, you'll be fine. If you're having trouble getting to sleep, ear plugs and an eyeshade may help. In extreme cases, a sleeping tablet can help – these are available on prescription from your doctor. Some doctors may be reluctant to prescribe them, but they should be helpful if you explain the situation. You need to take them half an hour or so beforehand and they last for six to eight hours.

• Jet lag can be a problem, particularly if you're flying long distances from west to east. You can feel tired, spaced out and below par, and your body clock will be completely out of sync. so that you don't feel like sleeping or eating at the right times. Some experts suggest that it takes a day to recover from each time zone you fly through – so, if you fly from the UK to India, six hours ahead, you'll be affected for six days. It helps if your flight lands in the afternoon, local time, so you just have time to relax, settle in and have a meal before you go to bed. Arriving in the morning means you have to struggle through a whole day feeling awful. Different people have different ways of fighting jet lag but there's no guaranteed solution. However, great claims are being made for melatonin supplements, which can be bought from health stores. Other homeopathic remedies include arnica and camomile tea. The more rested you are, the quicker you'll recover, which is why some people swear by sleeping tablets.

• Don't forget to reconfirm all flights three days in advance or you'll be bumped off if the flight's busy. If you can't speak the language, the hotel or hostel staff may do it for you, or visit the office in person – most airline offices are downtown. You should also double-check that any special meals (vegetarian, kosher, etc.) have been ordered.

• If there's a particular part of the plane you want to sit in, most scheduled airlines will accept pre-booking of seats on long-haul flights so you don't have to take pot luck at the check-in desk. Ask your travel agent to do this for you, then double-check with the airline that the request has gone through.

• A seat next to the window gives you more chance of getting to sleep as you have something to lean against. An aisle seat makes it easy for you to come and go without disturbing anyone else, but isn't good for trying to sleep – people in the inside seats will want to get past. Seats next to the emergency exits are best for leg-room. The worst seat to have is a middle seat in the middle block. Avoid seats near the toilets if you don't want to be constantly disturbed. If you want to watch the movie, try not to get the seat right behind the bulkhead where you'll be sitting directly under the screen.

• Sucking sweets, chewing gum, yawning or swallowing does help to clear your ears when the pressure changes, especially on take-off and landing. Flying with a cold can be very painful – take a decongestant shortly before take-off to help.

• Walk round the plane now and again to stop yourself getting stiff.

• Every travel expert around recommends that you avoid alcohol when you're flying, and there's no doubt that that's the sensible thing to do. But we have to come clean and admit that, for us, one way of coping with the tedium of long-haul flights is to hit the duty-free as soon as the trolley comes round. And if you're setting off on a big adventure, it seems miserable not to take advantage of the free champagne on offer! That said, moderation is, as ever, the key word. Avoid dehydration, which makes jet lag worse, by making sure that you drink plenty of water (still, not sparkling) and fruit juice too. Don't smoke, and don't take sleeping tablets if you have had any alcohol.

• If your ankles and stomach tend to swell, wear loose clothes and shoes, take regular walks round the plane and do leg and ankle stretches and rotations in your seat. Avoid fizzy drinks.

• To counteract the dehydrating effects of flying, moisturize your skin throughout the flight. Regular spritzes with a mineral-water spray are wonderfully refreshing.

• If you wear contact lenses, the cabin air will dry them out. Remove them for the flight and wear glasses instead. Keep your lens case and solutions in your hand luggage.

• Fear of flying is widespread. If you're a nervous flyer, try to distract yourself by taking a really gripping book with you, listening to your favourite calming music, watching the in-flight movie or listening to the comedy channel. Learn some relaxation or deep-breathing techniques before you go and use them on the plane. Sleeping tablets can help, but never mix them with alcohol. You could also try homeopathic remedies such as argent. nit. to calm you, or aconite. Or try pure essential oils: put one drop of lavender and one drop of geranium oil on a tissue and hold it to your nose.

• You know how disgusting airline food can be, so make sure you take some healthy snacks with you, especially if it's going to be a long flight.

• Always remove luggage tags and airport stickers each time you arrive somewhere new – if you leave them on as souvenirs, you run the risk of baggage handlers getting confused and sending your bags on somewhere else.

• Finally, make it easy on yourself by booking in somewhere comfortable for the first couple of days so that you can come round gently (most travel agents will do good deals on accommodation).

Train Journeys

Trains have to be the most civilized form of transport. They're also (outside Europe) one of the cheapest and definitely the most fun. You'll meet lots of people and have the chance to see some marvellous countryside and scenes of rural life.

• When buying a ticket, try to go with a local or someone who knows what they're doing. The system can be confusing, especially if you don't speak the language. You may have to queue at three different windows before you get your ticket (or, as we did in Canton, spend two days going to every single window and still not manage to work out how to get one. Travel tip: It's easier to get out of Canton by boat!).

• If people approach you trying to sell you a ticket, be careful – if you can't read or speak the language, it's easy to be palmed off with a ticket that's out of date, or going to a destination other than the one you want.

• Arrive early to make sure you get a seat – and to allow for the inevitable problems in finding out which platform the train is leaving from and if it really *is* the train you want.

• In most Third World countries, people besiege the train at every stop, selling food, drink and fans. We've also been offered slightly more unusual items such as live chickens and caged rats on an Indonesian train. On the Trans-Siberian, you'll even get the chance to snap up a patchwork leather jacket or fluorescent track suit from one of the Chinese traders on board or, rather more to our taste, Russian champagne for $2 a bottle.

• Unless you're on the most minimal of budgets, avoid Third Class on Third World trains – or save it for the shortest of journeys. Carriages are inevitably crowded, uncomfortable, noisy, smelly and dirty.

Cars

- Many travellers, especially in Australia and America, buy a car on arrival and sell it at the end of their trip. When buying a vehicle, don't admit you're a traveller who'll only be around for a couple of months. If the seller thinks you've come to live for a while (and that you'll therefore be able to come back if anything goes wrong), you're less likely to get ripped off. Choose a car that's in good working order and take it for a test drive before you buy.
- You can also contact car-hire companies and ask if they need a car delivered to another city. All you have to pay for is the petrol and accommodation costs *en route*, which makes it a very reasonable form of transport, especially in America, where petrol is cheap.
- If you're planning to drive while you're away, make sure you get an International Driving Permit before you go, because very few countries will accept your British driving licence alone. They're available from the AA, price £3.00, and are valid for one year. You'll need a passport photo and your driving licence.
- See chapter 11 for advice on staying safe on the road.

Boats

- Seasickness can be a real misery. If you're prone to it, make sure you carry a remedy such as Dramamine. It also helps to remain in the centre of the ship where there is least movement, avoid looking at the water (keep your eyes closed or fix them on the horizon instead) and be very careful about what you eat and drink. Other than that, all you can really do is lie down and pray for sleep. As a general rule, big boats are better than small ones. See also chapter 9 for travel sickness tips.
- In some Third World countries boats are potential death traps.

You may not always have a choice, but if possible try for the one that looks most seaworthy and has plenty of lifejackets. (If you can't see any, ask where they are.) If you think the boat is getting overloaded (they'll try to cram on as many paying passengers as possible), get off and take the next one.

Buses

Buses are usually the cheapest form of public transport – with good reason. In some countries they transport not only people, but live animals, bales of hay, pots and pans, enormous bags, beds, turkeys, sacks of oranges – it's amazing how much can be squeezed in . . . They're also the least reliable mode of transport. Road conditions in many developing countries are appalling, and even the word 'road' is an imaginative description of the pothole-filled, muddy track you find yourself juddering along. That said, there are many small towns and villages that are only accessible by bus, so you're bound to spend quite a bit of time on them.

• Try to keep hold of your luggage rather than letting someone whip it off you and put it on the roof. If it's going into a luggage compartment under the bus, wait to see the compartment closed before you get on.

• On overnight trips, try to get two seats to yourself – in some countries you probably won't have much chance, but in places like Australia it should be possible. Even if you're travelling with a friend, book yourself into solo seats rather than side by side.

• If you're prone to travel sickness, avoid the back seats. Sit near the front and keep your eyes on the road ahead rather than looking out of the side window. Or put your Walkman on and close your eyes until you reach your destination! Don't read. See also chapter 9 for travel sickness tips.

• In India, especially, roads are littered with burnt-out or crashed wrecks, so if you're a nervous passenger, don't take a window seat.

• If you're busing it round the Third World, you'll find a lot of your fellow passengers suffer badly from travel sickness (especially on mountainous, twisting roads) and throw up for much of the journey. It's wise to keep the windows shut, however hot you are – otherwise, when the person in front of you is sick out of the window, it will blow back in *your* window. (We speak from experience on this one.)

Hitchhiking

• Read guidebooks and ask around to find out if hitching is both accepted and generally safe in the country you're going to. In New Zealand, for example, it's very much the norm and millions of travellers have hitched safely there. In Islamic countries, and parts of South America and the States, it's probably not such a good idea.
• In less developed countries, hitchhikers are expected to give the driver some money.
• Check that you know the correct sign to make – a thumbs-up sign is considered very rude in some countries. You may have to point down and waggle your hand.
• Never hitch alone, especially if you're a woman.

Cycling

Cycling is a great way to get to out-of-the-way villages and places that can be hard to reach by public transport. It's also a good way to meet people, who'll be intrigued and probably highly amused by the sight of a foreigner pedalling by on a bike.
• Travel light. Cycling can be hard work, especially in hot climates and hilly countryside. The more you can keep your baggage down, the better. That said, you must carry enough tools with you to carry out emergency repairs, and enough clothes to keep you warm if you get stranded in the middle of nowhere.
• Make sure you always have plenty of water with you.

- Remember that you don't have to cycle everywhere – if you fancy a break, you can load your bike onto trains, buses or planes.
- Make sure you have a comfortable saddle, wear padded shorts and take over-trousers for rainy weather.
- Don't do any strenuous cycling in the heat of the day – take a siesta instead and get back on the bike when the sun is less fierce.
- The Cyclists' Touring Club (CTC), Cotterell House, 69 Meadrow, Godalming, Surrey GU7 3HS, produces information sheets on cycling itineraries including the Karakoram Highway, Panama to Tierra del Fuego and London to Tanzania. Members also get advice on technical problems, specialist insurance, a free bimonthly magazine and a handbook with accommodation, technical and touring advice. Membership is £25 per annum.

Travellers' Tales

My friend and I wanted to travel across the States and decided the cheapest way to do it would be to do a driveaway – you pick up a car in one city and deliver it to another. You don't pay for any rental; all you pay for is the petrol, which is very cheap in America. We went to a driveaway agency in New York (we found the address in our guidebook) and they had about five long-distance driveaways to choose from. Most of them were to Florida but we decided to take one to Seattle instead. We stopped off at a few places *en route* – Chicago, the badlands of North Dakota, Yellowstone, Banff National Park in Canada and Mount Ridgemore. The trip was cheaper than we expected. Unfortunately when we got to Seattle we parked the car illegally and it was towed away. We had to spend two days trying to find it – and £300 to get it out of the car pound!

Sharon Wilcock, 30

Travellers' Tales

I was meeting friends in Dali, a small town in Yunnan, south-west China. At the time, the only way to get there was to take a 14-hour bus ride from Kunming along the old Burma Road. My guidebook said the scenery was spectacular, but I didn't see any of it. The road was narrow and twisty with heart-stoppingly sheer drops, and far below us we could see the mangled wreckage of buses that hadn't made it. The buses were ancient – they were sent from Poland when the Poles considered they were no longer usable! Few had glass in the windows, so if it rained you got wet (we wondered why the driver was wearing one of those little umbrella hats when he got on!). To make things worse, the Chinese are very bad travellers and suffer from motion sickness. Half of them were sick on the floor; the other half were chomping chicken feet and God knows what else and spitting the bones out on to the floor. The bus halted a few times for a toilet stop, but there was no toilet – just a field where everyone, men and women, squatted down together. I could hardly enjoy my time in Dali, a very lovely little town, for thinking of having to endure the trip again at the end of my stay.

Diana McDermott, 29

Travellers' Tales

I adore trains, so for me the highlight of a recent trip round South-East Asia and China was coming home on the Trans-Siberian. We left Beijing at 7.30 on a Wednesday morning and arrived in Moscow the following Monday afternoon. The people on the train were a real mix of personalities and nationalities and we all got on very well. The buffet car was the social centre of the train. Everyone would meet there in the morning and spend the time swapping travel stories, playing cards and drinking cheap Russian champagne. We got off to stretch our legs and take photographs at Ulan Bator, Novosibirsk and Irkutsk. From Moscow, I travelled on by train to Warsaw, then to Berlin and Amsterdam. My aim was to travel from Beijing back to Glasgow by train all the way but I ran out of time in Amsterdam (I had a job to go back to) and had to fly from Amsterdam to Glasgow.

The most interesting thing about the trip, from a personal point of view, was that I was a bit older than other backpackers. But travelling's a great leveller – I was amazed at how easy it was to get on with people of all ages, backgrounds and nationalities and I kept in touch with quite a few people afterwards.

Elaine O'Shea, 38

Ten Surefire Topics of Conversation

The British Royal Family
Football (especially Manchester United or Liverpool)
The Beatles/Michael Jackson
Your husband/wife
Your tragic lack of husband/wife
Your age
How much you earn
Why you don't have children
Your curly hair/freckles/big feet
What you think of the country you're travelling in

Chapter 11 / **Staying Safe**

There has been much debate about the risks faced by young travellers. After recent media stories of tourist kidnappings in Cambodia and Kashmir, the murder of British backpacker Johanne Masheder by a Thai monk in early 1996 and the trial in Australia of the man who murdered several young hitchhikers, potential backpackers and their parents may be feeling a bit nervous. However, statistics from the Foreign and Commonwealth Office show that the most dangerous destinations for British tourists over the past five years have been the US, South Africa and Spain.

Common sense is your biggest asset when it comes to staying safe abroad. Most crime is opportunistic and by following a few basic rules you lessen the risk of falling prey to thieves or muggers. Remember, though, that no matter how tight a budget you may be on, you're rich compared to most of the people you meet in Third World countries, so you're an obvious target. Be particularly vigilant during the first week or two – you're at your most vulnerable when you've arrived in a strange country tired, jet-lagged and not yet in the travelling groove.

Reassure friends and family by talking through your route, showing how much thought and planning you've put into it, how aware you are of safety concerns, how sensible you're being and what your plans are for keeping in touch.

Your Belongings

• Keep a close hold on your daypack (even wearing it on your chest instead of your back to stop anyone snatching it). Never leave it hung over the back of a chair or lying at your feet.

- A bicycle lock is useful for attaching backpacks on to racks on trains and buses.
- Some travellers recommend lining your rucksack with plastic-coated chicken wire to thwart thieves who try to slash your pack. You can also buy Saklocks, especially designed for rucksack buckles (see chapter 13).
- Unfortunately, fellow travellers are among the main culprits when it comes to theft. Keep a close eye on your possessions when staying in dorms and camp-sites and don't leave valuables lying around. Don't leave anything unattended on the beach.
- Keep your camera in your daypack rather than around your neck.
- Budget accommodation often means faulty door locks or windows that don't close properly. To make your room more secure take a padlock with you and add it to the one supplied by the hotel whenever you go out. There are also various security devices available from travel shops that secure the door from within – or a simple door-wedge jammed underneath will help. Don't leave belongings within reach or sight of the window. Avoid rooms on the ground floor.
- Don't wear expensive jewellery or pull out wads of cash. Don't take items of jewellery that have sentimental value. The rule is: if you can't bear to lose it, don't take it.
- One of the worst things to lose is exposed film with all your precious souvenir photos on it. Rather than carrying it around, consider sending it home (by mail or with a fellow traveller returning to the UK). Alternatively, have it developed *en route*, then send the prints home (they're too heavy to carry). You can then keep the negatives, or send them home separately (in case one packet goes astray).
- Watches are very nickable, so don't bother taking a valuable one with you. Digital watches are said to be less tempting to thieves.
- It's not unheard-of for seemingly friendly strangers to offer travellers food and drinks, which turn out to be drugged. The first you know about it is when you wake up hours later to find

your belongings gone. Be careful about what you accept from others.

• Thieves love trains. The Foreign and Commonwealth Office advises that anyone travelling on long-distance or international train services, particularly in Eastern Europe and Russia, should keep their train carriage door securely locked from the inside by tying it shut with wire or strong cord.

Your Money

• Don't carry your money in one place – spread it around your body.

• Count money in private.

• A cotton money belt that ties round your waist (or a wallet that hangs round your neck), under your clothes, is the safest place to keep your passport, money and valuables.

• Always keep some money in a pocket or purse, so you don't reveal your money belt every time you buy something.

• Avoid getting caught up in crowds – they're heaven for pick-pockets. Remember that children, however appealing or pitiful they might look, are as likely to make off with your money as adults.

• Don't wear a shoulder bag on the shoulder nearest the road – someone on a bike or in a car could snatch it off.

• Watch as your credit-card vouchers are printed and make sure only one copy is taken. Don't let anyone out of sight with your card – they could be running off multiple copies. Always fill in the total box clearly.

• Take care changing money on the black market (see p. 49). You should be particularly alert in big cities.

Scams to Look Out For

Foreigners are an easy target in some countries. Here's how some con artists attempt to part travellers from their cash.

• A 'policeman' asks to see your passport, which you left in your hotel. He says he'll have to fine you. If he's only after a small amount of money, pay up. If he asks for an outrageous sum, say you're happy to pay it but you'll only do so at the police station. Chances are, he'll settle for less and you can go on your way.

• Another trick of 'policemen' is to fine you for an imaginary offence such as walking on the wrong side of the road. The same rule applies as above.

• A taxi or cyclo driver persuades you to hire him for an hour or more but won't agree the fare in advance. 'Whatever you think,' he'll tell you. At the end of your journey, what you think the fare should be and what he thinks it should be are two very different things. You'll have to spend half an hour wrangling about it. Always pre-arrange the price.

• Having just got off a bus or train, your tuk-tuk/cyclo/cab driver tells you the hotel you want to go to is full, but he can recommend somewhere else that's very clean, not too expensive. He's probably getting a rake-off, so insist on being taken to your original destination – it probably won't be full.

• At the entrance to the grounds of a temple, you're asked to sign your name in a visitors' book and pay a visitor's fee of $5. When you get to the temple entrance you're asked to sign again and charged the real fee – 20p. The person who took your five dollars will be long gone.

Yourself

• Read about the culture and traditions of the country before you go, so that you don't unwittingly offend people. Check up on any unusual laws that might affect you – in Thailand, for example, you can be arrested for joking about their Royal Family, while defacing the currency is a criminal offence in Kenya and Tanzania.

• If you are warned against travelling in a certain area, take heed. Insurrectionist and guerrilla groups are increasingly targeting tourists as a means of getting their voices heard internationally, so venturing into areas you've been told are high risk isn't a good idea. Keep abreast of the news when you can. Talk to other travellers so you're aware of events that might affect your travel plans. Don't travel into restricted areas (e.g., the Punjab area bordering Pakistan) without a permit.

• Steer clear of public demonstrations – crowd behaviour is unpredictable and things can quickly turn nasty.

• When you are due to arrive in a strange town, study the guide-book before you get there and work out a route to your prospective accommodation *before* you set out walking. Try not to stand out as a stranger or make it obvious that you're lost. Reading a map in the middle of a busy street advertises the fact that you're new in town. Walk confidently, as if you know where you're going.

• Try to avoid arriving in a strange city late at night. Always double-check the local arrival times of flights and whether or not there will be facilities open at the airport (toilets, cafés, bureaux de change). If you catch a taxi, make sure it's an official one and don't share it with strangers.

• Learn at least a few words of the local language so that you're not totally at the mercy of others.

• Avoid dark or badly lit streets. Steer clear of deserted beaches, alleys and parks at night.

- Only camp in official camp-sites.
- Don't try to fight muggers and thieves, especially if they're wielding weapons. Better to hand over your cash or whatever they want than to resist and risk losing your life.
- Don't go trekking without checking the weather conditions and forecast first. Always make sure someone knows where you're going and when you're expected to arrive or return.
- Don't take part in hazardous sports without first checking that good emergency medical facilities are available. Check that your insurance covers you for accidents (see chapter 8). Always follow any instructions or safety guidance the experts give you. And remember that activities like white-water rafting and bungee jumping *do* involve an element of risk. See also Water Safety, p. 117.
- However bolshie or unpleasant they're being, always keep your patience with officials.
- Be careful about what you photograph. Ask people's permission before snapping them. If you're in a politically sensitive area, don't even think about taking pictures of airfields, barracks, borders, bridges, etc., unless you want to be whisked off on suspicion of spying. Ask permission, too, before taking pictures in religious buildings.
- Remember you're bound not by the laws of the UK, but by the laws of the country you're in – however restrictive or ridiculous you may find them.
- You're more likely to be endangered by local transport than by the local people. Generally speaking, trains are safer than buses (especially overnight buses and especially in India, where the roadsides are littered with overturned vehicles). Any journey in a tuk-tuk or bemo means taking your life in your hands.
- If you change your travel plans, remember to let the folks back home know.
- Be sensitive to the local dress code. If they cover up, so should you – and that applies to men as well as women. Don't wear army-style clothes.
- Don't drink too much alcohol – you're an easy target if you're

drunk. Remember that in some countries (e.g. Egypt) you can be arrested for drunkenness. In Islamic countries such as Iran and Saudi Arabia, drinking any form of alcohol (if you can find it) is a serious offence.
• Consider investing in self-defence classes before you leave!

Just Say No!

In many countries, possession of drugs is a very serious crime, so the only sensible advice is to steer clear of them completely. Carrying even a small amount of drugs through Customs, especially in countries such as Singapore and Thailand, is a huge risk and punishments can be far more severe than in Europe, regardless of the quantity or type of drugs involved. Never agree to carry someone else's bags through Customs or put anything belonging to them in your rucksack. Life imprisonment or the death penalty can be the price you pay. In some places, such as Goa or Ko Phangan, the widespread use of drugs may lull you into a false sense of security, but remember that just because they're readily available doesn't mean they're legal.

On the Road

Many travellers, especially in America and Australia, buy a cheap car or motorbike to travel round in. It can be one of the best ways to see the country and gives you the freedom to get to places you can't reach by public transport. However, according to the Department of Health, traffic accidents are the major cause of death and injury among travellers, so make sure you stick to the basic rules of staying safe on the road.
• Don't drink and drive. Check the laws on alcohol limits for drivers in the relevant country – in some places, even one beer will put you over the legal limit.

- Always wear your seatbelt, whether or not it's a legal requirement.
- If you're on a motorbike, always wear a crash helmet – yes, it's great feeling the wind in your hair but it's not worth the risk. Make sure that your arms and legs are well covered – if you hit a pot-hole and come off your body will need as much protection as possible.
- Keep an eye open for wildlife. According to Richard Dawood's *Travellers' Health*, one survey of motorcycle accidents abroad found that 20 per cent involved collision with an animal.
- Before setting out, check that you are insured and that you're aware of the local driving laws. Take great care driving – conditions and habits differ abroad.
- Don't venture into the outback without plentiful supplies of water, food and spare cans of petrol.
- Keep the car in good condition so there's less risk of a breakdown. You should either have some basic knowledge of car maintenance or travel with someone who has. Make sure you carry tools and a spare tyre. A reflective warning triangle is also compulsory in many countries.
- Always lock car doors when you get out and when you're driving, especially in cities.
- Don't keep valuables on the seat – thieves can reach in through open windows (or smash closed ones). Never leave anything of value in a parked car.
- Keep the petrol tank as full as possible – don't leave it until the needle's in the red zone before stopping to get more.
- If anyone flashes you, or overtakes and signals that there is something wrong with your car and you should pull over, ignore them – it could be a scam. Keep driving until you reach a garage or other safe place to stop.
- When approaching your car, carry the keys in your hand and keep an eye out for other people around you. Check the back seat before you get in.
- If you think you're being followed, drive to a busy area where

there are plenty of people around, or to a police station. Do not lead the person back to where you're staying.
• Invest in a really good map, especially if you're going into rural areas.
• Learn the local words for petrol, oil, etc.
• Look out for specialist publications such as *Africa by Road* (Bradt) or *The Off-Road 4-Wheel-Drive Book* (Patrick Stephens Ltd).

Water Safety

Most travellers' accidents are caused through carelessness, especially when it comes to being in and around water. Staying safe is largely a matter of using your common sense.
• Never go swimming or take part in watersports or other activities when you've had too much to drink.
• Don't swim alone or at night. Midnight dips sound fun but are dangerous.
• Don't go swimming after a meal – you're more likely to get cramp.
• Don't dive into water without checking how deep it is first. Many people are paralysed every year as a result of diving into water that's too shallow.
• Before swimming in a strange sea, always check with locals or someone who's been there longer than you. Are there dangerous tides or a fierce undertow you should be aware of? Is the water heavily polluted?
• Never swim where there is a red flag flying.
• If using a lilo, take care not to drift out to sea.
• If you go scuba-diving while you're away, make sure you go with an operation that's recognized by a major diving association such as PADI (Professional Association of Diving Instructors), BSAC (British Sub-Aqua Club) or NAUI (National Association of Underwater Instructors).

Women Travellers

Outside Western societies, a woman, or women, travelling un-accompanied by a male will generate interest and, in rare cases, harassment. People of both sexes will immediately enquire as to the whereabouts of your husband. If you don't have one, the best defence is to invent one and say he's back at the hotel or you're on your way to meet him. Try saying he's on government business – that'll scare persistent men. Wearing a 'wedding' ring will help, as will carrying a photograph of a friend or relative's child and pretending it's yours. The status of wife and mother is often a form of protection.

Male-dominated Muslim countries can be hardgoing for women travellers – including parts of the Middle East, Africa (especially North Africa), Iran, Pakistan and areas of India. Some Latin American countries are also rather macho in their approach to Western female travellers. To avoid attracting unwelcome attention:

• Don't wear skimpy shorts or tight skirts. Cover arms and legs when entering a temple or any other place of worship. Watch how much the local women cover up and follow their lead.
• Be careful with make-up – even a small amount is a sign of being a 'loose' woman in some countries, as are smoking and drinking alcohol.
• Keep sunglasses on when talking to men and avoid making eye contact – they may construe it as a come-on. In some cultures it is also considered a sign of lack of respect.
• Without being rude, do not be over-friendly – it's open to misinterpretation.
• Walk confidently and speak assertively.
• Avoid night-time travel on your own.
• Don't discuss issues such as divorce, cohabitation or pregnancy with foreigners – your ideas may make you appear 'promiscuous'.

• The best thing to do with whispering and groping is to ignore it. If you start to get worried or scared, tell the person in a loud voice to leave you alone. Other people, especially women, will chastise him for being rude to a foreigner.

• If you're going camping on safari, or somewhere like northern Canada where there may be bears, try to go when you're not menstruating. Animals can smell your blood, so you need to be particularly cautious when out in the wilderness. You should also avoid wearing perfume and perfumed cosmetics.

• The Suzy Lamplugh Trust runs travellers' personal safety seminars around the country. As we went to press, they were also planning to publish a booklet on staying safe in 196 countries: call 0181 392 1839 for details.

Arresting Moments

When STA Travel and British Airways conducted a student survey early in 1996, they found that four per cent of respondents had been arrested while travelling. Reasons included:
• dancing in the nude in India;
• freeing lizards from a cage in a North African market;
• urinating behind a tree near the Kremlin;
• trying to cross the Swiss border in a caravan which was one inch longer than regulations permit;
• throwing tomatoes in Bulgaria;
• eating cookies on a bus in Texas.

Travellers' Tales

A girlfriend and I spent New Year in Goa. We'd heard about it being a good place for young people, with lots of parties, dancing on the beach, etc. What we hadn't heard is that the main part of tourist Goa is visited by the so-called Bombay Boob Bus, in which Indian men pay to come up from Bombay to see topless Westerners. Apparently they get their money back if they don't see any! They don't actually touch you, or even talk to you, but it was very irritating. Even if you're wearing a swimming costume, they'll sneak up and take your photograph. Because the drinking laws are more relaxed in Goa compared to other parts of India, things could get pretty heavy at night, though. Eventually we had to ask two British guys we met to pretend to be our boyfriends as it was the only way we could get any peace. Be warned!

Emma Marlin, 26

Travellers' Tales

I spent a year in southern and eastern Africa, five months of it in Zimbabwe. If you have only one big adventure during your time in Zimbabwe, make it a canoe trip down the Zambezi. It really is the best way to see wildlife and to be at one with nature. It's important to choose a reputable company with highly trained guides, because they will make or mar the trip. A good guide will open your eyes to all the marvels around you and alert you to the dangers – because a canoe safari is admittedly not without risks. Hippos, crocodiles and submerged tree stumps are the things to look out for! Hippos kill more people than any other mammal in Africa.

On an expensive trip, meals will be cooked for you and sundowners served. If you're roughing it, you'll all have to cook in rotation and set up your own camp. Either way, don't expect a toilet in the bush, or anything more than a bucket shower.

Hwange National Park is Zimbabwe's largest wildlife park. You can stay very cheaply in lodges, but you do need transport and, obviously, you can't camp independently or walk anywhere outside recognized areas.

The best way to arrive at Victoria Falls is by overnight steam train from Bulawayo then have breakfast at the colonial Victoria Falls Hotel. There's a caravan- and camp-site nearby. You can walk across the bridge into Zambia and spend a few hours in Livingstone.

If time is short, you'll find it difficult to get everywhere you want to go by local buses and trains. Remember that Africans are used to a journey taking days rather than hours, so there's no point in getting annoyed if a bus is delayed by a week or so. Travelling on a suspensionless bus is a wonderful way to get a feel for the country and strike up conversations.

Kathleen Corrigan, 42

Chapter 12 / **Keeping in Touch with Home**

Setting off on your big adventure, you may think the last thing you want to do is keep in touch with home – apart from sending postcards from exotic locations to make everyone feel jealous! But it doesn't have to be an emergency or a disaster that propels you towards a telephone. It could be on a parent's birthday, for example, or when you know your best friend is due to have a baby, that you feel the urge to get in touch. And, of course, it's important that friends and family can contact you in case of emergency.

Alternatively, if you're sentimental, you may worry about being so far from people you love for so long and missing them – but global communications are now so sophisticated that there's no reason for you to feel out of touch.

How Can Friends and Family Contact Me?

The Royal Mail will redirect your mail anywhere in the world if you are staying away in one place for a minimum of a month. Costs are £12 for one month; £26 for three months and £60 for a year. You can get an application form from the Post Office or telephone 0345 777888 to order a form or make a credit-card payment. If you're going away for up to two months, ask the Post Office about its Keepsafe service, which holds your mail for you so that envelopes don't pile up behind your letter-box advertising the fact that you're not around. Cost for up to two weeks is £5; for two months it's £15.

If you have no fixed address abroad but still want to receive letters from home, and you know roughly when you'll be in each place, ask friends to write to you c/o Poste Restante. This is a service that is available in main post offices in most of the world. The envelope should be addressed with your name (your surname should be in capitals and underlined), Poste Restante, Central Post Office, Bangkok (or wherever you're staying). There's usually no fee. When you're collecting mail, it's as well to check under your first name as well as your surname – letters can easily be misfiled.

There's no equivalent of Poste Restante in the States or Canada. If you're planning to stay in one place for any length of time you can rent a mailbox.

Type up a list of your destinations and approximate dates you'll be there and copy it to your friends and family. Drum into everyone the fact that mail can take weeks to reach its destination overseas and it's really not much use leaving it until three days before your birthday to post your cards to Bali.

If you have an American Express card, mail can be sent to an AmEx office and held until you collect it. Ask AmEx for an up-to-date list of their branches abroad before you go – speaking from experience, it can be extremely frustrating to turn up at a branch only to find it has moved. Be warned that most AmEx branches will only accept normal letter-size envelopes and won't take parcels. This service is also available to anyone using AmEx travellers' cheques. Telephone 0171 930 4411 for details.

How Can I Contact Home?

The simplest and cheapest way, of course, is to send letters and postcards home – and friends and family will never forgive you if you don't. Don't feel you have to write a six-page letter every week, though, or it can start to feel like a chore. Quick postcards are just as good to reassure your family that everything's going well.

Don't take your address book with you – it would be a disaster if you lost it. Copy the addresses out into a notebook instead, or take photocopies of the pages.

Telephone Cards

Some people believe the easiest way to ring home is simply to reverse the charges! However, if parents and friends are unwilling, or unable, to pay for your calls, you can take advantage of one of the increasing number of phone cards now available for travellers.

Most of them work on more or less the same principle. You are given a card, an account number and a PIN number which can be used in most countries. Each country will have a Freefone number which will connect you to an English answering service. All you have to do then is tap in your account number and PIN number, followed by the telephone number of whoever you're dialling. Calls can be made from private telephones, telephone boxes and most hotel phones. (Some hotels have cottoned on to this, however, and will add a few dollars charge for using your card.)

.The cost of calls depend on your card and where you're calling from. Some companies charge by the minute (so if your call lasts two minutes and seven seconds, you'll be charged for three minutes), others charge by the second. If you think you're going to be making lots of telephone calls, ring all the numbers given below and compare prices.

Different companies have different methods of payment. With BT and Mercury, charges can be put on to your normal home telephone bill. Interglobe, World Telecom, Sprint and AT&T insist that you pay on a previously authorized credit-card account. VisaPhone calls are charged to your credit card. World Telecom charge an annual fee of £20 – but then give you £20 worth of free calls. The other companies don't charge a fee.

Phone Card Charges and Contact Numbers

AT&T WorldPlus Service	5 mins from USA –	£7
(0500 897801)	5 mins from Aus	– £10
BT Chargecard	5 mins from USA –	£5
(0800 345144)	5 mins from Aus	– £8
Global Foncard Sprint	5 mins from USA –	£4
(0800 289751)	5 mins from Aus	– £5
Interglobe Phonecard	5 mins from USA –	£4
(0171 972 0800)	5 mins from Aus	– £7
Mercury Calling Card	5 mins from USA –	£5
(0500 100505)	5 mins from Aus	– £7
World Telecom Global Calling Card	5 mins from USA –	£3
(0171 384 5000)	5 mins from Aus	– £6
VisaPhone (details from card issuer)	5 mins from USA –	£3
	5 mins from Aus	– £5

Prices were correct at time of going to press, but ask the companies concerned for a current price list.

Airports and hotels often now have business centres from where you can send a fax. This is useful if you're in a different time zone and don't want to disturb the person at the other end. It's also cheaper than telephoning, but watch out for hotel surcharges. Ask the cost before you send anything.

Don't promise anyone that you'll ring home at specific times – e.g., every second Friday, or the last day of every month. Chances are, you'll find yourself paddling up the Orinoco that Friday, or on a bus in rural India, a hundred miles away from the nearest town. If you can't get to a phone, the person waiting for your call will worry that something's happened to you. Explain that you'll only ring when you can and that it probably won't be frequently.

Voicemail

Australia makes it easy for backpackers, offering several services you can use to help people keep track of where you are. You can set up voicemail so you and your family and friends can leave messages for each other or you can register with companies who will enter your movements on a database to keep note of where you are at any one time (you call in as you're going along).

Companies you can register with include:

Australia Backpackers Connection
PO Box 350, Mooroolbark, Victoria 3138
e-mail: austback@ozemail.com.au
ABC provide a fax and voice message forwarding service. They'll keep a record of your travel plans and will store any other important information such as your passport number and flight details.

BackTrackers Australia
PO Box 1490, Geelong Delivery Centre, Geelong, Victoria 3220
e-mail: backtrak@ne.com.au
On the Net at http://www.ne.com.au/~backtrak
BackTrackers' Travellers ring Free Call telephone number and give their route, which is then put on to the database. Message banks can be used by travellers and their families. A brochure is available in this country – telephone 01932 829030.

Travellers Contact Point
7th Floor, 428 George Street, Sydney
e-mail: tcpaus@ozemail.com.au
Agency that offers a mail and message service as well as providing information on work, accommodation and discount passes.

New companies are springing up every day – look for them in

backpacker publications such as TNT *Australia & New Zealand Travel Planner* (see chapter 16). For information on New Zealand, ring Contact Me on 0064 07827 3200 or Worldtel on 0064 09308 9357.

The Media

The BBC World Service, Voice of America and Australia Today are the three main international broadcasting stations that can be picked up on short-wave radios. *Worldwide*, a monthly magazine published by the BBC, gives listings.

Posting Parcels Home

If you want to send small gifts home (or send back guidebooks or clothes that you no longer need), surface mail is cheap and reliable, if slow. If you're staying away for a while, the fact that packages take up to three months to reach Europe shouldn't be a problem. Outside post offices in rural areas, there's very often a person who will take your parcel and wrap it up for you to comply with the local regulations, using lots of paper and intricately tied string, all finished off with a splendid seal. All you have to do then is get it weighed and attach your Customs declaration form, stating exactly what you're sending and how much it's worth.

Chapter 13 / **Good Kit Guide**

Rucksack/Backpack

Your choice of rucksack is vital – it's your key piece of equipment. You're going to be inseparable from it for months, maybe years, to come – you'll be carrying it for hours at a time, sitting on it, stuffing it into bus holds and on to train luggage racks, scrabbling through it . . . If you choose one that's uncomfortable to carry, fiddly to use or too flimsy to cope, you'll be cursing it all the way.

Don't cut corners on this one – it's worth investing in a high-quality pack that's durable and hard-wearing. Good names to look out for include Lowe Alpine, Berghaus, Karrimor and The North Face. Make sure that the straps and zips are sturdy (they'll be taking a battering) and check that the bag has a waist strap and chest strap, which help take the weight off your shoulders and distribute it more evenly. The pack should sit high on your shoulders, not slumped down on your lower back. Compression straps that will reduce the size of the pack when it's not full are useful – they make the pack neater and less bulky.

Try on several packs for size and comfort – they all vary in fit and size. If possible, put something in the pack to weigh it down so that you get a more representative idea of how it will feel. Ask the sales assistant to adjust the frame so that it's properly fitted to your body. The hip belt should sit snugly on your hip bone; the shoulder straps should curve round the shoulders (not sit above them). Watch it carefully as it's done (write the instructions down if you don't get any given to you) so that you'll know how to adjust it yourself if necessary.

Don't buy an enormous pack – remember, you have to carry it around and, if you have the space, it's terribly tempting to fill it. Rucksack capacity is measured in litres and most packs are between 55 and 100 litres. The averagely built man or woman going away for a year shouldn't look at anything bigger than 65 litres. If you're small, go for something below that. Even for a bloke, 75 litres would be pushing it. As a general rule of thumb, it's recommended that you carry no more than one-third of your body weight. If you're going to be camping and will be carrying a tent, sleeping bag, mat and cooking utensils, you'll obviously need more space than you will if you're going to be staying in hostels and hotels all the way (as many do).

If you're going to be doing a lot of trekking or will be carrying your pack for long periods, you should go for a conventional framed backpack. Some come with fixed-back systems; some with adjustable ones. If you can find a fixed-back system that happens to fit you it will be stronger and leave less room for things to go wrong. Otherwise, go for one with an adjustable-back system and have it fitted to your frame – this is also useful if you ever want to lend your rucksack to anyone else later or sell it on. Special 'ladies'' packs are available, with a shorter back. You may find some packs have an indication on the label as to what they're suitable for, e.g. inter-railing or adventure backpacking.

It's useful to get a rucksack with two separate compartments rather than one big one – it makes it easier to find things or means you can divide them into wet and dry, clean and dirty, etc. Or you can keep your sleeping bag in the bottom compartment. (It's always best to keep as much as possible inside your pack rather than strapped to the outside – that way it's less likely to be damaged or stolen.) Side pockets are useful but can also get in the way – once your rucksack is fully loaded, you may find you can't fit through doors, on to trains, and so on, without a real struggle.

If your trip doesn't involve much trekking, you may decide to go for one of the increasingly popular convertible rucksacks or travelpacks instead. These are packs that zip around the front and sides like a suitcase; they have padded frames and straps like normal rucksacks, but the straps can be zipped away behind a cover so that they turn into a soft suitcase – which stops the straps getting caught in luggage carousels and looks smarter if you're checking into somewhere a bit upmarket or going through border posts. One of the biggest advantages is that it's much easier to find things in a travelpack than in a conventional rucksack. Some travelpacks come with zip-off daypacks attached, but when zipped on full they make your backpack very bulky and are tempting to thieves. You're probably better off just getting a separate daypack.

You can buy a special big bag to put your rucksack into for protection when travelling – it keeps all the buckles and straps tucked away and also provides extra security (price around £15–18). When not in use, it folds up small. There are also bags that will cover up your pack but allow the shoulder and waist straps to be threaded through. These protect against wear and tear, keep out dust, dirt and water, and provide an extra barrier for thieves – and if you're trekking through the Borneo jungle, they will stop straps snagging on trees and creepers (prices vary according to your rucksack specifications but are around £20).

Most packs have waterproof fabric, but you can't make a pack wholly waterproof. Water tends to come in through stitching and zips. The bags mentioned above can help keep things dry, as can a rucksack liner. Or you can just make sure to pack everything in plastic bags.

Prices for backpacks start at around £70 and go up to £200, but you should expect to spend about £120 for a pack to take you on a year-long trip. Some packs come with a standard guarantee (which is basically your statutory rights); others may have a lifetime guarantee (but that applies only to you – if you sell it on to someone else the guarantee is negated).

You should also ensure that you can lock your bag. Look out for double zips that can be padlocked together – and when you're buying a luggage padlock, go for one with a combination lock rather than a key (too easy to lose). You can also now buy devices called Saklocks, which are specially designed to fit rucksack buckles and which stop people just clicking them open (cost is around £6 for a pack of two locks).

Daypack

You'll also need a daypack – a mini rucksack in which to carry the essentials from day to day (camera, water bottle, guidebook, etc.). Always keep a tight hold on your daybag – they're eminently nickable and are best carried in front of you rather than slung over your shoulder or on your back. Expect to pay between £20 and £30 for a sturdy one, though prices range from around £10 to £40. A small pack (say, 20 to 25 litres) would be OK for most travellers, but if you plan to go on any short treks (say, three to four days on the Inca Trail), leaving your main pack behind, you might consider getting a bigger daypack.

Sleeping Bag

Whether or not you think it's worth lugging a sleeping bag around depends on where you're going and when. If you're travelling through the Far East in the dry season, for example, you'll never take it out of its bag. The disadvantage of taking one is the weight and the amount of space it takes up. That said, it can be immensely comforting if you have to rough it – sleeping out in the desert where temperatures can plummet at night, or if you're doing overnight bus or train journeys where no bedding is provided. If you decide to go on a trek or organized tour while you're away, there are companies that hire out tents and sleeping bags.

Sleeping bags can be filled either with down or with synthetic material – each has its advantages and disadvantages. Down is one of the best insulating materials available and provides maximum warmth for minimum weight and bulk. High-quality down bags are unbeatable on insulation, are light and will pack up small. However, it's a problem if they get wet. Good synthetic bags, on the other hand, are catching up on down all the time. They're a bit heavier, but also cheaper and are not such a problem if they get wet, which is useful if you're travelling in very humid or wet places – and they'll dry faster.

It's important to keep your bag dry all the time, especially if it's down-filled, so make sure it's well protected in a waterproof bag. Hang it out to air when you get a chance, and when storing it for long periods take it out of the stuff sac and keep it loosely folded, somewhere dry. If squeezed into its sac it will lost its 'loft', the ability to trap air, which is what keeps you warm. If well cared for, a down bag may be good for 15–20 years' regular use; a man-made bag for 5–6 years.

The type of bag you buy depends on where and when you're going, and you should consult the staff of specialist shops for their advice. Bags come with a 'seasons' rating: 1-season (suitable for summer use); 2-season (summer/spring); 3-season (spring/autumn); 4-season (winter); 5-season (for serious polar explorers!). Remember that it's usually better to be too warm than too cold – if you're too hot you can just unzip the bag; if you're too cold you'll have a miserable night. Tapered, 'mummy'-shaped bags keep you warmer but can feel a bit claustrophobic, especially if you're a restless sleeper. You can even find 'ladies'' sleeping bags, which are shorter (why carry extra length you don't need?), slightly differently shaped, and come with extra lining at the bottom of the bag for cold feet.

Most travellers want something that's small, light, warm, and not too expensive – which can be tricky. As a general rule, small and light means high-tech materials and therefore a bigger price tag. And if a bag is small and light it's hard for it to be as warm as a bigger bag. Down bags are a good investment if you're a serious hiker and camper. However, synthetic bags are much cheaper and perfectly adequate for most backpackers. Two ranges of bags that would fit the bill for most travellers are the Snugpack Softie and Ajungilak Kompakt ranges. The Softie 3 weighs 750g and costs around £60; the Kompakt Ultra weighs 790g and costs around £90.

It's a good idea to use a sleeping-bag liner – this will keep the bag cleaner and is much more easily washed than the bag itself.

It also adds a bit of extra warmth, or, on hot nights, can be used on its own, like a sheet sleeping bag. If you've got a mummy-shaped sleeping bag, remember to get a mummy-shaped liner too.

If you already have a bag and can't afford to splash out on a new one, you can buy compression bags or harnesses that can reduce the bulk of your bag by up to 40 per cent.

Sheet Sleeping Bag

This is an absolute essential. If you're travelling somewhere hot, this will probably be all you need to sleep in. If you're staying in budget hotels where the sheets are less than pristine it's preferable to have your own – and some youth hostels insist that all travellers use a sheet sleeping bag. They cost around £12.

Sleeping Mat

This is probably another item that is best left at home unless you're doing a lot of camping out – but if you *are* camping out, you'll need something to protect you from the cold ground. A sleeping bag is only as good as the insulation beneath it and a sleeping mat has a big effect on how warm you are at night. Foam rolls are cheap (from around £13) but big and bulky to carry. An increasingly popular choice now is a Therm-a-rest self-inflating mat. They're a bit heavier than a foam mat (and, at £40–50, pricier) but they pack up smaller. They also come in different lengths so if you want to save a bit of weight and space you can get a three-quarter-length one.

Tent

A lightweight tent can be useful in Europe, where accommodation is often expensive, or in places like Australia and Canada, where it allows you to go off the beaten track more. However, many travellers, especially in Asia, will probably find a tent unnecessary. It means extra weight and less space, and cheap hotels and hostels can usually be easily found.

Don't buy a tent without putting it up first to see how it works and how simple it is. Would you be able to do it in the dark? Would it go up quickly in the rain or when your hands were frozen? Can you do it on your own or does it need someone to help you? Is there enough room between the inner tent and flysheet to store your backpacks? A-frames, the traditional triangular tents, are fairly stable and reliable but can be bulky to carry. Dome tents and tunnel tents are more roomy than traditional tents – but have lower wind resistance, which can be a problem on exposed mountain sides, for example. Geodesic tents are stronger but probably more than the average backpacker needs. If you're going to be camping in malarial areas, make sure the tent has a mosquito-net door.

Once you've bought a tent, practise putting it up and taking it down a few times before you go away. If you're travelling with a friend, split up bits of the tent between you – one can carry the tent, the other the pegs and poles. Try not to pack a tent when it's wet, and always brush off dirt, leaves, etc. before you roll it up.

For travel in hot countries, you'll probably be able to buy something fairly cheap – the YHA, for example, sells the popular Dome 2, suitable for late spring/summer use, for around £55, and there are similar tents around for up to £70. Otherwise, you're looking at £150 to £200 or even more.

Camping Gear

Again, most people don't really need to carry stoves and pans around, but if you're planning to do a lot of trekking or camping (outside organized trips), it might be worth investing in some cooking equipment. Bear in mind that some travellers have had stoves confiscated by Customs – there's not a lot you can do about it, though some have recommended dismantling them to pack.

Check out what kinds of fuel are going to be available in the countries you're going to. Things like Camping Gaz are widely available in Europe and the US but in the Third World you're more likely to find paraffin and petrol. Gas stoves start at around £17–20. Multi-fuel stoves that can run on different fuels (e.g., petrol, Coleman fuel, paraffin) start at £50–60 – as a general rule, the more fuels they burn, the more expensive they are. Check airline regulations before trying to take any form of fuel on board – most airlines ban all types of fuel in both hand and hold luggage.

When it comes to pans, aluminium is lighter and conducts the heat better; stainless steel is heavier and doesn't conduct heat as well – but there's no risk of Alzheimer's. The best bet is probably to go for aluminium pans with stainless-steel liners.

Cotswold have an advice line on outdoor stoves and food (01285 862140).

Water Bottle

Water bottles come in plastic and metal. Plastic is cheaper but may leak if not stored upright and can give the water a plastic taste. Metal is stronger and doesn't give an unpleasant taste. Sigg aluminium bottles are coated inside, and the coating won't crack if you drop or dent the bottle. Nalgene Trail Products produce unbreakable plastic bottles that have a liquid measure on the side (useful for purifying water), are guaranteed leakproof and can withstand extreme temperatures (so you could even use them as hot water bottles!).

Conventional water bottles take up room even if they're empty, but if space is at a premium you can buy collapsible water bottles that squeeze up small when not in use. They cost around £5 and can be used up to 1,000 times.

The best size of water bottle to buy is one litre, because most chemical water purification works on a one-litre basis.

Mosquito Net

Mozzie nets are essential if you're travelling in malarial areas. Many hotels will already have them over the beds, but you should carry your own just in case.

Look for a net that's been impregnated with Permethrin. As well as being an added insect deterrent, the impregnation allows the mesh to be wider, which gives a better flow of air through and makes the net less hot and humid to sleep in. (If it isn't impregnated, the mesh has to be smaller to keep out sandflies and other insects, which makes the net stuffy.) The Permethrin will break down eventually (through a combination of exposure to light and oil from your hands), so if you're travelling a lot and putting your net up and down every day, you'll need to reimpregnate it about every six weeks. When it's not being used, keep it in its bag.

Nets come in both single and double sizes, and in a variety of shapes. If you're carrying it round, you'll need one that's compact and lightweight. Prices for these start at around £20–25 for a single.

You won't always find hooks to hang your net on, so it's a good idea to carry some sticky plastic hooks to use if necessary. Alternatively, Travellers Gaffa Tape (about £2.50 a roll) can be used to stick your net to the wall – it also has a host of other uses, from sealing tears in rucksacks and jackets to closing doors.

Boots/Shoes

Many people find that trainers or walking shoes are perfectly adequate for their trip, so if you've already got a pair and are on a strict budget, stick with those. The only problem is that they're not waterproof.

However, if you know you're going to be doing a lot of serious trekking, invest in a good pair of hiking boots. At one time, these were always leather but now there are fabric boots too. Fabric boots are lighter and cooler to walk in, can be waterproof and are suitable for most travellers. Leather boots are not necessary unless you're planning lots of hill walking, scrambling, etc. Whichever type you go for, they need to be comfortable, provide good support to feet and ankles, cushion the feet from rough ground and keep your feet warm and dry. When trying them, take a pair of walking socks. For both leather and fabric boots you can pay anything from around £40 to £130, but many are between £60 and £90.

Whether you take boots or trainers, make sure you break them in *before* you go, rather than waiting until you hit the Inca Trail or Milford Track – you don't want to end up with blisters and bruises on the first day. Do a few trial hikes in them. Leather boots will need much more breaking in than fabric. Avoid Gore-Tex boots in very hot, humid or wet conditions (in the jungle, for instance) – they'll take ages to dry out; canvas jungle boots are better. Keep your toe-nails short to avoid bruising the toes; and after each day's walking, wash and dry your feet thoroughly and give them some fresh air.

Sports sandals or performance sandals are also worth considering. Basic models are around £15, but higher-range models, which are suitable for pretty serious walking, come in at around £40–60.

Outdoor Clothing

Fleeces are lighter than wool jumpers and just as warm. They are also easy to wash and quick to dry and, because they absorb so little water, can keep you warm even when wet. Polartec is a popular and effective fleece that comes in different weights; prices start at around £50–60. An alternative is a lightweight down jacket, which will pack up small, but is more expensive at over £100.

Even in hot countries, it's worth taking a lightweight waterproof (e.g., cagoule), preferably one that's breathable. These start at around £30. However, if you're looking at something that will protect you from wind, rain and cold, the price rises to between £150 and £300.

Reliable brands include Berghaus, The North Face, Lowe Alpine, Sprayway and Phoenix – but the array of fabrics and fibres on offer is baffling and ever-changing. They're getting lighter and more efficient all the time (and prices vary greatly), and the best outdoor clothing for you will depend on exactly what you'll be doing during your trip. It is best to go to an outdoor activity shop and ask for specific advice on the most suitable thing for your trip.

Bumbag

Bumbags are useful for keeping essential items to hand when you're out in the evening, or don't want to be encumbered by a pack. They should be big enough to take sunglasses, lip salve, sunblock, tissues, etc. It's safer to carry the pouch over your stomach than at your back. Costs vary but there are plenty at around £10–11. You can also buy Velcro-fastening wristband purses for times when even a bumbag is more than you want to carry.

Money Belt

This is one of the essential items and the best way to keep your passport, money, credit cards and other valuables. Money belts cost between £4 and £10. You can also buy 'normal'-looking belts, either fabric or leather, with a zip sewn in, in which you can keep an emergency stash of cash; they cost between £10 and £22. Or you could sew pockets in the lining of your clothes.

Security Gadgets

If you're worried about staying in rooms with dodgy locks, there are gadgets to secure doors and prevent them being opened when you're in the room – e.g. the Doorguard or Personal Door Lock (price around £6–8). Or some travellers recommend taking a simple door-wedge with you, to wedge under the door.

Torch

An absolute essential – for finding your way home along pitch-black lanes and beaches, for lighting things up when the inevitable power cuts happen, and for finding a toilet spot in the middle of the bush at night. The torch should be small but with a large enough beam to be useful and should also take a common size of battery (AA or AAA are both pretty widely available). It should also be strong enough to cope with knocks and bangs, and water-resistant. Maglites, which come in several different sizes, are our favourite and carry a lifetime guarantee. The Mini-Maglite comes, confusingly, in three different sizes: most popular is the one using two AA batteries, which costs around £16–17; the smaller one, which takes two AAA batteries, costs around £13–15. By unscrewing one end and putting it on the other, they can also be turned into free-standing lights, which can be useful.

We're also quite taken by headtorches – they may look silly but can be really useful if you're doing something where you need to keep both hands free, like cooking, erecting a tent at night, mending a car or writing postcards. The Petzl Zoom headtorch costs around £22–5, though cheaper models are also available.

Always keep your torch by your side at night, so that you don't have to scrabble round trying to find it. And remember to take a spare bulb with you – you probably won't be able to find them when you're away.

Penknife

An absolute essential, wherever you're going. There are lots of makes around but most travellers swear by their Swiss Army knives. Look for one that includes a corkscrew, bottle opener and scissors as well as the usual blades. Popular models include the Traveller, which costs around £20–21. Also good is the Huntsman, at around £24–6.

Camera

Most people like to take a camera travelling so they can record all the new sights and faces of the big trip. But cameras are eminently nickable, so you'll have to keep an eye on it at all times.

If you're a real enthusiast, you'll probably want to take a selection of lenses and other paraphernalia, but for most people an automatic compact camera is perfectly adequate – and takes up much less space. When you're buying a camera, weight and size are factors to bear in mind. Is it so heavy you'll get fed up lugging it everywhere? Is it small enough to fit in your pocket or bumbag? If you can afford it, go for a camera with a zoom lens. This is particularly useful on safaris or if visiting hill tribes, when you can't always get as close to your subject as you'd like.

If you buy a new camera, shoot a trial roll of film and get it developed before you go, so that you're sure you know how to operate it properly. Take the instruction leaflet away with you if you think you'll forget how to rewind, use the timer, etc. Keep your camera well wrapped up at all times – dust and moisture will do it no good at all.

You might also consider taking a disposable wide-angle or waterproof camera with you, if you're going somewhere with great scenic vistas or want to record your scuba-diving experience.

Don't worry about your film going through airport X-ray machines – most of them are now film-safe. However, if you're entering or leaving a country where the scanning equipment is very old, ask to take the film through by hand. Don't carry exposed film around in hot climates for too long – either process it locally if you're somewhere with good facilities, or post it home.

Equipment Stockists

There's no shortage of shops selling a wide selection of rucksacks, tents, sleeping bags and every little thing a traveller could possibly need. Prices can vary quite a bit, so it's always worth shopping around before you buy. You'll find branches of Blacks and YHA Adventure Shops around the country, but if you don't have a good shop near you, many of the companies listed below offer a mail-order service; call them for details.

- **LD Mountain Centre**, 34 Dean St, Newcastle upon Tyne NE1 1PG (0191 232 3561).
- **Blacks** have branches nationwide; ring 0191 417 0414 to find the one nearest you.
- **Call of the Wild**, 21 Station St, Keswick, Cumbria CA12 5HH (017687 71014).
- **Cotswold** have branches in London (Shepherds Bush), Manchester, South Cerney (near Cirencester), Southampton, Betws-y-Coed, St Albans and Reading. Call 01285 643434 for a catalogue.

- **Field & Trek** have shops in Brentwood, Croydon, Gloucester and Slough (01277 233122).
- **Karrimor International Ltd**, Petre Road, Clayton-le-Moors, Accrington, Lancs BB5 5JZ (01254 385911).
- **Nomad**, 3–4 Wellington Terrace, Turnpike Lane, London N8 0PX (0181 889 7014) and 4 Potters Road, New Barnet, Herts CN5 5HW (0181 441 7208).
- **Rohan**, 30 Maryland Road, Tongwell, Milton Keynes MK15 8HN (01908 618888).
- **SafariQuip**, The Stones, Castleton, Sheffield S30 2WX (01433 620320).
- **Survival Shop**, 11–13 Euston Station West Colonnade, London NW1 2DY (0171 388 8353).
- **Taunton Leisure**, 40 East Reach, Taunton, TA1 3ES (01823 331875).
- **Travelling Light**, Morland, Penrith, Cumbria CA10 3AZ (01931 714488).
- **YHA Adventure Shops** sell a large variety of travelling equipment (with a 10 per cent discount for YHA members). There are branches in Birmingham, Brighton, Bristol, Cambridge, Cardiff, Leeds, Liverpool, London, Manchester, Nottingham, Reading, Southampton (phone 01784 458625 for your nearest branch). Alternatively, they have a full mail-order service; call 0171 836 8541 for a copy of their catalogue. And they sell gift tokens if you want to get a present for a travelling friend.

Further Reading

If you're heading off for some serious trekking through the wilderness, you can find advice on equipment and survival in *The Backpacker's Handbook* by Hugh McManners (Dorling Kindersley).

Travellers' Tales

The first time I went on a long trip I borrowed a normal rucksack from a friend, but I got fed up having to unpack it every time I needed something that was at the bottom. The next time I was going away, I bought a convertible one, which makes finding things much easier. I also found it easier to pack. As I like to book into slightly more expensive places sometimes, it makes me look a bit more respectable, too. The other mistake I made the first time was to spend a fortune on very expensive hiking boots – a normal pair of trainers would have been just as good. The one thing I didn't take was a waterproof jacket – and I needed one almost everywhere I went.

Christina Ryan, 26

Chapter 14 / **What to Pack**

The luggage allowance on most international flights is limited to 20 kg per person. However, that doesn't mean you *have* to pack that much – it's best to keep it light, especially when travelling to hot climates where lugging a heavy rucksack around can be hell. If you're doing a trip round South-East Asia, for example, you don't need to take as much as you would for South America, where temperatures are more extreme and nights at high altitude can be cold. Remember that you can always send stuff home along the way (cold-weather clothes you don't need any more, for instance).

Clothes

Take clothes that are quick and easy to wash and dry (and that won't look *too* awful creased). Natural fibres are usually best for comfort. Patterned clothes don't show up dirt and creases as much as plain ones do. Dark clothes hide dirt, too – but they absorb heat, so light colours are better for hot climates.

Loose-fitting clothes are best for keeping you cool when it's hot, and can be layered on top of each other in cold climates. They also conceal the tell-tale bulge of your money belt. You should also wear loose-fitting clothes in countries where skin-tight items would offend local sensibilities. Clothes with pockets in are extremely useful, especially if the pockets are zipped.

Your list of what to take should include the following:

• Trousers. Loose-fitting cotton are best. Sweat pants are good if it's going to get chilly. A pair of leggings can also come in handy. Jeans aren't very good for travelling – denim is heavy and takes ages to dry.

• Shorts. Long and loose or cycling-style are both useful. Brief shorts may be O K on the beach or in Western countries but are not the thing for Third World travel.

• Skirts. Take a long one that reaches to at least mid-calf, for visiting temples. If you're in a situation where you have to go to the toilet in the open (by the side of the road on bus journeys, for example), it will also protect your modesty better than a pair of trousers.

• Long-sleeved shirt. For keeping warm, covering arms in temples, protecting them from the sun and avoiding mosquito bites.

• Scarf. To cover your head in temples, shield your scalp from the sun or, sprinkled with perfume and wrapped round your nose, protect you from the stench of Third World toilets! Also good as a dust mask.

• T-shirts. Pack three or four cotton ones. T-shirts with slogans (in English) are popular items for swapping and bartering with.

• One warm jumper or fleece (see chapter 13). It can get chilly even in hot climates and temperatures in desert areas can drop dramatically at night.

• Sarong. One of the most valuable items in your luggage, it can be anything you want it to be – skirt, towel, beach mat, sheet, scarf. Gives you instant modesty in temples and on beaches.

• Walking boots or trainers (see chapter 13).

• Sandals or flip-flops (can be bought on arrival but you may have a problem finding large sizes in Asian countries).

• Underwear (thermal for cold climates).

• Socks (you won't need many for hot climates; more if you're doing lots of trekking).

• Swimsuit.

• Hat. To shade you from the sun or keep you warm in the cold. Baseball caps are useful (and good for bartering, especially if they have logos or slogans on them). You can also get collapsible hats from Chinese stores that fold up flat to pack but open out into a wide-brimmed sunhat.

Remember that you can buy clothes along the way. Cities like Bangkok and Hong Kong are great for stocking up on T-shirts, cotton tops and shorts, sarongs, etc. You can even have silk items made to measure – you can usually collect the next day and they cost a fraction of the price you'd pay at home. If you're planning to work, remember to take some smart clothes with you. (It also helps to look as smart as possible when crossing borders, especially in places like Singapore and Russia where officials can be a bit fierce, so always try to keep at least one set of clean clothes to wear on such occasions.)

Equipment

See chapter 13 for advice on choosing and buying equipment. A tent and sleeping bag are optional, depending on where you're going and what you'll be doing there. You'll need a mosquito net in malarial regions. The following items are essential wherever you're going:
- sheet sleeping bag;
- torch;
- money belt;
- padlock (for doors and rucksacks);
- Swiss army knife (make sure it's got a corkscrew and bottle opener).

A camera isn't essential but most people like to take one. Film is fairly widely available (though you should always check the expiry date). You can stock up in airports, or in places like Singapore or Hong Kong. Slide film is more difficult to find. Take a spare camera battery in case yours runs out; it can be hard to find the right sort while you're away.

Toiletries

A medical kit is a must for any traveller – see chapter 9 for details of what to include.

- There's no need to load yourself down with enough suntan lotion, toothpaste, shampoo, soap and body lotion to last the whole trip. These are cheaper and easily available abroad, so just take enough to start you off. However, the choice of brands will probably be limited outside major cities so if you're fussy about your products, take your own supplies.
- Contact-lens solutions can usually be found in major cities so don't weigh yourself down by stocking up for the whole trip, unless you're fussy about the brand.
- Tampons are not always available so take enough to see you through or stock up in major cities *en route*. They can be very difficult to find in South America.

Sundries

Some of the items we take for granted are expensive or difficult to find on the road. You might like to pack some or all of the following.
- Universal sink plug (about £3). Some travellers say a squash ball does the job just as well – and because it looks out of place in a bathroom, you're probably less likely to leave it behind when you leave a hotel.
- Ear plugs. To help drown out the racket of busy streets, noisy neighbours, videos on buses, etc.
- Eye shades. To help you sleep when it's light.
- Sunglasses (UV-protective).
- Travel alarm clock. How else will you wake up in time for those early-morning buses and trains?
- Towel. These take up a lot of room, so don't take a large one. On the beach, use a sarong instead – it's lighter, smaller and dries faster.
- Blow-up travel pillow (about £5). This can be a godsend on long journeys and make the difference between some sleep and none at all.

- Mug or cup (tin or plastic). In countries like China and Russia, trains have boiling water for passengers to make hot drinks as they travel.
- Mini sewing kit and safety pins.
- Transparent plastic ziplock bags for keeping papers, books, passport, etc. dry. GO Travel Products do a pack of three PVC pac-a-pouches in different sizes for £4.99.
- Toilet paper.
- Scrubbing brush. You'll be amazed at how dirty you and your clothes can get; a scrubbing brush will help get things a bit cleaner.
- Books. Don't take too many – they're very heavy. You can swap with fellow travellers along the way (though you won't necessarily have the same taste in writers) or in hostel libraries or second-hand bookshops. A good guidebook is invaluable – but if you're only going to certain definite areas and don't mind mutilating it you can cut down the weight by ripping out and taking only the relevant pages.
- Diary or notebook and pens. To record your impressions.
- Telephone charge card.
- Sticky hooks. Useful for hanging up mosquito nets, or hanging clothes up in rooms with no hooks or rails.
- Walkman and tapes. Some will say this is a luxury, but in our book it's an essential and worth every ounce and square inch it takes up. It will get you through interminable delays and long journeys, and help you tune out beach hawkers. And if you get a pair of mini speakers that plug into your headphone socket, you can have a party in your room. It helps if your travelling companion shares your taste in music – and check before you go what they're taking so that you don't duplicate tapes.
- Batteries for Walkman, torch, etc. But don't go mad – they're heavy to carry and you can usually stock up *en route*. If you use an unusual size of battery, though, take enough to see you through.
- If you want to take presents for people, take something useful like pens. (If you can get hold of them, BBC pens are highly appreciated around the world!) Children everywhere, but especially in country places, love balloons. It's also nice to take photos

or postcards of your home town to show people (postcards of the British royal family go down a treat, too). Johnnie Walker and American cigarettes are well received just about everywhere, with the obvious exception of 'dry' countries.

• In some countries the food can be relentlessly bland and boring, so some travellers carry a bottle of soy or chilli sauce to add a bit of interest to their food.

Documentation

Whatever you do, don't leave home without the following:
• passport and visas;
• tickets;
• money (travellers' cheques, cash, credit cards);
• insurance documents;
• photocopies of all the above;
• vaccination certificate;
• discount cards;
• passport photographs for any visas you're getting along the way (it can be difficult or expensive to get these done abroad);
• addresses – your friends and family will never forgive you if you don't send them cards;
• if you're planning to drive at all, a UK and/or international driving licence.

Luxury Items

• No, you won't *need* perfume, mascara or lipstick – but there may be times when you'll be really glad you have them and they don't take up much space, so allow yourself the odd luxury or two.

• Binoculars are expensive (especially if you go for the lightweight ones) but invaluable if you're planning any safari trips while you're away.

- Wet-wipes. They're bulky to carry but there are times on a trip when the thing that makes you most happy is a clean, cool wet-wipe!
- Playing cards and miniature travel games (e.g. dice, Pass the Pigs, roll-up backgammon) don't take up much room but can pass hours.

What to Leave at Home

Don't even think about taking a travel hairdryer or travel iron – you don't need them. Leave jewellery behind, too, especially if it has great sentimental or monetary value. It's safer and more fun to pick things up as you go along.

Packing Tips

Don't overdo it. The classic traveller's packing tip is to lay out on your bed everything you're planning to take with you – then halve the amount of clothes and double the money. Just because you have a certain amount of space doesn't mean you have to fill it – and anyway you need to leave room for all the things you'll doubtless end up acquiring along the way. So be ruthless about chucking things out – then ask for a second opinion.

Pack so that when the rucksack is on your back the heaviest items are nearest the top and close to your back. Make sure that anything you're going to want to get out is packed readily to hand, not right at the bottom. Items that you'll need frequently, such as lip salve, pen, sunblock and tissues, are best kept in a bumbag or daypack.

Use lots of plastic bags to keep things waterproof – either transparent ones so you can see what's in each, or different colours to distinguish them. Roll clothes rather than folding them to help prevent creasing.

If you're travelling with a friend (and don't anticipate splitting up with them before the end of the trip), you don't need one of everything each, so sit down with a list and divide things up. You take the antiseptic cream if they carry the alarm clock, etc. If you're happy to share toiletries that will help too. You can also divide bits of a tent between you, one taking the tent itself while the other carries the poles and pegs.

Once you've filled your pack, pick it up and carry it round for a while. You might think it's not too bad at first but it doesn't take long for the true weight to tell. Remember that liquid is heavy – an empty water bottle won't make much difference to the weight of your pack, but a full one is a different story.

Put a note of your name and address inside the pack as well as on the outside, in case the outer label is ripped off and your baggage goes astray. Penknives are better packed in check-in luggage – they may be confiscated from hand luggage. On some flights you also have to hand in any batteries at check-in (they're returned to you later on).

Avoid carrying anything in glass bottles, which may smash. Transfer the contents into plastic containers instead – available in chemists (or empty film containers are good). The exception is tablets or other medicines, which will look suspicious to Customs and other officials if repackaged – leave them in their original containers.

When you return from a trip, make a note of what you took and what you used or didn't use, and what you were missing. Next time you'll know . . .

Chapter 15 / **How to Be a Good Traveller**

Take only photographs, leave only footprints.

Tourism is the world's largest industry, affecting the lives of millions of people. Hundreds of millions of tourists travel abroad every year and the impact they make *en masse* on their destination countries is immense. Sometimes it can be for the good – they may encourage the preservation of native habitats and wildlife and may provide much-needed cash for the local economy. But while the development of tourism brings rewards to some, the benefits are seldom spread evenly. People living in many tourist destinations are now counting the cost of having an industry that often fails to put their interests and rights on a par with those of their visitors. Tourists use up precious reserves of water, electricity and food. Forests are felled to build new roads; villages bulldozed to make way for a modern hotel; tribes displaced, as in Kenya's Masai Mara, which is now a National Park. The revenue generated from the tourists often goes straight into the hands of multinational companies or a few local bigwigs rather than benefiting the whole populace. Countries such as Myanmar (Burma) have even forced their people into virtual slavery to build roads, hotels and other facilities in order to attract the dollar-wielding tourist.

There are some simple steps you can take to help preserve the area you're visiting. If you are interested in finding out more about these and other travel issues, contact the organizations at the end of this chapter.

Protecting the Environment

- To help limit deforestation, don't make open fires when camping or hiking. Where firewood is scarce, use as little as possible; it's better to take your own fuel supplies. Take great care when discarding matches and cigarettes.
- Always take all your litter away with you – not only is it unsightly, but it can be harmful to animals.
- Don't pollute streams and rivers by using detergents or other pollutants. Take only environmentally-friendly, biodegradable shampoos and washing products with you.
- If there are no toilet facilities, bury or cover all waste, and make sure you are at least thirty metres away from water sources.
- Don't pick flowers or take cuttings from plants; in many areas, this is illegal as well as destructive to the environment.
- Don't buy animal or marine products, such as ivory, furs, butterflies, coral or turtle shells – you're endangering the natural environment and in many cases importing such articles into the UK is illegal.
- Treat coral with care – it is fragile and takes centuries to grow, but you can damage it in an instant. Don't step on it, break it or anchor a boat to it.
- Stick to marked paths, whether on foot or in the car. Unsupervised off-road driving can damage soil and vegetation.
- Try to save water. If you're staying somewhere upmarket, for example, tell them you don't need clean towels every day. Hotels could save millions of gallons if they washed guests' towels every other day, rather than every day.
- Remove all unnecessary packaging and wrapping from the products you're taking with you – the country you're going to may not have a waste-disposal system that's up to dealing with the increased pressures of tourists.
- Switch off lights and air conditioning when you leave a room.

- On safari, keep your distance from animals – getting too close or making too much noise distresses them and can disrupt their breeding and feeding cycles. In some cases, animals can contract human diseases to which they have no immunity.
- Don't encourage or take part in entertainments and events that cause suffering to animals – bull-fighting, dancing bears, photographers' monkeys, etc.

Respecting Local Cultures

- Read up on the local culture before you go and make sure that you respect all local customs.
- In Muslim countries, use only your right hand for eating and greeting, never your left.
- Respect other people's privacy when taking photographs. Always ask permission first.
- Show respect for holy places. Do not touch or remove any religious artefacts. Follow whatever rules are given, such as removing shoes or covering heads when visiting temples. Don't shout, run about or laugh excessively.
- How you deal with beggars is largely down to your personal moral code. However, many people who work in countries where begging is widespread advise that any money given would be more constructively spent if it were donated to a health centre, school or aid project.
- In Thailand and other Buddhist countries it's rude to point your feet at someone or touch their head.
- If you visit someone in their home, watch how they behave and copy them (taking off shoes before entering, etc.).
- Don't touch other people – handshakes, for example, are not appropriate in many cultures, especially between men and women.
- Avoid public displays of affection with your partner – public kissing and even hand-holding are unacceptable in some countries.

- Always dress modestly. Loose-fitting clothes are less offensive than body-hugging, skimpy and revealing ones. Even bare arms can cause offence in some countries so make sure you're sensitive to the local dress code.

- Always pay a fair price for what you buy. If you allow yourself to be overcharged it makes it harder for those who come after you to avoid being overcharged, too. If you beat local prices down too much, you are only getting your bargain at great expense to others who can ill afford it.

- Don't give money or sweets to children; pens, books or balloons are a better choice.

- Always be patient, friendly and sensitive. You are a guest in a foreign country.

- Buy locally produced foods and drinks rather than the imported versions, to help countries maintain individual cultures and boost the local economy. And spend your money in locally owned shops, hotels and restaurants rather than in those owned by huge international companies.

- Buying quality arts and crafts will support local skills and help maintain the indigenous culture – buying mass-produced tourist tat will help kill it off.

- In areas with repressive governments, make sure that you don't unwittingly put anyone in danger by quizzing them about human rights abuses, for example, or by asking awkward questions about politics and pro-democracy movements.

Further Information

- **Actionaid**, Chataway House, Leach Road, Chard, Somerset TA20 1FA. Africa, Asia and Latin America are popular with travellers, yet the people in these areas live in dreadful poverty. For more information on Actionaid's schemes in developing countries, and how you can help them, ring 01460 62972.

- **CERT** (Campaign for Environmentally Responsible Tourism), PO Box 4246, London SE21 7ZE (0181 299 6111). Aims to put resources into practical measures to help protect and look after the world's natural heritage.

- **Coalition on Child Prostitution and Tourism**, Anti-Slavery International, The Stableyard, Broomgrove Rd, London SW9 9TL (0171 924 9555). The rise of tourism in some countries has coincided with an explosion in the child-sex industry. CCPT seeks an end to child-sex tourism in all the tourist-destination countries of Asia, Africa, Europe and Latin America.
- **Department of the Environment** (DOE), Freepost (BS 9156), Houlton St, Bristol BS2 9BR. Publishes a free fact-sheet, *Check it Out*, on buying exotic souvenirs abroad. Write to the address above, or ring 0117 987 8691 for advice on birds, reptiles and fish, 0117 987 8168 for advice on plants and mammals.
- **Friends of Conservation**, Sloane Square House, Holbein Place, London SW1W 8NS (0171 730 7904). International conservation charity working to preserve endangered wildlife and habitat in East and Southern Africa.
- **Green Globe**, 20 Grosvenor Place, London SW1X 7TT (0171 930 8333). A world-wide environmental management and awareness programme for the travel and tourism industry.
- **Population Concern**, 178–202 Great Portland Street, London W1N 5TB (0171 631 1546). Campaigns in eighteen countries world-wide that have some of the highest rates of population increase in the world.
- **Sight Savers International**, 13 Cheap St, Frome, Somerset BA11 1BN (01373 452272). As many as 1 in 100 people in countries such as India, Pakistan, Bangladesh and Sri Lanka are blind – 4 out of 5 of these are needlessly blind. A donation of £10 will restore the sight of one adult. £25 will give an incurably blind person the training required to make a living and support themselves.
- **Survival International**, 11–15 Emerald St, London WC1N 3QL (0171 242 1441). A world-wide organization supporting tribal peoples in their efforts to protect their lives, lands and human rights.
- **Tourism Concern**, Southlands College, Wimbledon Parkside,

London SW19 5NN (0181 944 0464). Campaigns on behalf of people displaced by the travel industry and works to make tourism more responsible, sensitive and just. Membership (£18 waged, £9 unwaged) includes a subscription to *In Focus*, a quarterly magazine that looks at various tourism-related topics.

• **World Wide Fund for Nature**, Panda House, Weyside Park, Godalming, Surrey GU7 1XR. Has a Buyer Beware! campaign against illegal imports of wildlife souvenirs by tourists.

Chapter 16 / **Genning Up Before You Go**

Finding out as much as you can about the places you'll be visiting adds greatly to the enjoyment of a country. Part of the fun of preparing for your trip is reading books about your destination, watching films set there, going to relevant exhibitions and museums and poring over maps.

Learning the Language

If you're planning to spend a few months in one country, learning as much of the language/s as you can before you go will ensure you get more out of your trip – and make the whole experience of travelling around much easier. At the very least, you should master a few basic phrases for every country (thank you, please, hello). Contact your Local Education Authority for details of language courses or check out the self-taught courses available in bookshops, published by Berlitz, the BBC, Linguaphone, Hugo, and others.

Guidebooks

As the travel market has boomed, so the number of guidebooks has expanded enormously and any good bookshop will stock a wide selection. Faced with so many, it can be confusing knowing which to go for, but the acknowledged leaders in the backpacker market are Lonely Planet guides (their *South East Asia on a Shoestring* is clutched by every backpacker making the trip from Bangkok to Bali) and the Rough Guide series. Between them, they cover the globe and are generally very reliable, although prices may be slightly out of date, especially in countries just opening up to tourists. Footprint (formerly Trade & Travel) Handbooks, although expensive, are also very good and are all updated annually. Their award-winning *South American Handbook* is *the* acknowledged bible for that area.

Let's Go Guides are aimed specifically at the budget traveller and are updated every year. Other guides are also worth reading for background information. In particular, Cadogan books are intelligent and well-written (but rather heavy to carry round), while Blue Guides can be a bit dry but tell you all you want to know about the cultural aspects of a country. APA Insight Guides have lots of glossy pictures that are great to look at both before you go and when you come back. The Culture Shock! series (published by Kuperard) give a good general introduction to the culture and customs of a country – particularly useful if you're planning to live abroad. Other books to look out for aimed at the independent traveller include Bradt and Moon handbooks.

On the internet you could check out the Lonely Planet web site at http://www.lonelyplanet.com/ and Condé Nast Traveler at http://www.travel.epicurious.com.

Maps

If you're planning to do any trekking, buy good maps in the UK – they're difficult to find abroad. It's a good idea to try out your orienteering skills before you leave, too, practising with a map and compass in countryside near your home. (You can break in your hiking boots and get used to carrying a full rucksack at the same time.)

Fiction and Travelogues

Guidebooks will give you the hard facts, but for a more personal flavour of the country check out works of fiction and travellers' accounts. The list below starts off with general, world-wide books, then goes into an alphabetical list of countries and continents. If you can't find anything for the country you're going to, look under the relevant continent. For example, if you're going to Laos, check out Asia (general) as well as Laos itself.

General/World-wide

Around the World in Eighty Days, Jules Verne (Alan Sutton)
Around the World in Eighty Days, Michael Palin (BBC Books)
Pole to Pole, Michael Palin (BBC Books)
Last Chance to See, Douglas Adams (Pan)
Video Night in Kathmandu, Pico Iyer (Transworld)
Heroes, John Pilger (Pan)
Holidays in Hell, P. J. O'Rourke (Picador)
Lost Cowboys: From Patagonia to the Alamo, Hank Wangford (Victor Gollancz)
The Great Railway Bazaar, Paul Theroux (Penguin)
A Thousand Miles from Nowhere, Graham Coster (Penguin)
Letters Home, Robert Byron (John Murray)
Worst Journeys: The Picador Book of Travel, ed. Keath Fraser (Picador)
Danziger's Travels, Nick Danziger (Flamingo)
The Wind in My Wheels, Josie Dew (Warner Books)
Full Tilt, Dervla Murphy (Flamingo)
The Picador Book of the Beach, ed. Robert Drewe (Picador)
Our Man in . . . Heaven and Hell, Clive Anderson (BBC Books)
Great Journeys (BBC Books)
The Virago Book of Women Travellers, ed. Mary Morris with Larry O'Connor (Virago)

More Women Travel (Rough Guides)
The Blessings of a Good Thick Skirt, Mary Russell (Flamingo)
Unsuitable for Ladies: An Anthology of Women Travellers, selected by
   Jane Robinson (Oxford University Press)
Spinsters Abroad: Victorian Lady Explorers, Dea Birkett (Gollancz)
Travels, Michael Crichton (Pan)

Africa (General) *see also individual countries*

Running with the Moon: A Boy's Own Adventure, Jonny Bealby (William
   Heinemann)
Black Mischief, Evelyn Waugh (Penguin)
Scoop, Evelyn Waugh (Penguin)
Men at Arms, Evelyn Waugh (Penguin)
The Music Programme, Paul Micou (Black Swan)
A Good Man in Africa, William Boyd (Penguin)
Heart of Darkness, Joseph Conrad (Penguin)
The Heart of the Matter, Graham Greene (Penguin)
The Ukimwi Road, Dervla Murphy (Flamingo)
Blood on the Tracks, Miles Bredin (Picador)
On Foot Through Africa, Ffyona Campbell (Orion)
The White Nile, Alan Moorehead (Penguin)
African Silences, Peter Matthiessen (Harvill)
Travels with Pegasus: A Microlight Journey across West Africa, Christina
   Dodwell (Sceptre)
The Coup, John Updike (Penguin)
Venture to the Interior, Sir Laurens van der Post (Penguin)
Travels with Myself and Another, Martha Gellhorn (Eland Books)
The Weather in Africa, Martha Gellhorn (Eland Books)
North of South: An African Journey, Shiva Naipaul (Penguin)
Travels in the Interior of Africa, Mungo Park (Eland Books)
Travels in West Africa, Mary Kingsley (Everyman)
Tales from the Dark Continent, Charles Allen (Abacus)

Algeria

The Outsider, Albert Camus (Penguin)
The Plague, Albert Camus (Penguin)

Argentina

The Book of Imaginary Beings, Jorge Luis Borges (Penguin)
Kiss of the Spider Woman, Manuel Puig (Vintage)
The Honorary Consul, Graham Greene (Penguin)
The Whispering Land, Gerald Durrell (Penguin)
The Drunken Forest, Gerald Durrell (Penguin)

Asia (General) *see also individual countries*

On the Road Again, Simon Dring (BBC Books)
In Xanadu, William Dalrymple (Flamingo)
Lands of Charm and Cruelty, Stan Stesser (Picador)
Tales from the South China Seas, ed. Charles Allen (Abacus Travel)
The Lost Heart of Asia, Colin Thubron (Penguin)

Australia

Oscar and Lucinda, Peter Carey (Faber and Faber)
Picnic at Hanging Rock, Joan Lindsay (Penguin)
Kangaroo, D. H. Lawrence (Penguin)
My Brilliant Career, Miles Franklin (Virago)
Voss, Patrick White (Penguin)
Tracks, Robyn Davidson (Vintage)
Ancestors, Robyn Davidson (Vintage)
The Dead Heart, Douglas Kennedy (Abacus)

Sean and David's Long Drive, Sean Condon (Lonely Planet)
The Chant of Jimmie Blacksmith, Thomas Keneally (Penguin)
A River Town, Thomas Keneally (Sceptre)
A Secret Country, John Pilger (Vintage)
The Thorn Birds, Colleen McCullough (Warner Books)
The Songlines, Bruce Chatwin (Picador)
In the Land of Oz, Howard Jacobson (Penguin)
Sydney, Jan Morris (Penguin)
Girls' Night Out, Kathy Lette (Picador)
Daddy, We Hardly Knew You, Germaine Greer (Penguin)
Australiaville, Andy Soutter (Abacus)
The Great World, David Malouf (Picador)
Flight of the Kingfisher, Monica Furlong (HarperCollins)
Blue Meridian – the Search for the Great White Shark, Peter Matthiessen
 (Harvill)

Austria

The Third Man, Graham Greene (Penguin)

Bali *see Indonesia*

Bangladesh

Songs of the River's Edge: Stories from a Bangladeshi Village, Katy
 Gardner (Virago)

Belgium

The Folding Star, Alan Hollinghurst (Vintage)

Bhutan

Dreams of the Peaceful Dragon: Journey into Bhutan, Katie Hickman (Coronet)

Bolivia

The General in his Labyrinth, Gabriel García Marquez (Penguin)
Before the Rainy Season, Gert Hoffman (Minerva)

Borneo

Into the Heart of Borneo, Redmond O'Hanlon (Penguin)
Queen of the Head-Hunters, Sylvia, Lady Brooke (Oxford University Press)
An Empire of the East, Norman Lewis (Picador)

Botswana

The Lost World of the Kalahari, Laurens van der Post (Penguin)
A Woman Alone, Bessie Head (Heinemann)
The Cardinals, Bessie Head (Heinemann)
Okavango – Jewel of the Kalahari, Karen Ross (BBC Books)
Starlings Laughing, June Vendall-Clark (Transworld)
Jamestown Blues, Caitlin Davies (Penguin)
Cry of the Kalahari, Mark Owens and Delia Owens (Flamingo)

Brazil

Rebellion in the Backlands, Euclides da Cunha (Picador Travel Classics)
Dona Flor and Her Two Husbands, Jorge Amado (Serpent's Tail)
Mad White Giant: A Journey to the Heart of the Amazon Jungle, Benedict Allen (Flamingo)

Burma *see Myanmar*

Cambodia *see Vietnam*

Cameroon

A Plague of Caterpillars, Nigel Barley (Penguin)
The Innocent Anthropologist, Nigel Barley (Penguin)
Cameroon with Egbert, Dervla Murphy (Flamingo)
Mission to Kala, Mongo Beti (Heinemann)
Houseboy, Ferdinand Oyono (Heinemann)
Talking Drums, Shirley Deane (John Murray)
A Zoo in My Luggage, Gerald Durrell (Penguin)

Canada

The Shipping News, E. Annie Proulx (Fourth Estate)
Black Robe, Brian Moore (Flamingo)
The Deptford Trilogy, Robertson Davies (Penguin)
The Salterton Trilogy, Robertson Davies (Penguin)
The Progress of Love, Alice Munro (Flamingo)
The Beggar Maid, Alice Munro (Penguin)

Cat's Eye, Margaret Atwood (Virago)
Surfacing, Margaret Atwood (Virago)
Shadows on the Rock, Willa Cather (Virago)
The Stone Diaries, Carol Shields (Fourth Estate)
St Urbain's Horseman, Mordecai Richler (Vintage)
Solomon Gursky Was Here, Mordecai Richler (Vintage)

Caribbean

The Crown of Columbus, Michael Dorris and Louise Erdrich (Flamingo)
Wide Sargasso Sea, Jean Rhys (Penguin)
A House for Mr Biswas, V. S. Naipaul (Penguin)
Indigo, Marina Warner (Vintage)
The Violins of Saint-Jacques, Patrick Leigh Fermor (Oxford University Press)
Tar Baby, Toni Morrison (Picador)
A High Wind in Jamaica, Richard Hughes (Panther)
The Middle Passage, V. S. Naipaul (Picador Travel Classics)
The Traveller's Tree, Patrick Leigh Fermor (Penguin)
A Small Place, Jamaica Kincaid (Virago)
The Dragon Can't Dance, Earl Lovelace (Longman)
The Weather Prophet: A Caribbean Journey, Lucretia Stewart (Vintage)
Omeros, Derek Walcott (Faber and Faber)

Central America (General) *see also individual countries*

The Old Patagonian Express, Paul Theroux (Penguin)
Reality is the Bug that Bit Me in the Galapagos, Charlotte du Cann and Mark Watson (Flamingo)
Nothing to Declare: Memoirs of a Woman Travelling Alone, Mary Morris (Penguin)
So Far from God: A Journey to Central America, Patrick Marnham (Penguin)

Chile

Travels in a Thin Country, Sara Wheeler (Abacus)
House of the Spirits, Isabel Allende (Black Swan)
Of Love and Shadows, Isabel Allende (Black Swan)
Eva Luna, Isabel Allende (Penguin)
The Stories of Eva Luna, Isabel Allende (Penguin)
Memoirs, Pablo Neruda (Penguin)
Selected Poems, Pablo Neruda (Penguin)

China

Wild Swans, Jung Chang (Flamingo)
The Kitchen God's Wife, Amy Tan (Flamingo)
The Joy Luck Club, Amy Tan (Minerva)
China to Me, Emily Hahn (Virago)
Farewell to My Concubine, Lilian Lee (Penguin)
The Good Earth, Pearl S. Buck (Mandarin)
Life and Death in Shanghai, Nien Cheng (Flamingo)
Riding the Iron Rooster, Paul Theroux (Penguin)
Red Star over China, Edgar Snow (Penguin)
Peking, Anthony Grey (Pan)
The Dream of the Red Chamber, Cao Xueqin (Penguin)
Red Azalea, An Chi Minh (Victor Gollancz)
Empire of the Sun, J. G. Ballard (Flamingo)
*From Emperor to Citizen: The Autobiography of Pu Yi, the Last Emperor
    of China* (Oxford University Press)
Behind the Wall: A Journey through China, Colin Thubron (Penguin)
Half of Man is Woman, Zhang Xianliang (Penguin)
Rice, Su Tong (Touchstone/Simon & Schuster)
Raise the Red Lantern, Su Tong (Touchstone/Simon & Schuster)
The Yangtze and Beyond, Isabella Bird (Virago)

Red Sorghum, Mo Yan (Minerva)
The Woman Warrior, Maxine Hong Kingston (Picador)

Colombia

Love in the Time of Cholera, Gabriel García Marquez (Penguin)
One Hundred Years of Solitude, Gabriel García Marquez (Picador)
Señor Vivo and the Coca Lord, Louis de Bernières (Minerva)
Condor and Humming-bird, Charlotte Mendez (The Women's Press)
The Fruit Palace, Charles Nicholl (Picador)

Congo

A Burnt-Out Case, Graham Greene (Penguin)
Brazzaville Beach, William Boyd (Penguin)

Costa Rica

Jurassic Park, Michael Crichton (Arrow)

Cuba

Islands in the Stream, Ernest Hemingway (Flamingo)
Our Man in Havana, Graham Greene (Penguin)
The Mambo Kings Play Songs of Love, Oscar Hijuelos (Penguin)
Los Gusanos, John Sayles (Penguin)
Driving through Cuba: An East-West Journey, Carlo Gebler (Abacus)
Dreaming in Cuban, Cristina Garcia (Flamingo)

Cyprus

Bitter Lemons, Lawrence Durrell (Faber and Faber)
Journey into Cyprus, Colin Thubron (Penguin)

Czech Republic

The Unbearable Lightness of Being, Milan Kundera (Faber and Faber)
The Book of Laughter and Forgetting, Milan Kundera (Faber and Faber)
Utz, Bruce Chatwin (Picador)
Dracula, Bram Stoker (Penguin)
The Trial, Franz Kafka (Minerva)
The Good Soldier Svejk, Jaroslav Hasek (Penguin)
The Piper on the Mountain, Ellis Peters (Headline)
The Engineer of Human Souls, Josef Skvorecky (Vintage)
A Stricken Field, Martha Gellhorn (Virago)
Letters to Olga, Vaclav Havel (Faber and Faber)
Saxophone Dreams, Nicholas Royle (Penguin)
Magic Prague, Angelo Maria Ripellino (Picador)

Denmark

Miss Smilla's Feeling for Snow, Peter Høeg (Harvill)
The History of Danish Dreams, Peter Høeg (Harvill)
Winter's Tales, Isak Dinesen (Karen Blixen) (Penguin)
Classic Fairy Tales, Hans Christian Anderson (Gollancz)

Ecuador

The Origin of Species, Charles Darwin (Penguin)
Voyage of the Beagle, Charles Darwin (Penguin)
Nostromo, Joseph Conrad (Penguin)

Egypt

Moon Tiger, Penelope Lively (Penguin)
The Cairo Trilogy (Palace Walk, Palace of Desire and *Sugar Street)*,
   Naguib Mahfouz (Black Swan)
The Alexandria Quartet, Lawrence Durrell (Faber and Faber)
The Hidden Face of Eve, Nawal El Saadawi (Zed Press)
Woman at Point Zero, Nawal El Saadawi (Zed Books)
God Dies by the Nile, Nawal El Saadawi (Zed Books)
The Levant Trilogy, Olivia Manning (Penguin)
The Balkan Trilogy (final two books), Olivia Manning (Mandarin)
Letters from Egypt, Lucie Duff Gordon (Virago)
Beyond the Pyramids: Travels in Egypt, Douglas Kennedy (Abacus)
Harem Years: The Memoirs of an Egyptian Feminist, Huda Sha'rawi
   (Virago)

Estonia

The Christening, Denise Neuhaus (Faber and Faber)

Ethiopia

Waugh in Abyssinia, Evelyn Waugh (Penguin)
In Ethiopia with a Mule, Dervla Murphy (Flamingo)
Cry Wolf, Wilbur Smith (Mandarin)

Europe (General) *see also individual countries*

The Pillars of Hercules, Paul Theroux (Hamish Hamilton)
Neither Here Nor There: Travels in Europe, Bill Bryson (Minerva)
A Time of Gifts, Patrick Leigh Fermor (Penguin)
Between the Woods and the Water, Patrick Leigh Fermor (Penguin)
Stalin's Nose: Across the Face of Europe, Rory MacLean (Flamingo)
Exit into History, Eva Hoffman (Minerva)
States of Change: A Central European Diary, Lynne Jones (Merlin Press)

Finland

One Night Stand, Rosa Liksom (Serpent's Tail)
The Downfall of Gerdt Bladh, Christer Kilman (Peter Owen)

France

Any nineteenth-century French novel (Balzac, Zola (e.g. *L'Assommoir, Nana, Germinal*), Hugo (e.g. *Les Misérables*), Flaubert (e.g. *Sentimental Education, Madame Bovary*), Stendhal)
A Tale of Two Cities, Charles Dickens (Penguin)
Jean de Florette and *Manon of the Springs*, Marcel Pagnol (Picador)
Le Grand Meaulnes, Alain-Fournier (Penguin)
Selected Short Stories, Guy de Maupassant (Penguin)
Tender is the Night, F. Scott Fitzgerald (Penguin)
Jericho, Dirk Bogarde (Penguin)
Perfume, Patrick Suskind (Penguin)
A Moveable Feast, Ernest Hemingway (Arrow)
Down and Out in Paris and London, George Orwell (Penguin)
Jigsaw, Sybille Bedford (Penguin)
The Collected Stories of Colette, Colette (Penguin)
The Autobiography of Alice B. Toklas, Gertrude Stein (Penguin)

Flaubert's Parrot, Julian Barnes (Picador)
The Girl at the Lion d'Or, Sebastian Faulks (Vintage)
Birdsong, Sebastian Faulks (Vintage)
Bonjour Tristesse, Françoise Sagan (Penguin)
Daughters of the House, Michèle Roberts (Virago)
Don't Tell Alfred, Nancy Mitford (Penguin)
The Blessing, Nancy Mitford (Penguin)
The Dud Avocado, Elaine Dundy (Virago)
A Year in Provence, Peter Mayle (Pan)
Toujours Provence, Peter Mayle (Pan)
Hotel Pastis, Peter Mayle (Penguin)
Travels with a Donkey in the Cévennes, Robert Louis Stevenson
   (Everyman)
Long Ago in France, M. F. K. Fisher (Flamingo)
Letters from my Windmill, Alphonse Daudet (Penguin)
A Motor-Flight through France, Edith Wharton (Picador Travel
   Classics)
Granite Island, Dorothy Carrington (Penguin)
France and the French, John Ardagh (Penguin)
Across the Channel, Julian Barnes (Cape)
Quartet, Jean Rhys (Penguin)
The Horseman on the Roof, Jean Giono (Harvill)
The Frontenac Mystery, François Mauriac (Penguin)

Germany

Hopeful Monsters, Nicholas Moseley (Minerva)
Buddenbrooks, Thomas Mann (Penguin)
The Innocent, Ian McEwan (Picador)
The Berlin Novels, Christopher Isherwood (Minerva)
All Quiet on the Western Front, Erich Maria Remarque (Penguin)
The Tin Drum, Günter Grass (Picador)
Germany and the Germans, John Ardagh (Penguin)
The Glass Bead Game, Hermann Hesse (Penguin)

Ghana

All God's Children Need Travelling Shoes, Maya Angelou (Virago)

Greece

The Odyssey, Homer (Penguin)
The Iliad, Homer (Penguin)
The Magus, John Fowles (Picador)
Zorba the Greek, Nikos Kazantzakis (Faber and Faber)
Captain Corelli's Mandolin, Louis de Bernières (Minerva)
Pascali's Island, Barry Unsworth (Penguin)
The Balkan Trilogy, Olivia Manning (Mandarin)
An Island Apart, Sara Wheeler (Abacus)
My Family and Other Animals, Gerald Durrell (Penguin)
Roumeli, Patrick Leigh Fermor (Penguin)
Mani, Patrick Leigh Fermor (Penguin)
The Unwritten Places, Tim Salmon (Lycabettus Press)
The Two Faces of January, Patricia Highsmith (Penguin)
The Double Tongue, William Golding (Faber and Faber)

Greenland

Miss Smilla's Feeling for Snow, Peter Høeg (Harvill)

Guatemala

Up Above the World, Paul Bowles (Paul Owens)

Gulf States

Arabia Through the Looking Glass, Jonathan Raban (Picador)
Arabian Sands, Wilfred Thesiger (Penguin)
Seven Pillars of Wisdom, T. E. Lawrence (Penguin)

Guyana

Ninety-Two Days, Evelyn Waugh (Penguin)

Haiti

The Comedians, Graham Greene (Penguin)
'Bonjour Blanc': A Journey through Haiti, Ian Thomson (Penguin)
The Kingdom of this World, Alejo Carpentier (Deutsch)

Honduras

The Mosquito Coast, Paul Theroux (Penguin)

Hong Kong

An Insular Possession, Timothy Mo (Picador)
The Monkey King, Timothy Mo (Vintage)
The Honourable Schoolboy, John Le Carré (Hodder)
Tai-Pan, James Clavell (Coronet)
Noble House, James Clavell (Coronet)
Hong Kong: Epilogue to an Empire, Jan Morris (Penguin)

Hungary

Under the Frog, Tibor Fischer (Penguin)
Between the Woods and the Water, Patrick Leigh Fermor (Penguin)

India

The Raj Quartet (The Jewel in the Crown, The Day of the Scorpion, The Towers of Silence and *A Division of the Spoils)*, Paul Scott (Pan)
Staying On, Paul Scott (Mandarin)
A Passage to India, E. M. Forster (Penguin)
Midnight's Children, Salman Rushdie (Vintage)
The Siege of Krishnapur, J. G. Farrell (Phoenix)
A Suitable Boy, Vikram Seth (Phoenix)
The Far Pavilions, M. M. Kaye (Penguin)
Heat and Dust, Ruth Prawer Jhabvala (Penguin)
A Backward Place, Ruth Prawer Jhabvala (Penguin)
The Heart of India, Mark Tully (Viking)
Third-Class Ticket, Heather Wood (Penguin)
Up the Country: Letters from India, Emily Eden (Virago)
A House in Pondicherry, Lee Langley (Minerva)
Plain Tales from the Raj, Charles Allen (Abacus)
Clear Light of Day, Anita Desai (Penguin)
Baumgartner's Bombay, Anita Desai (Penguin)
No Full Stops in India, Mark Tully (Penguin)
City of Djinns, William Dalrymple (Flamingo)
Grandmother's Footsteps, Imogen Lycett Green (Pan)
A Son of the Circus, John Irving (Black Swan)
On a Shoestring to Coorg, Dervla Murphy (Flamingo)
Where the Indus is Young, Dervla Murphy (Flamingo)
Three-Quarters of a Footprint, Joe Roberts (Black Swan)
Chasing the Monsoon, Alexander Frater (Penguin)
Karma Cola, Gita Mehta (Minerva)

Malgudi Days, R. K. Narayan (Penguin)
The Vendor of Sweets, R. K. Narayan (Penguin)
Bhowani Junction, John Masters (Ulverscroft)
The Jungle Book, Rudyard Kipling (Penguin)
Plain Tales from the Hills, Rudyard Kipling (Penguin)
An Area of Darkness, V. S. Naipaul (Picador Travel Classics)
India, V. S. Naipaul (Minerva)
City of Joy, Dominique Lapierre (Arrow)
A Fine Balance, Rohinton Mistry (Faber and Faber)
A Goddess in the Stones, Norman Lewis (in the *Norman Lewis Omnibus*)
    (Picador)
Indian Balm, Paul Hyland (Flamingo)
A Journey in Ladakh, Andrew Harvey (Picador)
Ancient Futures: Learning from Ladakh, Helena Norberg-Hodge (Rider)
*May You be the Mother of a Hundred Sons: A Journey among the Women
    of India*, Elisabeth Bumiller (Random House)

Indonesia *see also Borneo*

A Tale from Bali, Vicki Baum (Oxford University Press, Asia)
The Year of Living Dangerously, Christopher Koch (Minerva)
Victory, Joseph Conrad (Penguin)
Lord Jim, Joseph Conrad (Penguin)
The Last Paradise, Hickman Powell (Oxford University Press, Asia)
In Search of Conrad, Gavin Young (Penguin)
Not a Hazardous Sport, Nigel Barley (Penguin)
Distant Voices, John Pilger (Vintage)
Skulduggery, Mark Shand (Penguin)

Iran

The Valleys of the Assassins, Freya Stark (Arrow)
The Blindfold Horse, Shusha Guppy (Minerva)
Javady Alley, Manny Sharazi (The Women's Press)

Nine Parts of Desire (The Hidden World of Islamic Women), Geraldine
  Brooks (Hamish Hamilton)
The Road to Oxiana, Robert Byron (Penguin Travel Library)
Whirlwind, James Clavell (Coronet)

Iraq

The Marsh Arabs, Wilfred Thesiger (Penguin)
Arabian Sands, Wilfred Thesiger (Penguin)
Desert, Marsh and Mountain, Wilfred Thesiger (Flamingo)
Return to the Marshes, Gavin Young (Penguin)
Baghdad Sketches, Freya Stark (The Marlboro Press)

Israel

The Mandelbaum Gate, Muriel Spark (Penguin)
Roots Schmoots, Howard Jacobson (Penguin)
Jerusalem, Colin Thubron (Penguin)
The Yellow Wind, David Grossman (Picador)
Jerusalem: City of Mirrors, Amos Elon (Flamingo)
This Year in Jerusalem, Mordecai Richler (Vintage)

Italy

A Room with a View, E. M. Forster (Penguin)
Stone Virgin, Barry Unsworth (Penguin)
Cara Massimina, Tim Parks (Minerva)
Mimi's Ghost, Tim Parks (Minerva)
Summer's Lease, John Mortimer (Penguin)
In the Valley of the Fireflies, Peter Hobday (Michael Joseph)
A Small Place in Italy, Eric Newby (Picador)
Love and War in the Apennines, Eric Newby (Picador)
The Agony and the Ecstasy, Irving Stone (Methuen)

A Valley in Italy, Lisa St Aubin de Teran (Penguin)
The Slow Train to Milan, Lisa St Aubin de Teran (Penguin)
Death in Venice, Thomas Mann (Penguin)
Don't Look Now and Other Stories, Daphne Du Maurier (Penguin)
Christ Stopped at Eboli, Carlo Levi (Penguin)
Watermark, Joseph Brodsky (Hamish Hamilton)
The Passion, Jeanette Winterson (Penguin)
Romola, George Eliot (Penguin)
The Golden Honeycomb, Vincent Cronin (Harvill)
Old Calabria, Norman Douglas (Picador Travel Classics)
Venice, Jan Morris (Faber and Faber)
The Leopard, Guiseppe di Lampedusa (Harvell Press)
The Decameron, Boccaccio (Penguin)
Isolina, Dacia Maraini (Peter Owen)
Journeys to the Underworld, Fiona Pitt-Kethley (Chatto and Windus)
Inspector Zen series, Michael Didbin (Faber and Faber)
The Wings of the Dove, Henry James (Penguin)
The Aspern Papers, Henry James (Penguin)
Two Lives, William Trevor (Penguin)
Sea and Sardinia, D. H. Lawrence (Olive Press)

Japan

Shogun, James Clavell (Coronet)
Gai-Jin, James Clavell (Coronet)
Snow Country and *Thousand Cranes*, Yasunari Kawabata (Penguin)
Sailor Who Fell from Grace, Yukio Mishima (Penguin)
Silence, Shusako Endo (Penguin)
The Hard Boiled Wonderland and the End of the World, Haruki Murakami (Hamish Hamilton)
Pictures from the Water Trade, John David Morley (Abacus)
A Personal Matter, Kenzaburo Oë (Picador)
Unbeaten Tracks in Japan, Isabella Bird (Virago)
The Lady and the Monk, Pico Iyer (Black Swan)

The Makioka Sisters, Junichiro Tanizaki (Picador)
The Pillow Boy of the Lady Onogoro, Alison Fell (Serpent's Tail)
On the Narrow Road to the Deep North, Lesley Downer (Sceptre)
Lost Japan, Alex Kerr (Lonely Planet)
Inspector Otani series, James Melville (Secker)
The Shooting Gallery and Other Stories, Yuko Tsushima (The Women's
    Press)
Lizard, Banana Yoshimoto (Faber and Faber)

Kenya

West with the Night, Beryl Markham (Virago)
The Flame Trees of Thika, Elspeth Huxley (Penguin)
A Small Town in Africa, Daisy Waugh (Large Print Books)
Out of Africa, Karen Blixen (Penguin)
An Ice-Cream War, William Boyd (Penguin)
I Dreamed of Africa, Kuki Gallmann (Penguin)
African Nights, Kuki Gallmann (Penguin)
Devil on the Cross, Ngugi wa Thiong'o (Heinemann)
My Kenya Days, Wilfred Thesiger (Flamingo)
The Weather in Africa, Martha Gellhorn (Eland)
The Jacaranda Flower, Toril Brekke (Methuen)
Ripples in the Pool, Rebeka Njau (Heinemann)
Elephant Memories, Cynthia Moss (Fontana/Collins)
No Man's Land, George Monbiot (Picador)

Korea

I Am the Clay, Chaim Potok (Penguin)

Laos *see Vietnam*

Lebanon

The Hills of Adonis, Colin Thubron (Penguin)
The Rock of Tanios, Amin Maalouf (Abacus)

Liberia

Journey Without Maps, Graham Greene (Penguin)

Madagascar

Madagascar Travels, Christina Dodwell (Hodder and Stoughton)
Muddling Through in Madagascar, Dervla Murphy (Flamingo)

Malaysia and Singapore *see also Borneo*

Collected Short Stories, Volume Four, W. Somerset Maugham
    (Mandarin)
Far Eastern Tales, W. Somerset Maugham (Mandarin)
The Borneo Stories, W. Somerset Maugham (Mandarin)
The Singapore Grip, J. G. Farrell (Phoenix)
The Shadow-Line, Joseph Conrad (Penguin)
Lord Jim, Joseph Conrad (Penguin)
Turtle Beach, Blanche d'Alpuget (Penguin)
The Malayan Trilogy, Anthony Burgess (Penguin)
King Rat, James Clavell (Coronet)

Mexico

The Power and the Glory, Graham Greene (Penguin)
Air and Fire, Rupert Thomson (Penguin)
The Plumed Serpent, D. H. Lawrence (Penguin)
Mornings in Mexico, D. H. Lawrence (Penguin)
Like Water for Chocolate, Laura Esquivel (Black Swan)
Under the Volcano, Malcolm Lowry (Picador)
Nostromo, Joseph Conrad (Picador Classics)
A Trip to the Light Fantastic: Travels with a Mexican Circus, Katie
    Hickman (Flamingo)
A Visit to Don Otavio, Sybille Bedford (Eland)

Middle East

The Levant Trilogy, Olivia Manning (Penguin)
The Seven Pillars of Wisdom, T. E. Lawrence (Penguin)
Among the Believers, V. S. Naipaul (Penguin)
The Crossing Place: A Journey among the Armenians, Philip Marsden
    (Flamingo)
The Price of Honour, Jan Goodwin (Warner Books)
Coming Up Roses, Michael Carson (Black Swan)
Eothen: Traces of Travel Brought Home from the East, Alistair Kinglake
    (Picador Travel Classics)

Mongolia

The Last Disco in Outer Mongolia, Nick Middleton (Phoenix)
Storm from the East, Robert Marshall (Penguin)

Morocco

Hideous Kinky, Esther Freud (Penguin)
The Spider's House, Paul Bowles (Abacus)
The Sheltering Sky, Paul Bowles (Flamingo)
By Bus to the Sahara, Gordon West (Black Swan)
See Ouarzazate and Die: Travels through Morocco, Sylvia Kennedy (Abacus)
Tangier, Iain Finlayson (Flamingo)

Mozambique

Kalashnikovs and Zombie Cucumbers, Nick Middleton (Phoenix)

Myanmar (Burma)

The Lacquer Lady, F. Tennyson Jesse (Virago)
Burmese Days, George Orwell (Penguin)
Golden Earth, Norman Lewis (Eland)
Freedom from Fear, Aung San Suu Kyi (Penguin)
Kim, Rudyard Kipling (Penguin)

Namibia

The Burning Shore, Wilbur Smith (Pan)

Nepal

The Snow Leopard, Peter Matthiessen (Harvard Press)
The Waiting Land, Dervla Murphy (Arrow)
Against a Peacock Sky, Monica Connell (Penguin)

Netherlands

The Diary of Anne Frank (Macmillan)
Nicolas Freeling's Van der Valk detective novels (Penguin)

New Guinea

Islands in the Clouds, Isabella Tree (Lonely Planet)

New Zealand

Dunedin, Shena Mackay (Penguin)
Collected Stories, Katherine Mansfield (Penguin)
The Bone People, Keri Hulme (Pan)
Once Were Warriors, Alan Duff (Vintage)
Owls Do Cry, Janet Frame (The Women's Press)
Living in the Manioto, Janet Frame (The Women's Press)
Scented Gardens for the Blind, Janet Frame (The Women's Press)
Crime Story, Maurice Gee (Faber and Faber)
River Lines, Elspeth Sandys (Sceptre)
The Picador Book of Contemporary New Zealand Fiction, ed. Fergus
   Barrowman (Picador)

Nigeria

Dangerous Love, Ben Okri (Phoenix)
Stars of the New Curfew, Ben Okri (Penguin)
Anthills of the Savannah, Chinua Achebe (Picador)
No Longer at Ease, Chinua Achebe (Heinemann)
The Interpreter, Wole Soyinka (Heinemann)

Norway

The Wanderer, Knut Hamsun (Souvenir)
Dina's Book, Herbjorg Wassmo (Black Swan)

Pacific Basin

The Happy Isles of Oceania, Paul Theroux (Penguin)
Paradise News, David Lodge (Penguin)
Slow Boats Home, Gavin Young (Penguin)
Island of Dreams, Tony Williams (Signet)
In Search of Tusitala: Travels in the Pacific after Robert Louis Stevenson,
    Gavin Bell (Picador)
Transit of Venus: Travels in the Pacific, Julian Evans (Minerva)
Tales of the Pacific, Jack London (Penguin)
Typee, Herman Melville (Oxford)

Pakistan

The Golden Peak: Travels in Northern Pakistan, Kathleen Jamie
    (Virago)
Where the Indus is Young, Dervla Murphy (Flamingo)
Daughter of the East, Benazir Bhutto (Mandarin)

Panama

Getting to Know the General, Graham Greene (Penguin)

Papua New Guinea

Into the Crocodile Nest, Benedict Allen (Flamingo)
The Proving Grounds, Benedict Allen (Flamingo)
Under the Mountain Wall, Peter Matthiessen (Harvill)

Paraguay

The Drunken Forest, Gerald Durrell (Penguin)

Peru

Aunt Julia and the Scriptwriter, Mario Vargas Llosa (Faber and
   Faber)
Overthrown by Strangers, Ronan Bennett (Penguin)
Eight Feet in the Andes, Dervla Murphy (Flamingo)
Inca-Kola: A Traveller's Tale of Peru, Matthew Parris (Phoenix)
Three Letters from the Andes, Patrick Leigh Fermor (Penguin)

Philippines

The Blue Afternoon, William Boyd (Penguin)

Poland

Schindler's List (originally called *Schindler's Ark*), Thomas Keneally
   (Sceptre)
If Not Now, When? Primo Levi (Abacus)
Wartime Lies, Louis Begley (Picador)
Scum, Isaac Bashevis Singer (Penguin)

Portugal

Lucio's Confession, Mario de Sa-Carneiro (Dedalus)
Passport to Portugal, Mike Gerrard and Thomas McCarthy (Serpent's Tail)
The Last Guests of the Season, Sue Gee (Arrow)
The Relic, Eça de Quieroz (Dedalus European Classics)

Romania

Saxophone Dreams, Nicholas Royle (Penguin)

Russia

War and Peace, Leo Tolstoy (Penguin)
Anna Karenina, Leo Tolstoy (Penguin)
Crime and Punishment, Fyodor Dostoyevsky (Penguin)
The Time: Night, Ludmilla Petrushevskaya (Virago)
Immortal Love, Ludmilla Petrushevskaya (Virago)
Dr Zhivago, Boris Pasternak (Harvill)
A Month in the Country, I. S. Turgenev (Penguin)
The Portable Chekhov (Penguin)
The Gulag Archipelago, Aleksandr Solzhenitsyn (Harvill)
One Day in the Life of Ivan Denisovich, Aleksandr Solzhenitsyn (Penguin)
Among the Russians, Colin Thubron (Picador Travel Classics)
On the Golden Porch and Other Stories, Tatyana Tolstaya (Penguin)
Oblomov, Ivan Goncharov (Penguin)
The Russian Album, Michael Ignatieff (Penguin)
Journey Into Russia, Laurens Van Der Post (Penguin)
The Big Red Train Ride, Eric Newby (Picador)
Gorky Park, Martin Cruz Smith (Pan)

Volga, Volga: A Voyage Down the Great River, Lesley Chamberlain (Picador)

First Russia, Then Tibet, Robert Byron (Penguin)

Beyond Siberia, Christina Dodwell (Sceptre)

A Dry Ship to the Mountains: Down the Volga and Across the Caucasus in My Father's Footsteps, Daniel Farson (Penguin)

The Penguin Book of New Russian Writing, ed. Victor Erofeyev (Penguin)

Journey into the Mind's Eye, Lesley Blanch (Pimlico, out of print)

Rwanda

Gorillas in the Mist, Dian Fossey (Penguin)

Samoa

Rain, W. Somerset Maugham (in *Short Stories*) (Minerva)

Tales of the South Pacific, James Michener (Corgi)

Return to Paradise, James Michener (Mandarin)

Rascals in Paradise, James Michener and Arthur Grove Day (Mandarin)

Saudi Arabia

Eight Nights on Ghazzah Street, Hilary Mantel (Penguin)

The Southern Gates of Arabia, Freya Stark (John Murray)

Sierra Leone

Our Grandmother's Drums, Mark Hudson (Mandarin)

Singapore *see Malaysia*

Solomon Islands

Tales of the South Pacific, James Michener (Corgi)
Rascals in Paradise, James Michener and Arthur Grove Day
  (Mandarin)

South Africa

The Life and Times of Michael K, J. M. Coetzee (Penguin)
Age of Iron, J. M. Coetzee (Penguin)
Cry, the Beloved Country, Alan Paton (Penguin)
A Chain of Voices, André Brink (Minerva)
A Dry White Season, André Brink (Minerva)
Selected Stories, Nadine Gordimer (Penguin)
A World of Strangers, Nadine Gordimer (Penguin)
The Power of One, Bryce Courtenay (Mandarin)
Buckingham Palace District Six, Richard Rive (Heinemann)
My Traitor's Heart, Rian Malan (Vintage)
The Penguin Book of Contemporary South African Short Stories (Penguin)
Long Walk to Freedom, Nelson Mandela (Abacus)
The Story of an African Farm, Olive Schreiner (Virago)
Where the Lion Feeds, Wilbur Smith (Mandarin)
The Sound of Thunder, Wilbur Smith (Mandarin)

South America (General) *see also individual countries*

The Tiger, Lisa St Aubin de Teran (Penguin)
The Motorcycle Diaries: A Journey around South America, Ernesto Che
  Guevara (Fourth Estate)
Through Jaguar Eyes, Benedict Allen (Flamingo)
Dream Catching: On the Road Reluctantly, Dyan Sheldon (Little Brown)
In Patagonia, Bruce Chatwin (Picador)

Señor Vivo and the Coca Lord, Louis de Bernières (Minerva)
The Troublesome Offspring of Cardinal Guzman, Louis de Bernières (Minerva)
The War of Don Emmanuel's Nether Parts, Louis de Bernières (Minerva)

Spain

As I Walked Out One Midsummer Morning, Laurie Lee (Penguin)
Homage to Catalonia, George Orwell (Penguin)
Fiesta / The Sun Also Rises, Ernest Hemingway (Arrow)
For Whom the Bell Tolls, Ernest Hemingway (Arrow)
Don Quixote, Miguel de Cervantes (Penguin)
Homage to Barcelona, Colm Tóibín (Penguin)
The South, Colm Tóibín (Picador)
Voices of the Old Sea, Norman Lewis (Picador)
Spain, Jan Morris (Penguin)
Between Hopes and Memories: A Spanish Journey, Michael Jacobs (Picador)
Here We Go: A Summer on the Costa del Sol, Harry Ritchie (Penguin)
The Face of Spain, Gerald Brenan (Penguin)
South from Granada, Gerald Brenan (Penguin)
Desperately Seeking Julio, Maruja Torres (Fourth Estate)
Leo the African, Amin Maalouf (Abacus)
Morvern Callar, Alan Warner (Vintage)
The Windfall, Prue Carmichael (Warner Books)

Sri Lanka

Reef, Romesh Gunesekera (Granta/Penguin)
Monkfish Moon, Romesh Gunesekera (Granta/Penguin)
Running in the Family, Michael Ondaatje (Pan)

Sweden

My Life as a Dog, Reidar Jönsson (Farrer, Straus & Giroux)
Blackwater, Kerstin Ekman (Vintage)

Switzerland

Hotel du Lac, Anita Brookner (Penguin)
Dr Fischer of Geneva or The Bomb Party, Graham Greene (Penguin)

Syria

Mirror to Damascus, Colin Thubron (Penguin)
The Gates of Damascus, Lieve Joris (Lonely Planet Journeys)

Taiwan

Death in a Cornfield, Ching Hsi Pserng and Chiu-Kuei Wang (Oxford University Press)

Tanzania

No Man's Land, George Monbiot (Picador)

Thailand

Borderlines, Charles Nicholl (Picador)
An English Governess at the Court of Siam, Anna Leonowens (Oxford
   University Press)
The Beach, Alex Garland (Viking)

Tibet

First Russia, Then Tibet, Robert Byron (Penguin)
From Heaven Lake, Vikram Seth (Phoenix)
Tibetan Foothold, Dervla Murphy (Flamingo)
Seven Years in Tibet, Heinrich Harrer (Flamingo)
*Journey to Lhasa: The Personal Story of the Only White Woman Who
   Succeeded in Entering the Forbidden City*, Alexandra David-Neel
   (Virago)

Turkey

Mooncranker's Gift, Barry Unsworth (Penguin)
The Towers of Trebizond, Rose Macaulay (Flamingo)
A Fez of the Heart, Jeremy Seal (Picador)
Dervish, Tim Kelsey (Hamish Hamilton)
Portrait of a Turkish Family, Irfan Orga (Eland)
A Proper Holiday, Ann Oakley (Flamingo)

USA

American novels are too numerous to list. Take your pick from
the big-name classic writers – Edith Wharton, Henry James,
John Steinbeck, Dorothy Parker, F. Scott Fitzgerald, Carson

McCullers, Mark Twain, Jack London. Or try crime, from vintage writers like Dashiel Hammett and Raymond Chandler or contemporary writers such as Sara Paretsky and Elmore Leonard. There's a rich vein of black writing from the likes of Maya Angelou, James Baldwin, Alice Walker and Terry Macmillan. As far as contemporary writers go, you can't go wrong with anything by Alice Hoffman, Alison Lurie, John Irving, Anne Tyler.

So we've restricted ourselves to listing a selection of travel writing, plus some fiction particularly relevant to travelling or to specific areas.

General
The Great American Bus Ride, Irma Kurtz (Fourth Estate)
Bury My Heart at Wounded Knee, Dee Brown (Vintage)
USA, John Dos Passos (Penguin)
The Lost Continent, Bill Bryson (Abacus)
Dances with Wolves, Michael Blake (Penguin)
On the Road, Jack Kerouac (Penguin)
America Observed, Alistair Cooke (Penguin)
From Sea to Shining Sea, Gavin Young (Penguin)
American Heartbeat, Mick Brown (Penguin)
Into the Badlands, John Williams (Flamingo)
Old Glory, Jonathan Raban (Picador)
Travels in a Strange State, Josie Dew (Warner Books)
The Oxford Book of American Short Stories, ed. Joyce Carol Oates (Oxford University Press)
The Kinky Friedman Crime Club, Kinky Friedman (Faber and Faber)
Where I'm Calling From, Raymond Carver (Harvill)

Deep South and Florida
The Sound and the Fury, William Faulkner (Vintage)
As I Lay Dying, William Faulkner (Vintage)
Gone With the Wind, Margaret Mitchell (Pan)
To Kill a Mockingbird, Harper Lee (Mandarin)
Midnight in the Garden of Good and Evil, John Berendt (Vintage)
A Confederacy of Dunces, John Kennedy Toole (Penguin)

Beloved, Toni Morrison (Picador)

In God's Country: Travels in the Bible Belt, USA, Douglas Kennedy (Abacus)

The Color Purple, Alice Walker (The Women's Press)

Strip Tease, Carl Hiaasen (Pan)

Double Whammy, Carl Hiaasen (Pan)

Skin Tight, Carl Hiaasen (Pan)

Miami, Joan Didion (Flamingo)

To Have and Have Not, Ernest Hemingway (Arrow)

Miami Blues, Charles Willeford (No Exit Press)

New York and East Coast

The Catcher in the Rye, J. D. Salinger (Penguin)

Bonfire of the Vanities, Tom Wolfe (Picador)

Bright Lights, Big City, Jay McInerney (Flamingo)

Slaves of New York, Tama Janowitz (Picador)

The Secret History, Donna Tartt (Penguin)

Jazz, Toni Morrison (Picador)

A Tree Grows in Brooklyn, Betty Smith (Mandarin)

The Novels of Old New York (The Age of Innocence; The Custom of the Country; The House of Mirth), Edith Wharton (Penguin)

The New York Trilogy, Paul Auster (Faber and Faber)

The Heart of the World, Nik Cohn (Vintage)

Flesh and Blood, Michael Cunningham (Penguin)

Our Noise, Jeff Gomez (Penguin)

West Coast and South-West

Tales of the City series, Armistead Maupin (Black Swan)

Los Angeles without a Map, Richard Rayner (Flamingo)

Snow Falling on Cedars, David Guterson (Bloomsbury)

The Joy Luck Club, Amy Tan (Minerva)

Tortilla Curtain, T. Coraghessan Boyle (Bloomsbury)

The Postman Always Rings Twice, James M. Cain (Chivers)

Double Indemnity, James M. Cain (Hale)

Mildred Pierce, James M. Cain (Hale)

The Black Dahlia, James Ellroy (Arrow)

Get Shorty, Elmore Leonard (Penguin)
The Loved One, Evelyn Waugh (Penguin)
Pigs in Heaven, Barbara Kingsolver (Faber and Faber)
Even Cowgirls Get the Blues, Tom Robbins (Bantam)
Generation X, Douglas Coupland (Penguin)
Dead Man's Walk, Larry McMurtry (Phoenix)
Lonesome Dove, Larry McMurtry (Phoenix)
Motel Nirvana, Melanie McGrath (Flamingo)

Mid-West
The Beet Queen, Louise Erdrich (Flamingo)
Lake Wobegon Days, Garrison Keillor (Faber and Faber)
A Lady's Life in the Rocky Mountains, Isabella Bird (Virago)
Moo, Jane Smiley (Flamingo)
A Thousand Acres, Jane Smiley (Flamingo)
Who Will Run the Frog Hospital? Lorrie Moore (Faber and Faber)
A Map of the World, Jane Hamilton (Black Swan)

Uzbekistan

Samarkand, Amin Maalouf (Abacus)

Venezuela

The Creature in the Map, Charles Nicholl (Jonathan Cape)
In Trouble Again (A Journey between the Orinoco and the Amazon),
    Redmond O'Hanlon (Penguin)

Vietnam, Cambodia and Laos

The Quiet American, Graham Greene (Penguin)
The Lover, Marguerite Duras (Fontana)
The Sorrow of War, Bao Ninh (Minerva)

River of Time, Jon Swain (Minerva)
Derailed in Uncle Ho's Victory Garden, Tim Page (Touchstone/Simon & Schuster)
Three Moons in Vietnam, Maria Coffey (Abacus)
Novel without a Name, Duong Thu Huong (Picador)
Dispatches, Michael Herr (Pan)
Swimming to Cambodia, Spalding Grey (Picador)
Bridge Across My Sorrows, Christina Noble (Corgi)
A Good Scent from a Strange Mountain, Robert Olen Butler (Minerva)
A Phoenix Rising: Impressions of Vietnam, Zoë Schramm-Evans (Flamingo)
A Dragon Apparent, Norman Lewis (Eland)
Bright Shining Lie, Neil Sheehan (Picador)
Lord Jim, Joseph Conrad (Penguin)

Yemen

The Southern Gates of Arabia, Freya Stark (Large Print Books)

Zimbabwe

Under my Skin, Doris Lessing (HarperCollins)
The Grass is Singing, Doris Lessing (Flamingo)
African Laughter, Doris Lessing (Flamingo)
Nervous Conditions, Tsitsi Dangaremga (The Women's Press)
The Leopard Hunts in Darkness, Wilbur Smith (Mandarin)
A Time to Die, Wilbur Smith (Pan)
Mukiwa: A White Boy in Africa, Peter Godwin (Picador)

Travel Magazines

- *Wanderlust*, PO Box 1832, Windsor, Berks SL4 6YP (01753 620426). Bi-monthly, £2.50. Subscription: £15 (6 issues).

- *Independent & Specialist Travel*, 3 Clive House, Prospect Hill, Redditch, Worcestershire B97 4BY (01527 584500). Subscription: £15 (6 issues); £30 (12 issues).
- *Traveller*, published by WEXAS International, 45–9 Brompton Road, London SW3 1DE (0171 589 0500). Annual subscription: £39.58 (UK); £50.42 (overseas).
- *Business Traveller*, Compass House, 22 Redan Place, London W2 4SZ (0171 229 7799). Annual subscription: £39.30 (UK); £43.30 (Eire); £60.10 (Europe).
- *Planet Talk* is a free quarterly newsletter produced by Lonely Planet (0181 742 3161).
- *TNT Magazine*, free every Monday (London and Edinburgh). They also produce an *Australia & New Zealand Travel Planner* every two months – you can pick them up free in London or at travel shows like Independent Travellers' World, or take out a subscription (£2.50 for three editions; £5 for six editions). Send your name, address and cheque/postal order, made out to TNT Magazine, to TNT Planner Subscriptions, TNT Planners, 14–15 Child's Place, London SW5 9RX (0171 373 3377). Other travellers' magazines, such as *Traveller Magazine* and *Southern Cross*, also appear free in dispensing stands every week in London.
- *GO New Zealand*, *GO Australia* and *GO Canada*, useful, information-packed booklets, available free from GO Publishing Distribution, 70 Brunswick Street, Stockton-on-Tees, Cleveland TS18 1DW. Just send a self-addressed, 9″ by 6″ envelope, with two first-class stamps, and write in the top left-hand corner the name of the booklet you require (if you want all three, send three s.a.e.s).

Travel Bookshops

Most good bookshops now carry a range of guidebooks and travel literature, but there are also several specialist travel bookshops around if you want a wider selection. All of the following shops carry guidebooks and maps and some have a mail-order service.

- **The Travel Bookshop**, 13 Blenheim Crescent, London W11 2EE (0171 229 5260).
- **Daunt Books**, 83 Marylebone High St, London W1M 3DE (0171 224 2295).
- **Stanfords**, 12–14 Long Acre, London WC2E 9LP (0171 836 1321/1915). Also at British Airways, 156 Regent Street, London W1R 5TA (0171 434 4744) and at Campus Travel, 52 Grosvenor Gardens, London SW1W 0AG (0171 730 1314).
- **The Map Shop**, 15 High Street, Upton-on-Severn, Worcestershire WR8 0HJ (01684 593146). Has a mail-order service.
- **Blackwell's Map & Travel Shop**, 53 Broad Street, Oxford OX1 3BQ (01865 792792).
- **Heffers Map Shop**, 19 Sidney Street, Cambridge CB2 3HL (01223 568467). Has a mail-order service.

Chapter 17 / **A–Z Country Guide**

Tourist-Information Offices in Great Britain

Many countries, especially some of the smaller African states or Pacific islands, for example, don't have tourist-information offices. If no tourism-information contact is given for the country or countries you plan to visit, consult a good guidebook instead or try the embassy/consulate/high commission to see if they can help.

Embassies and Consulates in Great Britain

The visa situation changes all the time. In many countries, UK citizens won't need a visa. In some, you may not need a visa for tourism but will if you intend to work or if you plan to spend longer than a certain amount of time (often three months). Other countries may at certain times refuse to issue visas at all. The best course is always to check with the relevant embassy or consulate. Many of the offices are only open during limited hours, so if at first you don't get an answer, keep trying. Where no embassy contact is given, visas are usually issued on arrival or at the embassies in neighbouring countries; enquire on the spot or consult the most up-to-date guidebook.

World Weather

We've given a rough idea of the weather patterns in each country, but for more detailed information, consult a good guidebook or call the Meteorological Office Overseas Enquiry Bureau on 01344

420242 and ask about the countries you're interested in. Calls are charged at premium rate (49p per minute peak rate; 39p per minute all other times).

Afghanistan

Climate Extreme, with hot, dry summers and cold winters with lots of snow.

Contacts Afghan Embassy, 31 Prince's Gate, London SW7 1QQ (0171 589 8891).

Albania

Climate Mediterranean on the coast with warm, dry summers (May to September) and cool, damp winters. Most rain falls November to April. Sea breezes and moderate temperatures in coastal areas. The climate in the mountains is harsher, with snow and rain in winter.

Contacts Albanian Embassy, 4th Floor, 38 Grosvenor Gardens, London SW1W 0EB (0171 730 5709).

Algeria

Climate Hot. Warm and temperate on the coast, with temperatures ranging from 12°C in winter to 25°C in summer. Temperatures inland are higher. Rainfall is erratic – desert regions receive next to nothing but the northern mountains can get heavy rain. Most rain falls in winter.

Contacts Algerian Embassy, 6 Hyde Park Gate, London SW7 5EW (0171 221 7800)

Andorra

Climate Alpine, with warm, dry summers, mild, wet springs, and long winters with plenty of snow.

Contacts Andorran Delegation and Tourist Office, 63 Westover Road, London SW18 2RF (0181 874 4806).

Angola

Climate Mix of temperate and tropical. Generally hot year-round with temperatures ranging from around 23°C in winter (June to September) to 30°C in summer. Rainy season runs from November to April. Desert climate in the south but hot, humid and equatorial in the north, which gets more rain. Cooler and drier on the coast.

Contacts Angolan Embassy, 98 Park Lane, London W1Y 3TA (0171 495 1752).

Anguilla (UK Dependent Territory)

Climate Tropical and generally pleasant. Hot and humid much of the year, but trade winds relieve the humidity, especially from January to April. The rainiest months are usually May to November and it is wetter on the windward (north-east) sides of the

island and in the interior. The
hurricane season runs from June to
November, with August and
September the riskiest months.

Contacts Anguilla Tourist Office,
3 Epirus Road, Fulham, London
SW6 7UJ (0171 937 7725).
British Dependent Territories Office,
Clive House, Petty France, London
SWIH 9HD.

Antigua and Barbuda

Climate Tropical and generally
pleasant, with hot, sunny winters and
even hotter summers (August to
October), though the trade winds and
sea breezes provide relief, especially
from January to April. Average
temperatures year-round are around
27°C. Low rainfall, most of it in
November; it is wetter on the
windward (north-east) sides of the
island and in the interior. The
hurricane season runs from June to
November, with July and August the
riskiest months.

Contacts Antigua and Barbuda
Tourist Information, Antigua House,
15 Thayer St, London WIM 5LD
(0171 486 7073).
Antigua and Barbuda High
Commission, as above.

Argentina

Climate Temperate, with mild
winters and warm summers. Hot and
subtropical in the north-east
rainforests. Dry in the western
lowlands. The central Pampas plains
are mild, with rain in summer.
Buenos Aires has warm, sunny
summers (it can be very hot and humid
from December to February) and mild
winters. The best time to visit is
during the winter months (June to
October). Tierra del Fuego, in the far
south of the country, has a sub-arctic
climate: cold, wet and stormy.

Contacts Tourist Information,
Argentinian Consulate, 100
Brompton Road, London SW3 :ER
(0171 589 3104).
Argentinian Embassy, 53 Hans Place,
London SWIX OLA (0171 584 6494).

Armenia

Climate Continental, with warm
summers and very cold winters. Rain
falls year-round but is heaviest in
summer.

Contacts Armenian Embassy, 25A
Cheniston Gardens, London W8 6TH
(0171 938 5435).

Australia

Climate In such a huge country, the
climate varies from one area to the
next, from cool and temperate to
tropical monsoon. In the southern half
of the country, summer months (the
best time to visit) are November to
March; winter months (June to
August) can be cold and wet. In the
northern half, the climate is tropical
and the seasons basically divide into
wet (November to April) and dry (May
to October). Places like Cairns and
Darwin are pretty hot year-round

(though nights in the desert are cold). Tropical cyclones with high winds and torrential rain are fairly frequent in the north-east and north-west. The western half of the country is mostly arid desert. Rain decreases from the coast inland. The north-east has the highest rainfall. If you want fine weather, aim to spend winter in the north and summer in the south.

Contacts Australian Tourist Commission, Gemini House, 10–18 Putney Hill, London SW15 6AA (0181 780 2227).
For a free traveller's guide to Australia, call 01793 707093.
Australian High Commission, Australia House, Strand, London WC2B 4LA (0171 379 4334).
Australian Visa Information Service: 0891 600333.

Austria

Climate Climate is changeable and varies with the altitude, but as a general rule summers are warm and sunny, springs are wet and winters are cold and snowy. Rain falls throughout the year (especially May to August) and snow falls from December to March.

Contacts Austrian National Tourist Office, 30 St George St, London WIR OAL (0171 629 0461).
Austrian Embassy, 18 Belgrave Mews West, London SWIX 8HU (0171 235 3731).

Azerbaijan

Climate Continental, with warm summers and cold, dry winters. Low rainfall, mostly in summer. On the Black Sea coast, summers (June to September) are warm and humid. Temperatures are more extreme in the steppe regions – hotter in summer, colder in winter (November to April).

Contacts Azerbaijan Embassy, 4 Kensington Court, London W8 5DL (0171 938 3412).

Bahamas

Climate Subtropical, with hot summers, low humidity and mild (sometimes cool) winters. Plenty of rain, especially in summer. Hurricane season runs from July to December.

Contacts Bahamas Tourist Office, 3 The Billings, Walnut Tree Close, Guildford, Surrey GUI 4UL (01483 448900).
Bahamas High Commission, 10 Chesterfield St, London WIX 8AH (0171 408 4488).

Bahrain

Climate Very hot, humid summers (May to October), with daytime temperatures as high as 40°C or more. Mild winters (November to March) with warm days and cool nights. This is the best time to visit. Extremely low rainfall.

Contacts Bahrain Embassy and Tourist Information, 98 Gloucester

Road, London SW7 4AU
(0171 370 5132/3).

Bali see Indonesia

Bangladesh

Climate Hot and humid. Heavy
monsoon rains in summer months
frequently cause floods; cyclones are
also possible at that time of year.

Contacts Bangladesh Embassy, 28
Queen's Gate, London SW7 5JA
(0171 584 0081).

Barbados

Climate Moderate tropical and
generally pleasant climate. Warm and
sunny year-round, with temperatures
between 25°C and 28°C. Atlantic
breezes have a cooling effect,
especially from January to April. The
driest months are December to June.
Most rain falls from July to
November, which is also hurricane
season though they usually miss the
island.

Contacts Barbados Tourism
Authority, 263 Tottenham Court Rd,
London WIP OLA (0171 636 9448).
Barbados Embassy, 1 Great Russell
Street, London WC1B 3NH
(0171 631 4975).

Belarus (Belorussia)

Climate Continental, with warm,
wet summers and long, cold, dry
winters (December to April), with

temperatures below freezing and lots
of snow. The warmest month is July.
Moderate rainfall; wettest months are
June to August.

Contacts Embassy of Belarus, 6
Kensington Court, London W8 5DL
(0171 937 3288).

Belgium

Climate Maritime, temperate and
very changeable, but with no real
extremes. Mild winters, cool to warm
summers (June to September) and lots
of rain, especially on the coast.

Contacts Belgian Tourist Office, 29
Princes Street, London WIR 7RG
(0171 629 3977 or 0891 887799).
Belgian Embassy, 103 Eaton Square,
London SW1W 9AB (0171 470 3700).

Belize

Climate Most of the country is hot,
humid and tropical throughout the
year, with temperatures pretty
consistent at about 23–7°C. In the
mountains, it can get cool at night.
The rainforests of southern Belize are
very humid because of the heavy
rainfall. The dry season runs from
October to May, which is the best
time to travel round. Winter
(mid-December to April) is a busy
tourist season. The rainy season runs
from May to December with July,
September and October the wettest
months and a risk of hurricanes from
June to November.

Contacts Belize High Commission

and Tourist Information Office,
22 Harcourt House, 19 Cavendish
Square, London WIM 9AD
(0171 499 9728).

Benin

Climate Hot year-round. The south
has two rainy seasons: April to
mid-July (most rain falls in June) and
mid-September to late October. In the
north there is only one rainy season –
June to late October. The climate in
the north is tropical and temperatures
can reach 46°C. In the south
temperatures range from 18–35°C.
The hottest months are March to
June. Dusty winds in the dry season
(December to March).

Contacts Benin Consulate, Dolphin
House, 16 The Broadway, Stanmore,
Middlesex HA7 4DW (0181 954 8800).

Bermuda

Climate Subtropical. Great climate
with hot summers and warm winters.
Rain falls year-round but less in
summer.

Contacts Bermuda Tourism,
1 Battersea Church Rd, London
SW11 3LY (0171 734 8813).
British Dependent Territories Office,
Clive House, Petty France, London
SW1H 9HD.

Bhutan

Climate Changes with the altitude:
weather in the northern highlands is
always cold and harsh; the centre is

temperate; the southern lowlands are
subtropical. Warmer in the east than
the west in the central valleys.
Monsoon rains fall from June to
August.

Contacts Bhutan Tourism
Corporation (BTCL), PO Box 159,
Thimphu, Bhutan (00 975 24045).

Bolivia

Climate High plateau has extreme
tropical climate. Hot and humid in
the north and west. Wettest in the
summer months, from November to
February. La Paz gets rain daily and
can get cold winds from the Altiplano.
Snow in mountains. The winter
months of April to October are drier
and temperatures pleasant, though it
can be cold at night. The western
plains are arid in the south; humid
and tropical in the north.

Contacts Bolivian Embassy, 106
Eaton Square, London SW1W 9AD
(0171 235 4248/2257).

Borneo

Climate Wettest months are
October to December.

Contacts See Malaysia, Indonesia or
Brunei (Borneo is divided into
Kalimantan, a province of Indonesia;
Sabah and Sarawak, which form
Eastern Malaysia; and Brunei).

Bosnia/Herzegovina

Climate Warm summers, cold winters with snow, especially at altitude.

Contacts The Embassy of the Republic of Bosnia and Herzegovina, 320 Regent Street, London WIR 5AB (0171 255 3758).

Botswana

Climate Mostly dry. Rainfall is low and erratic but there is a wet season in the summer (November to March). These months are also very humid and hot, with daytime temperatures up to 40°C. Winter months are late May to August, which are very dry and can be subject to droughts. Winter can be the best time to view the wildlife as it clusters round the water holes. Winters are warm and sunny, with cool nights. Night-time temperatures in the Kalahari can be bitterly cold in June and July, with occasional frosts.

Contacts Botswana High Commission and Tourist Information, 6 Stratford Place, London WIN 9AE (0171 499 0031).

Brazil

Climate The Amazon basin is hot and humid year-round, with a rainy season from April to July. The south has hot summers and cool winters. Wettest months are December to March. Rio is hot and tropical, with sunny summers and mild winters. The rainy season is November to April,

when it's also hot and humid. Winter months are June to August, when temperatures range from 13–18°C. Summer months are December to February when temperatures can rise up into the 30s and 40s. It can be very humid in many places. Rain falls year round. In the north, winters are cooler, with rainfall in summer. The north-east can have droughts.

Contacts Brazilian Embassy, 32 Green Street, London WIY 4AT (0171 499 0877). Brazilian Consulate, 6 St Alban's Street, London SWIY 4SQ (0171 930 9055).

British Virgin Islands

Climate Tropical and generally pleasant. Hot and humid much of the year but trade winds relieve the humidity, especially from January to April. It's wetter on the windward (north-east) sides of the islands and in the interior, with May to November seeing the highest rainfall. The hurricane season runs from June to November, with August and September the riskiest months.

Contacts British Virgin Islands Tourist Board, 110 St Martin's Lane, London WC2N 4DY (0171 240 4259). British Dependent Territories Office, Clive House, Petty France, London SWIH 9HD.

Brunei

Climate Tropical and humid. Temperatures are stable at between

26° and 31°C all year. Heavy rainfall, especially during the north-east monsoon from September to January.

Contacts Brunei High Commission, 20 Belgrave Square, London SW1X 8PG (0171 581 0521).
Visa Section, 19 Belgrave Mews West, London SW1X 8HT (0171 581 0521).

Bulgaria

Climate Temperate, with cold, damp winters (when temperatures can fall to below freezing) and warm, dry summers. The mountains get most rain. In winter, snow is likely everywhere. Most rain falls in the summer months.

Contacts Bulgarian Embassy, 186–8 Queen's Gate, London SW7 5HL (0171 584 9400/9433).

Burkina Faso

Climate Tropical. Dry and cool from November to February; the hottest months are March to early June. Rainfall is erratic and the region is prone to droughts.

Contacts Burkina Faso Embassy, 5 Cinnamon Row, Plantation Wharf, London SW11 3TW (0171 738 1800).

Burma see Myanmar

Burundi

Climate Temperate but very humid. Hottest and most humid in lowland regions, and near Lake Tanganyika, with temperatures around 30°C. In the northern highlands, temperatures are cooler. Plenty of rain, especially from October to May (with a brief dry period in December/January).

Contacts No embassy or tourist-information office in the UK.

Cambodia

Climate Tropical. Hot year-round, with average temperatures over 25°C. Summer (May to October) is hot and humid, with temperatures around 33°C and humidity as high as 90 per cent; this is also the time of the heavy monsoon rains.

Contacts No embassy or tourist-information centre in the UK. Visas for travel to Cambodia are issued in Saigon, Moscow or Bangkok.

Cameroon

Climate Rainfall varies from north to south. The south has an equatorial climate, with lots of rain. The rainy seasons here are March/April and May to November. Floods are possible in July and August. There is less rain inland. In the north, the rainy season runs from June to September. The far north can have droughts.

Contacts Cameroon High Commission and Tourist Information, 84 Holland Park, London W11 3SB (0171 727 0771).

Canada

Climate Winters and summers are both more extreme in the interior of the country. Temperatures on the Pacific coast are generally milder. Wettest months are November to January. Montreal has hot, sunny summers and very cold winters with lots of snow and ice from December to March. Toronto is similar. Vancouver has a similar climate to the UK, with warm summers and mild, wet winters; it rains year-round but especially from November to February. Newfoundland has heavy fog and icebergs. On the whole, the climate is continental – hot summers and harsh winters – but climate varies according to altitude, latitude and proximity to the sea.

Contacts Visit Canada Centre, 62–5 Trafalgar Square, London WC2N 5DY (0891 715000). Canadian High Commission (visa section), 38 Grosvenor St, London WIX OAA (0171 258 6600). Immigration Information Service: 0891 616644.

Cape Verde Islands

Climate Cooler than mainland West Africa. July to October are the hottest months, when temperatures go up to 27°C. It can get very cool from December to March. Rainfall is erratic: most occurs between late August and early October. The rest of the year is very dry and subject to long droughts and can be very windy, especially from December to February.

Contacts No embassy or tourist-information office in the UK.

Cayman Islands (UK Dependent Territory)

Climate Pleasant year-round, with average temperatures of around 25°C. Most rain falls between May and October.

Contacts Cayman Islands Government Office and Department of Tourism, 6 Arlington Street, London SWIA IRE (0171 491 7771). British Dependent Territories Office, Clive House, Petty France, London SWIH 9HD.

Central African Republic

Climate Hot and dry in the north (Sahara desert), where temperatures can go up to 40°C from February to May. Equatorial in the south, with fairly heavy rain year-round, especially from June to October. High humidity.

Contacts French Consulate General, 6A Cromwell Place, London SW7 2EW (0171 838 2050/1). Visa Information Service: 0891 887733.

Chad

Climate Desert climate in the north, on the edge of the Sahara; tropical in the south; semi-arid in-between.

Hottest months are March to May, with daytime temperatures at 45°C and even higher. Milder from December to February, when nights can be chilly. Heavy rains in the south from June to September.

Contacts No embassy or tourist-information office in the UK.

Chile

Climate Generally temperate, with mild winters and warm summers, but there are great variations from top to bottom, and depending on the altitude. Generally hot and dry in the north. The far south is pretty constantly cold and can be stormy and windy. Central regions have hot, dry summers and mild winters. Snow year-round on high mountain peaks. Wettest months are April, June, December. Santiago has a Mediterranean climate, with hot, sunny, dry summers and mild, temperate winters – average temperatures around 28°C in January, 10°C in July. Nights can be cold and can get bitter winds from the mountains. Rainy season is May to August. Most rain falls in the winter months, when there may also be frost and snow inland. Easter Island is hot and dry.

Contacts Embassy of Chile and Tourist Information Office, 12 Devonshire St, London WIN 2DS (0171 580 6392).

China

Climate Such a huge country obviously has very different weather conditions from one area to the next. The north has an extreme continental climate – winters (December to March) are harsh and very cold (temperatures can drop as low as −30°C) but dry and sunny. Summers (May to August) are hot (temperatures can go up to the high 30s) and rainy (most rain falls in July and August). North-western areas have hot, dry summers. Spring and autumn are the best times to visit, with temperatures between 20°C and 30°C, though nights can be cold. Central regions have hot and humid summers (April to October); winters are cold and wet, with temperatures below freezing. In the south, summers (April to September) can be hot (temperatures up to 38°C), humid and wet. Typhoons are possible in coastal regions from July to September. The winter months are January to March. Autumn and spring are the best times to visit. Temperatures in the desert areas can be very hot. In winter it is very cold with temperatures falling to −10°C.

Contacts China National Tourist Office, 4 Glentworth St, London NWI 5PG (0171 935 9427/9787). Chinese Embassy, Visa Section, 31 Portland Place, London WIN 3AG (0171 631 1430). Chinese Embassy Visa and General Information Service: 0891 880808.

Colombia

Climate Tropical, though temperatures vary with the altitude. Hot and wet on the coast; cooler in the highlands. Bogota temperatures stay fairly constant (18–19°C) year-round. Warm and sunny days but the nights can be cool. Most rain falls from March to May and October to November.

Contacts Colombian Embassy, Flat 3A, 3 Hans Crescent, London SW1X 0LN (0171 589 9177). Colombian Consulate, Suite 14, 140 Park Lane, London W1Y 3AA (0171 495 4233).

Comoros

Climate Hot and humid year-round. Moderate rainfall, most of it in the summer months of November to April, which is also cyclone season. Temperatures at this time of year are around 35°C. It is cooler and drier from May to October, with south-east trade winds.

Contacts No embassy or tourist-information office in the UK. Comoros visas can be obtained from the French Embassy.

Congo

Climate Hot, tropical and humid year-round. The rainy season is October to November and February to April/May. Rainfall is especially heavy in the north of the country. Temperatures range from 21°C to 27°C. The best time to visit is from June to September, the driest months. Travel in the rainy season can be difficult.

Contacts No embassy or tourist-information office in the UK.

Cook Islands

Climate December to April are the rainiest and hottest months. It is coldest from June to September. The hurricane season runs from November to March. The best time to visit is between May and October, but the climate is pleasant year-round, with no real extremes of temperature.

Contacts Tourism Council of the South Pacific, 375 Upper Richmond Road West, London SW14 7NX (0181 392 1838).

Costa Rica

Climate Temperatures are affected by altitude. Hot, humid and tropical along the coast; more temperate in the highlands. The dry season runs from late December to April. The rest of the year is wet, with the Caribbean region wetter than the rest of the country. The dry season is particularly dry in the highlands and on much of the Pacific coast, with negligible rainfall. On the southern Pacific coast there is rain year-round. The Caribbean coast is particularly hot.

Contacts Costa Rica Embassy and Tourist Information Office, Flat 1, 14

Lancaster Gate, London W2 3LH
(0171 706 8844).

Croatia

Climate The Adriatic coast has a
Mediterranean climate, with hot, dry
summers and mild, rainy winters. Sea
breezes create moderate temperatures
along the coast in spring and summer.
Spring and autumn are the best times
to visit this region. The interior has a
temperate continental climate, with
cold winters and warm summers.

Contacts Croatia National Tourist
Office, 2 The Lanchesters, 162–4
Fulham Palace Road, London W6
9ER (0181 563 7979).
Embassy of the Republic of Croatia,
21 Conway Street, London W1P 5HL
(0171 387 1144).

Cuba

Climate Subtropical – hot and sunny
year-round. The coolest months are
December to March, with average
temperatures of 26°C. In the hottest
months (July and August) average
temperatures rise to 32°C. Most rain
falls between May and October,
especially in September and October,
when humidity is also high.
Hurricanes are rare but possible in
autumn (August to November).

Contacts Cuban Embassy and
Tourist Office, 167 High Holborn,
London WC1V 6PA (0171 379 1706).
Cuban Consulate Visa, Tourism and
General Information Service: 0891
880820.

Cyprus

Climate Mediterranean, with hot,
dry, sunny summers (May to
September) and mild winters, with
snow in the mountains. Most rain
falls in the winter.

Contacts Cyprus Tourist Office, 213
Regent Street, London W1R 8DA
(0171 734 9822/2593).
Cyprus Consulate, 93 Park Street,
London W1Y 4ET (0171 629 5350).

Cyprus, Northern see Northern Cyprus

Czech Republic

Climate Mix of temperate and
continental climates. Winters are cool
to cold; temperatures can go below
freezing and thick fogs are likely.
Summers are warm (this is also when
most of the rain falls). Prague has
changeable weather, with cold, icy
winters and mild, sunny summers. The
wettest months are spring and
summer.

Contacts Embassy of the Czech
Republic, 28 Kensington Palace
Gardens, London W8 4QY (0171 243
1115).
Information Service (inc. visa
enquiries): 0891 171267.
Czech Centre, 30 Kensington Palace
Gardens, London W8 4QY.
24-hour information service (inc.
tourism enquiries): 0891 171266.

Denmark

Climate Cool and temperate, very like the British climate, with no real extremes. It's mild, equable and changeable. Mild summers; cold, wet winters; moderate rainfall year-round, especially in summer and autumn.

Contacts Danish Embassy, 55 Sloane Street, London SW1X 9SR (0171 235 1255 or 333 0200). Danish Tourist Board, 55 Sloane Street, London SW1X 9SY (0171 259 5959). Information Service: 0891 600109.

Djibouti

Climate Hot and dry year-round and very hot in June to August. Temperatures range from 25–35°C. The coolest months are October to April, when there may also be a little rain.

Contacts French Consulate General, 6A Cromwell Place, London SW7 2EW (0171 838 2050/1). Visa Information Service: 0891 887733.

Dominica

Climate Tropical and generally pleasant, with average temperatures over 25°C. It is hot and humid much of the year, but trade winds relieve the humidity, especially from January to April. The rainiest months are usually May to November and it is wetter on the windward (north-east) sides of the island and in the interior.

The hurricane season runs from June to November, with August and September the riskiest months.

Contacts Dominica Tourist Office, 1 Collingham Gardens, Earl's Court, London SW5 0HW (0171 835 1937). Dominica High Commission, 1 Collingham Gardens, Earl's Court, London SW5 0HW (0171 370 5194).

Dominican Republic

Climate Hot, humid and tropical around the coast; cooler in the highlands. Plenty of rain (especially in the north-east).

Contacts Honorary Consulate of the Dominican Republic, 6 Queens Mansions, Brook Green, London W6 7EB (0171 602 1885).

Dubai

Climate Warm and hot year-round. Very low rainfall, mostly from December to February. High humidity.

Contacts Dubai Tourism Promotion Board, 125 Pall Mall, London SW1Y 5EA (0171 839 0580). UAE Embassy (visa section), 48 Prince's Gate, London SW7 1PT (0171 581 1281). Consular department: 0171 589 3434.

Easter Island see Chile

Eastern Caribbean
(St Kitts and Nevis; St Lucia; St Vincent and the Grenadines)

Climate Tropical and generally
pleasant, with temperatures between
16°C and 33°C. It is hot and humid
much of the year, but trade winds
relieve the humidity, especially from
January to April. There is lots of rain
year-round, especially from May to
November; it is wetter on the
windward (north-east) sides of the
island and in the interior. Spring is the
driest time. The hurricane season runs
from June to November, with August
and September the riskiest months.

Contacts Eastern Caribbean High
Commission, 10 Kensington Court,
London W8 5DL (0171 937 9522).
Tourist offices for St Kitts and Nevis
(0171 376 0881), and St Vincent and
the Grenadines (0171 937 6570), are
also at this address.

Ecuador

Climate Tropical, hot and humid on
the coast; cooler in the mountains.
The wettest months are January to
May. Very changeable weather. The
Galapagos and coastal areas are hot
and rainy from January to April. The
Amazon area is pretty constantly
rainy and also hot. The highlands have
a dry season from June to September
and December, and cooler
temperatures. Can get landslides on
mountain roads in the wet season.

Contacts Embassy of Ecuador, Flat
3B, 3 Hans Crescent, London SW1X
0LS (0171 584 2648).

Egypt

Climate Generally has hot summers
(June to September) and mild winters.
In the south, it's hot year-round but
cooler at nights. Hot Saharan winds
can blow between March and June.
The best time to visit is May or
October/November. Little rain apart
from in the coastal region. Cairo is
hot and sunny year-round – it has a
desert climate, with next to no rain.

Contacts Egyptian Tourist Office,
Egyptian House, 170 Piccadilly,
London W1V 9DD (0171 493 5282).
Information Service: 0891 600299.
Egyptian Consulate General, 2
Lowndes Street, London SW1X 9ET
(0171 235 9719).
Visa Information Service: 0891
887777.
Egyptian Embassy, 26 South Street,
London W1Y 6DD (0171 499 2401).

El Salvador

Climate Tropical and hot, with
temperatures fairly constant, from
30–34°C. The coastal plain is hotter
than the rest of the country. Highland
regions are cooler and more
temperate. Winter (May to October)
is the wet season but it may only rain
for about an hour a day; summer
(November to April) is dry and can be
dusty.

Contacts Embassy of El Salvador,
Tennyson House, 159 Great Portland
Street, London W1N 5FD
(0171 436 8282).

Equatorial Guinea

Climate Hot, wet and humid year-round, with heavy rainfall. The rainy season runs from July to January and is especially wet from July to October. The mainland is slightly drier and cooler than Bioko Island, with most of its rain in April/May and October to December.

Contacts No embassy or tourist-information office in the UK.

Eritrea

Climate Hot in the desert; warm in the mountains. The coast is hot but temperatures are lower inland. Erratic rainfall and subject to droughts.

Contacts Eritrean Consulate, 96 White Lion Street, London N1 9PF (0171 713 0096).

Estonia

Climate Temperate, with very cold winters (November to February), warm summers (May to September), and steady rain throughout the year. Hottest and wettest months are July and August. Snow is likely from December to March.

Contacts Estonian Embassy and Tourist Information, 16 Hyde Park Gate, London SW7 5DG (0171 589 3428).

Ethiopia

Climate The east of the country is mostly arid plateaux, hot and dry

with serious droughts. The highlands are warm and usually get good rains in summer (June to September), though subject to occasional droughts. Can get snow on the mountains.

Contacts Ethiopian Embassy, 17 Prince's Gate, London SW7 1PZ (0171 589 7212).

Falkland Islands (UK Crown Colony)

Climate Temperate and can be windy. Temperatures rarely reach the mid-20°Cs. In the winter months of December and January it is wet and cold.

Contacts Falkland Islands Government Office (inc. tourist information), Falkland House, 14 Broadway, London SW1H 0BH (0171 222 2542).

Fiji

Climate Tropical. High temperatures all year. Rain falls year-round but the wettest months are November/December and March/April, which are also hot and humid. It's cooler and dryer between May and October, and also better on the coast because of the sea breezes. Sunny year-round, with fairly constant temperatures between 20°C in July/August and 29°C from November to April.

Contacts Fiji Embassy, 5th Floor, New Zealand House, Haymarket,

London SW1Y 4TQ (0171 839 2200).
Tourism Council of the South Pacific,
375 Upper Richmond Road West,
London SW14 7NX (0181 392 1838).

Finland

Climate Long and very cold winters,
with lots of snow. Short, warmer and
sunny summers (with lots of
mosquitoes). The north has a
particularly harsh climate with very
little sunlight in winter. Low rainfall,
especially in the north.

Contacts Embassy of Finland, 38
Chesham Place, London SW1X 8HW
(0171 235 9531/838 6200).
Finnish Tourist Board, 32−5 Pall
Mall, London SW1Y 5LP
(0171 839 4048).

France

Climate The north is temperate,
damp and changeable − summers quite
warm and sunny; winters cold and
frosty (most rain falls in summer).
The south has a Mediterranean
climate: hot, sunny summers with
very little rain, and mild winters with
some rain.

Contacts French Consulate General,
6A Cromwell Place, London SW7 2EW
(0171 838 2000/2050/1).
Visa Information Service: 0891
887733.
French Embassy, 58 Knightsbridge,
London SW1X 7JT (0171 201 1000).
French Tourist Office, 178 Piccadilly,
London W1V 0AL (0891 244123).

French Guiana
(Overseas Department of
France)

Climate Tropical, hot, wet and
humid in the lowlands, with cooling
breezes on the coast. Cooler in the
highlands. The rainy season runs
from December to June, with
especially heavy rainfall in May.

Contacts French Consulate General,
6A Cromwell Place, London SW7 2EW
(0171 838 2000/2050/1).
Visa Information Service: 0891
887733.

French Polynesia (inc. Tahiti)
(Overseas Territory of France)

Climate Hot and can be humid.
Sunny all year and fairly constant
temperatures, between 20°C and
32°C. Rain falls year-round, especially
from November to April. It's dryer
and cooler from May to October, with
average temperatures of around 25°C.

Contacts French Consulate General,
6A Cromwell Place, London SW7 2EW
(0171 838 2000/2050/1).
Visa Information Service:
0891 887733.

Gabon

Climate Hot and tropical
year-round, with temperatures
around 30°C. High humidity. Cooler
on the coast. Heavy rain most of the
year (with a rainy season from January
to May). The driest months are June
to September.

Contacts Gabonese Embassy, 27 Elvaston Place, London sw7 5nl (0171 823 9986).

The Gambia

Climate Hot and tropical with temperatures usually around 30°C. The wettest months are between July and September, when it rains most days and humidity is high. The hottest months are October to November and mid-February to late June. In between these two hot periods, the weather is dry and pleasantly warm. Coastal areas are generally cooler than inland.

Contacts Gambia High Commission, 57 Kensington Court, London w8 5dg (0171 937 6316/8). Gambia Tourist Information Office, address as above (0171 376 0093).

Georgia

Climate Generally warm though colder at altitude. The west gets the most rain. Subtropical on the coast.

Contacts Georgian Embassy, 45 Avonmore Road, London w14 8rt (0171 603 5226).

Germany

Climate Temperate in north and central areas; more extreme in the south. The east is colder. Frankfurt and Munich have mild, warm summers and chilly winters. Rains year-round, especially in summer.

Contacts German National Tourist Office, Nightingale House, 65 Curzon St, London w1y 7pe (0891 600100). German Embassy (Visa Section), 23 Belgrave Square, London sw1x 8pz (0171 235 5033). Visa Information Service: 0891 331166.

Ghana

Climate Tropical, with temperatures from 21°C to 32°C year-round. Rainfall is heaviest in the rainforests; the north and coastal regions are drier. The north has one wet season from May to September.

Contacts Ghana Tourist Information, 102 Park Street, London w1y 3rj (0171 493 4901). Ghana High Commission, 104 Highgate Hill, London n6 5he (0181 342 8686).

Greece

Climate Mainly Mediterranean, with hot, dry summers (with winds on the islands) and mild, wet winters. Alpine in northern mountain areas, which can get snow. Low rainfall, mostly between November and January.

Contacts National Tourist Organization of Greece, 4 Conduit St, London w1r 0dj (0171 734 5997). Greek Embassy, 1A Holland Park, London w11 3tp (0171 221 6467). Greek General Consulate Visa Information Service: 0891 171202.

Greenland see Denmark

Grenada

Climate Tropical and generally pleasant. It is hot and humid much of the year, but trade winds relieve the humidity, especially from January to April. There is plenty of rain, mostly in the summer months (July to November), and it is wetter on the windward (north-east) sides of the island and in the interior. The hurricane season runs from June to November, with August and September the riskiest months.

Contacts Grenada Board of Tourism, 1 Collingham Gardens, Earl's Court, London sw5 0HW (0171 370 5164).
Grenada High Commission, address as above (0171 373 7809).

Guadeloupe
(Overseas Department of France)

Climate Tropical and generally pleasant. It is hot and humid much of the year, but trade winds relieve the humidity, especially from January to April. The rainiest months are usually May to November and it is wetter on the windward (north-east) sides of the island and in the interior. Hurricane season runs from June to November, with August and September the riskiest months.

Contacts See France.

Guam
(External Territory of USA)

Climate Tropical oceanic climate. Warm and humid year-round, with temperatures ranging from around 21°C to 32°C (average daily temperature is 27°C). The best time to visit is between December and March, the driest, least humid and coolest months. Typhoons are possible between August and December.

Contacts See USA.

Guatemala

Climate The dry season runs from October to May, when the climate is warm and pleasant in the central highlands. On both Pacific and Caribbean coasts and in the northern lowlands, the climate is tropical, hot (temperatures can go up to 38°C), humid and rainy. Most rain falls in the summer.

Contacts Embassy of Guatemala and Tourist Information, 13 Fawcett Street, London sw10 9HN (0171 351 3042).

Guinea

Climate Tropical, with heavy annual rainfall on the coast, especially in July and August. The central mountains are drier, with rainfall between May and October. Hot Sahara winds blow in the dry season.

Contacts No embassy or tourist-information office in the UK.

Guinea-Bissau

Climate Tropical, with a rainy season from late May to early November. The coast is much wetter than the interior. It is humid almost year-round, especially just before the rainy season. December to April are dry, with hot winds. The best time to visit is between November and February.

Contacts Guinea-Bissau Consulate, Flat 5, 8 Palace Gate, Gloucester Road, London w8 5NF (0171 589 5253).

Guyana

Climate Tropical, hot, wet and humid in the lowlands, with cooling breezes on the coast. Cooler in the highlands. There are two rainy seasons, from April to August and November to late January.

Contacts Guyana High Commission, 3 Palace Court, Bayswater Road, London w2 4LP (0171 229 7684).

Haiti

Climate Tropical. Hot and humid on the coast; more temperate in highland regions. Rainy year-round.

Contacts No embassy or tourist-information office in the UK.

Hawaii see USA

Honduras

Climate Tropical, hot and humid in coastal regions. The Caribbean coast gets rain all year round, especially from September to January/February. In these months there are sometimes floods in the north. In the rest of the country, the summer rainy season runs from May to October. It's relatively dry from November to April. Cooler, drier and more temperate inland in the mountains. The coolest months are December and January.

Contacts Honduras Embassy, 115 Gloucester Place, London w1H 3PJ (0171 486 4880).

Hong Kong
(UK Dependent Territory until June 1997)

Climate Subtropical, with hot, humid, wet summers and cool but usually dry winters. Most rain falls from May to September. The typhoon season is July/August. The best time to visit is between October and February – temperatures and humidity fall and there are lots of clear, sunny days.

Contacts Hong Kong Tourist Association, 125 Pall Mall, London sW1Y 5EA (0171 930 4775). Hong Kong Embassy, 6 Grafton St, London w1X 3LB (0171 499 9821).

Hungary

Climate Temperate continental climate. Winters are very cold, with snow. Warm summers from June to August. Rain year-round but especially in May/June and November. The west is wetter than the east.

Contacts Hungarian National Tourist Office, PO Box 4336, London SW18 4XE.
Information Service: 0891 171200.
Hungarian Embassy, 35B Eaton Place, London SW1X 8BY
(0171 235 2664/4048).
Visa Information Service: 0891 171204.

Iceland

Climate Changeable and moderate, with cold winters and cool, short summers. Wettest times of year are autumn and winter.

Contacts Iceland Tourist Information, Icelandair, 172 Tottenham Court Rd, London W1P 9LG (0171 388 5599).
Iceland Brochure Unit: 0171 388 7550.
Embassy of Iceland, 1 Eaton Terrace, London SW1W 8EY (0171 730 5131/2).

India

Climate Varies hugely, but on the whole tropical with monsoons in summer. The south-west monsoon brings the rainy season to most of India, starting in the south-west and spreading north and east from mid-May through to early July. The best time to visit is generally between November and April (although early June is the best time for trekking in the northern regions). From February to the start of the south-west monsoon in May, the northern Indian plains are very hot, but northern hill stations are cooler (they usually have a severe winter). The pre-monsoon season is extremely hot – temperatures in central India can reach 45°C. Most of the country has three seasons – hot, wet and cool. Winter temperatures in the far south are pleasantly warm but it can get chilly at night in Delhi and in the north, especially in December and January.

Contacts India Tourist Office, 7 Cork St, London W1X 2LN (0171 437 3677).
Indian High Commission, India House, Aldwych, London WC2B 4NA (0171 836 8484).
Visa Information Service: 0891 880800.

Indonesia

Climate Varies slightly across the islands but is generally hot and humid, with tropical monsoons bringing wet seasons from October to March/April. The dry season (which is cooler) is usually May/June to August/September (the best time to visit). The nearer you get to Australia, the longer the dry season lasts. Travel can be difficult in the rainy months. The hottest months are February/March. Temperatures are fairly constant, ranging from 23°C to 31°C, though hilly areas are cooler. Typhoons are possible, though rare, in Timor.

Contacts Indonesian Tourist Office, 3–4 Hanover Street, London WIR 9HH (0171 493 0030).
Indonesian Embassy, 38 Grosvenor Square, London WIX 9AD (0171 499 7661).

Iran

Climate Harsh, desert climate, with extremes – very hot summers and very cold winters. Temperatures range from −20°C to 50°C. More temperate around the Caspian Sea. Low humidity and little rain (most of it in winter, between December and April). The coast is humid but relieved by sea breezes. Hot, dry, dusty desert winds blow at the start and end of the summer.

Contacts Iranian Embassy, 50 Kensington Court, London W8 5DB (0171 937 5225).

Iraq

Climate Very hot, dry summers and mild winters, with some rain in the south. Dry summers and harsh winters in the north. Low rainfall.

Contacts Iraqi Embassy, 21 Queen's Gate, London SW7 5GJ (0171 584 7141).

Israel

Climate Mostly Mediterranean, with warm, sunny summers (which can get very humid) and mild, wet winters. The hottest months are July and August. Rain falls mostly in winter, especially between December and February. The Negev Desert in the south is very hot and dry.

Contacts Israel Tourist Office, 18 Great Marlborough St, London WIV IAF (0171 434 3651).
Embassy of Israel, 2 Palace Green, London W8 4QB (0171 957 9500).

Italy

Climate Mostly Mediterranean, with warm summers and mild winters, with some rain. Extremes in the north and mountains. Milan has hot summers and very cold winters, with snow and frost; most rain falls in late spring and October/November. Rome has a Mediterranean climate, with hot, sunny, mostly dry summers and mild winters; there's little rain, most of it between October and January.

Contacts Italian State Tourist Office, 1 Princes St, London WIR 8AY (0171 408 1254).
Italian Consulate General Visa Section, 38 Eaton Place, London SWIX 8AN (0171 235 9371).
Visa Information Service: 0171 259 6322.

Ivory Coast

Climate Hot year-round. In the south, there is heavy rain from May to October. The north is drier, with a shorter rainy season from June to September. Humidity in the south is high but temperatures rarely go over 32°C. Dusty desert winds can blow from the Sahara in the northern mountains from early December to February.

Contacts Ivory Coast Embassy, 2 Upper Belgrave Street, London SWIX 8BJ (0171 235 6991).

Jamaica

Climate Tropical, hot and humid around the coast but more temperate inland. The hurricane season is from June to November. Wetter in the mountains. In the south of the island rains fall mostly in May and October. Temperatures are fairly constant, around 30°C.

Contacts Jamaica Tourist Board, 1 Prince Consort Road, London SW7 2BZ (0171 224 0505).
Jamaica High Commission, 2 Prince Consort Road, London SW7 2BZ (0171 823 9911).

Japan

Climate Temperate oceanic, with warm, sunny springs; hot, humid summers with rain. Winters are generally mild though in the north it can be very cold, with heavy snow. Rain falls year-round but especially in June, September and October. Japan is subject to frequent earthquakes, monsoons, typhoons and tidal waves. Except for Hokkaido, the large cities are very hot in summer. The best times to visit are spring and autumn.

Contacts Japan National Tourist Organization, 20 Savile Row, London WIX IAE (0171 734 9638). Japanese Embassy, 101 Piccadilly, London WIV 9FN (0171 465 6500).

Jordan

Climate The eastern valleys are hot and dry, with average temperatures above 36°C (they can go up to 49°C) and little rain. West and east of the valleys the climate is milder and wetter, but summer temperatures are still around 30–35°C; the short winters in this area can be cool and wet. Below sea level it's especially hot in summer and warm in winter. Desert areas have very high temperatures in summer, very cold winters and little rain. The best times to visit the country are spring and autumn.

Contacts Jordanian Tourist Office, 211 Regent St, London WIR 7DD (0171 437 9465).
Jordanian Embassy, 6 Upper Phillimore Gardens, London W8 7HB (0171 937 3685).

Kazakhstan

Climate Dry and continental, with hot summers and very cold winters. Summers are hottest in the desert south; winters coldest in the northern steppes.

Contacts Kazakhstan Embassy and Consulate, 114A Cromwell Road, London SW7 4ES (0171 244 0011).

Kenya

Climate Hot, humid and tropical year-round on the coast, though sea breezes provide relief. Temperatures are consistent, at between 22°C and 30°C. The central plateau is temperate. North of the equator, much of the land is arid semi-desert, with temperatures ranging from 20°C to 40°C. Hot summers from December to March. Mild winters, but chilly at nights. In the central highlands and Rift Valley, the climate is temperate and pleasant. Two rainy seasons: March to May ('the long rains') are hot and wet; October to December ('the short rains') are warm and wet. Generally, January and February are hot and dry; from June to October it is warm and dry. Rain can fall any time at high altitude.

Contacts Kenya Tourist Office, 25 Brooks Mews, London W1Y 1LG (0171 355 3144).
Kenya High Commission, 45 Portland Place, London W1N 4AS (0171 636 2371/5).

Kiribati

Climate Central islands have a maritime equatorial climate. Northern and southern islands are tropical, with constant high temperatures. Low rainfall.

Contacts Kiribati Honorary Consulate, 7 Tufton Street, London SW1P 3QN (0171 222 6952).
Tourism Council of the South Pacific, 375 Upper Richmond Road West, London SW14 7NX (0181 392 1838).

Korea see North and South Korea

Kuwait

Climate Desert climate, with very hot, dry summers (April to September) when temperatures can reach 52°C. Rainfall is negligible. Cooler, mild winters, with some rain and maybe even frost. Can be very humid, especially near the coast. Sandstorms year-round, especially in spring.

Contacts Kuwait Tourist Information, 30 Old Burlington Street, London W1X 1LB (0171 734 0017).
Kuwait Embassy, 45–6 Queen's Gate, London SW7 5HR (0171 589 4533).

Kyrgyzstan (Kirghizia)

Climate Hostile, with hot summers and very cold winters. Low regions are hot deserts. Snow and deserts in the high regions.

Contacts Embassy of the Russian Federation, 5 Kensington Palace Gardens, London W8 4QS (0171 229 8027).

Russian Consulate Information Service: 0891 171271.

Laos

Climate Hot. Monsoon rains from May to October, when temperatures are in the 30°Cs. The winter months (November to March) are cool and dry. Temperatures in the highland areas are lower and can drop to freezing in December and January.

Contacts No embassy or tourist-information office in the UK. Visas can be granted in Bangkok.

Latvia

Climate Very cold winters (November to February), warm summers (May to September), steady rain. The hottest and wettest months are July and August. Snow is likely from December to March.

Contacts Embassy of Latvia, 45 Nottingham Place, London WIM 3FE (0171 312 0040).

Lebanon

Climate Hot, dry summers (May to October), humid on the coast. Sometimes gets hot desert winds in early/late summer. Mild winters, though can get cool and may rain.

Contacts Lebanon Tourist Office, 90 Piccadilly, London WIV 9HB (0171 409 2031).
Lebanese Embassy, 15 Palace Garden

Mews, Kensington, London W8 4RA (0171 229 7265).

Lesotho

Climate Temperate, warm and pleasant. Hot and wet in summer, when temperatures can be in the 30°Cs. Cold winters with frosts and snow on the mountains in winter. Rainy season runs from October to April.

Contacts Lesotho High Commission, 7 Chesham Place, Belgravia, London SWIX 8HN (0171 235 5686).

Liberia

Climate Average daily temperatures are over 25°C year-round and can rise to 33°C. There is lots of rain: the wet season runs from May to October and June and July are especially wet. Coastal regions are much wetter than the interior. The dry season, from November to April, is the best time to visit.

Contacts Embassy of Liberia, 2 Pembridge Place, London W2 4XB (0171 221 1036).

Libya

Climate Hot and dry year-round. In the south, temperatures can get as high as 45°C. On the coast the climate is more temperate – summer temperatures are around 30°C and it may be humid; winters are mild and damp. Spring and autumn are pleasant but dusty desert winds can blow at this time.

Contacts No embassy or tourist-information office in the UK.

Liechtenstein

Climate Temperate, with warm, dry summers and cold winters with snow from December to March.

Contacts Switzerland Tourism, Swiss Centre, Swiss Court, London WIV 8EE (0171 734 1921).
Swiss Embassy, 16 Montagu Place, London WIH 2BQ (0171 723 0701).

Lithuania

Climate Temperate, with cold winters, cool summers and steady rain.

Contacts 84 Gloucester Place, London WIH 3HN (0171 486 6401).

Luxembourg

Climate Temperate and moist, with warm summers and cold winters. Heavy snow in highland areas in winter.

Contacts Luxembourg Tourist Office, 122 Regent Street, London WIR 5FE (0171 434 2800).
Luxembourg Embassy, 27 Wilton Crescent, London SWIX 8SD (0171 235 6961).

Macau

Climate Subtropical, with hot, humid, wet summers and cool but usually dry winters. The typhoon season is July/August. Late September to early December is the best time to visit – temperatures and humidity have fallen and there are lots of clear, sunny days.

Contacts Macau Tourist Office, 6 Sherlock Mews, London WIM 3RH (0171 224 3390).
For visa information, contact the Portuguese Embassy (Macau is a Chinese territory under Portuguese Administration).

Macedonia

Climate Wet springs, dry autumns, hot, dry summers and very cold winters, with snow in the mountains.

Contacts Macedonian Embassy, 19A Cavendish Square, London WIM 9AD (0171 499 5152).

Madagascar

Climate Tropical. Generally, there is a wet season from October to April but it varies according to latitude and altitude. The wettest months are December to February/March, which is also cyclone season in the east and north. Parts of the south receive very little rain; rainfall is heavier in the north. In the mountains, winter temperatures can drop to −15°C and snow may fall.

Contacts Madagascar Consulate, 16 Lanark Mansions, Pennard Road, London W12 8DT (0181 746 0133).

Malawi

Climate Subtropical. Hot and humid in the south; cooler in the highlands. Rainfall varies. The dry season runs from May to October. The rainy season runs from October to April, with December to February the wettest months.

Contacts Malawi High Commission, 33 Grosvenor St, London W1X ODE (0171 491 4172).

Malaysia

Climate Tropical – hot, sunny and very humid year-round, with temperatures rarely dropping below 22°C. On the east coast of the peninsular and in Sabah and Sarawak, October to January/February is the wettest period. The west coast gets more rain from September to November/December. However, rain can fall year-round. Typhoons are very rare in East Malaysia.

Contacts Tourism Malaysia, 57 Trafalgar Square, London WC2N 5DU (0171 930 7932).
Malaysian High Commission, 45 Belgrave Square, London SW1X 8QT (0171 235 8033).

Maldives

Climate Tropical, hot and humid year-round. Temperatures range from 24–33°C but are moderated by sea breezes. Rains year-round but especially during the south-west monsoon (April to November), when there can be violent storms. The sunniest months are October to April/May, which is high season.

Contacts High Commission of the Maldives, 22 Nottingham Place, London W1M 3FB (0171 224 2135).

Mali

Climate Hot year-round, especially from March to May. Average temperatures are around 30°C but can rise to 40°C. There is virtually no rain in the north (over half the country is arid desert) but rain falls in the south in summer (June to September). The region does get droughts and dry desert winds blow from December to February. October and November are the best months to visit.

Contacts No embassy or tourist-information office in the UK.

Malta

Climate Mediterranean, with hot, dry, sunny summers, little rain and mild winters. Cooling sea breezes. Spring and autumn can get siroccos (hot winds).

Contacts Malta High Commission, Malta House, 36–8 Piccadilly, London W1V OPQ (0171 292 4800).

Marshall Islands

Climate Tropical, oceanic climate. Warm and humid year-round, but cooled by trade winds. Temperatures range from around 21°C to 32°C (average daily temperature is 27°C). The best time to visit is between January and March, the driest, coolest and least humid months. The northern islands are quite dry; the southern islands get more rain. The wettest months are August to November and typhoons, though rare, are also possible at that time.

Contacts No tourist office or consulate in the UK; visas are issued on arrival.

Martinique
(Overseas Department of France)

Climate Tropical and generally pleasant. It is hot and humid much of the year, but trade winds relieve the humidity, especially from January to April. The rainiest months are usually May to November and it is wetter on the windward (north-east) sides of the island and in the interior. The hurricane season runs from June to November, with August and September the riskiest months.

Contacts See France.

Mauritania

Climate The weather is generally hot and dry, with dusty winds and sometimes droughts. Rainfall is

sporadic: there is very little in the north but the south has a short rainy season from July to September. Summers (April to October) are very hot; winters are mild. Coastal regions are cooled by sea breezes. December to March are the most pleasant months.

Contacts No embassy or tourist-information office in the UK.

Mauritius

Climate Tropical, with hot, sunny days and warm nights. Sea breezes help temper the humidity. Rain falls year-round but especially from December to April, when there may be cyclones and the weather is very hot and humid. The winter months (July to September) are drier and less humid, with temperatures around 24°C – this is also good surfing time.

Contacts Mauritius High Commission, Passport Section, 32–3 Elvaston Place, London sw7 5nw (0171 581 0294).
Mauritius Tourist Office, address as above (0171 584 3666).

Mexico

Climate The north and north-west are dry; the tropical far south has heavy rainfall. On the west coast the climate is tropical. The wettest months are July to September, when it can also be very humid. It is warm and sunny most of the year. The central plateau is mild temperate.

The coastal plain is hot and humid. The best time to visit is the winter dry season (October to March). The mountains and plains on the Caribbean side get plenty of rain year-round, especially from September to February. The mountains and plains on the Pacific side get little rain from December to April. The central and northern regions have a longer dry season and, even in the wet season, rain is limited. Temperatures are affected by altitude – the high heat and humidity at the peak of the wet season is uncomfortable at lower altitudes.

Contacts Mexican Tourist Office, 60–61 Trafalgar Square, London WC2N 5DS (0171 734 1058). Mexican Consulate, 8 Halkin Street, London SW1X 7DW (0171 235 6393). Mexican Embassy, 42 Hertford Street, London W1Y 7TF (0171 499 8586).

Moldavia (Moldova)

Climate Warm summers; mildish winters; moderate rainfall.

Contacts Represented by Russian Federation: Embassy of the Russian Federation, 5 Kensington Palace Gardens, London W8 4QS (0171 229 8027). Russian Consular Information Service: 0891 171271.

Monaco

Climate Mediterranean – hot, dry summers; mild, sunny winters.

Contacts Monaco Tourist Office, 3–18 Chelsea Garden Market, Chelsea Harbour, London SW10 0XE (0171 352 9962). Consulate of Monaco, 4 Cromwell Place, London SW7 2JE (0171 225 2679).

Mongolia

Climate Continental. Summers (June to August) are mild and can have thunderstorms. Spring and autumn are cool. Winters are long, dry and very cold, with lots of snow.

Contacts Mongolian Embassy, 7 Kensington Court, London W8 5DL (0171 937 0150).

Montserrat (UK Crown Colony)

Climate Tropical and generally pleasant. It is hot and humid much of the year, but trade winds relieve the humidity, especially from January to April. The rainiest months are usually May to November and it is wetter on the windward (north-east) sides of the island and in the interior. The hurricane season runs from June to November, with August and September the riskiest months.

Contacts Montserrat Tourist Board, Suite 433, High Holborn House, 52–4 High Holborn, London WC1V 6RB (0171 242 3131). British Dependent Territories Office, Clive House, Petty France, London SW1H 9HD.

Morocco

Climate Variable. Coastal areas have a temperate, Mediterranean climate, with mild winters and hot, sunny summers. Much of the country is dry and arid. Can get cold temperatures and snow in the mountains. Summers can get very hot. Temperatures are most extreme in the Sahara – can go up to 50°C in summer and down to 3°C in winter. Freezing nights can follow extremely hot days. The lowlands are warm to hot in winter (around 30°C) though temperatures drop at night. In summer they are very hot in the day and still around 23°C at night. Rainfall is light; most of it falls in winter, between November and April.

Contacts Moroccan Tourist Office, 205 Regent St, London W1R 7DE (0171 437 0073).
Moroccan Embassy, 49 Queen's Gate Gardens, London SW7 5NE (0171 581 5001).

Mozambique

Climate Tropical. The dry season runs from April to September. The wet months, October to March, are hot and humid with temperatures rising to 29°C on the coast. Inland areas are cooler.

Contacts Mozambique Embassy, 21 Fitzroy Square, London W1P 5HJ (0171 383 3800).

Myanmar (Burma)

Climate Tropical monsoon climate. The coast and lowland regions are hot and tropical year-round. The coast is also very humid. The monsoon season runs from May to October. In central regions, the wettest months are August to September/October, when floods are possible. Most rain falls in the mountains in the north and east. November to April/May is dry, with temperatures rising from February onwards. The hottest months are March to May, when temperatures can rise above 40°C. In highland regions, temperatures can go below freezing in December and January. November to February are the best months to visit.

Contacts Myanmar Embassy, 19A Charles Street, London W1X 8ER (0171 499 8841/629 6966).

Namibia

Climate Sunny pretty well year-round throughout the country. The most pleasant time to visit is in winter (May to September). It can get extremely hot between December and March, when it is probably best avoided. The country is generally arid, especially in the central Namib, but there are two rainy seasons – the 'little' rains from October to December and the 'big' rains from January to March/April. In these months, roads in the Caprivi Strip can become unpassable owing to floods. The coast gets very foggy.

Contacts Namibia High Commission, 6 Chandos Street, London WIM OLQ (0171 636 6244). Namibia Tourism, address as above (0171 636 2924).

Nauru

Climate Equatorial, with sea breezes. Sometimes gets droughts.

Contacts Nauru Government Office, 3 Chesham Street, London SWIX 8ND (0171 235 6911).

Nepal

Climate Warm monsoon climate from July to October. Dry, sunny and mild the rest of the year. The best time to go trekking is October/November, just after the monsoon, but February to April is also good. The wettest months are June to August. Subtropical on the plain; arctic on the peaks. March is pleasant (rhododendrons in bloom).

Contacts Nepalese Embassy, 12A Kensington Palace Gardens, London W8 4QU (0171 229 6231/1594).

The Netherlands

Climate Mild, maritime climate similar to that of the UK. Winters are mild and rainy; summers are cool. North Sea gales in autumn/winter.

Contacts The Netherlands Board of Tourism, 18 Buckingham Gate, London SWIE 6LB (0171 931 0661). Royal Netherlands Embassy,

38 Hyde Park Gate, London SW7 5DP (0171 584 5040). Visa Information: 0891 171217.

New Caledonia (Overseas Territory of France)

Climate Temperate year-round, with an average annual temperature of 23°C. Warm and humid from November to February; the coolest time of the year is July/August. Humidity is pretty high most of the year, especially between February and April, which are the wettest months. May is the driest month but there is no dry season as such – heavy downpours can happen at any time of year. The west coast is drier than the east.

Contacts See France. Tourism Council of the South Pacific, 375 Upper Richmond Road West, London SW14 7NX (0181 392 1838).

New Zealand

Climate Temperate and damp. The far north is almost subtropical, with mild winters and warm, humid summers. Southern winters are cold. The weather is changeable, rather like the British climate, but there's plenty of sun. The best time to visit is probably in the late spring/summer months of November to March. May to October is the ski season. The best time to swim with the dolphins is October to April. The wettest months are May to August; the west coast is much wetter than the east.

Christchurch has an equable climate, with no real extremes of temperature; warmest months are December to February; moderate rainfall year-round. Auckland's weather is changeable but has no real extremes; it can get humid in summer; moderate rain year-round, especially between May and August. North Island is temperate. South Island has cooler winters and upland snow. Rain throughout the year. Year-round snowfields in the south and snow falls in most areas in winter. The best time to visit is at the height of summer (December to March).

Contacts New Zealand Tourism Board, New Zealand House, 80 Haymarket, London SW1Y 4TQ (0171 930 1662).
New Zealand High Commission, address as above (0171 930 8422).
New Zealand Visa and Immigration Service: 0891 200288.

Nicaragua

Climate Climate varies according to altitude. The Pacific lowlands are hot and tropical. May to November are the rainiest months, and also very humid. The dry season runs from December to April – March and April can be particularly hot. The Caribbean lowlands are hot and wet, with heavy annual rainfall – there is a brief dry season from March to May but even then there can be heavy rain. In the mountains, the weather is much cooler.

Contacts Embassy of Nicaragua, 36 Upper Brook Street, London W1Y 1PE (0171 409 2825/2536).

Niger

Climate Hot year-round. March to June are the hottest months, especially April, when temperatures can go up to 45°C. The coolest months are December to February, when temperatures in the desert can drop to freezing. The south of the country gets some rain in late May but the country as a whole is extremely dry, especially in the Sahara regions of the north.

Contacts No embassy or tourist-information office in the UK.

Nigeria

Climate Tropical, with temperatures high and fairly even year-round. The north is hot and dry, with one wet season from May to September. From March to May, temperatures can rise to 45°C. The south is slightly cooler but humidity is high and rainfall heavier. Rain in these areas falls mainly from April to July and from September to October.

Contacts Nigeria High Commission, 9 Northumberland Avenue, London WC2N 5BX (0171 839 1244).

Niue see South Pacific

Northern Cyprus

Climate Mediterranean – hot, dry, sunny summers (May to September); mild winters, with snow in the mountains. Most rain falls in the winter.

Contacts North Cyprus Tourist Office, 28 Cockspur Street, London SWIY 5BN (0171 930 5069). Embassy of Turkish Republic of Northern Cyprus, address as above (0171 839 4577).

North Korea

Climate Continental – warm summers and cold winters; snow in the north. Temperatures vary from −10°C in winter to 30°C in summer. Most rain falls during the summer months.

Contacts No embassy or tourist-information office in the UK. Visas can be obtained in Macau or China.

Norway

Climate Mild on the coast; more extreme inland. Warm summers and cold, snowy winters. Warmer summers and colder winters inland. Rain throughout the year but heaviest from June to October. Coast modified by the North Atlantic Drift. Lots of rain in the northern mountains.

Contacts Norwegian Tourist Board, Charles House, 5–11 Lower Regent St, London SWIY 4LR (0171 839 6255/2650).
Norwegian Embassy, 25 Belgrave Square, London SWIX 8QD (0171 235 7151).

Oman

Climate Very hot in the north, especially in summer. Monsoon rains fall in the southern uplands from June to September. Hot and mostly dry; the coast is more humid than the interior. October to February/March is the best time to visit.

Contacts Omani Embassy, 167 Queen's Gate, London SW7 5HE (0171 225 0001).

Pakistan

Climate Temperatures are generally warm year-round and can be very high in the south and west; very low in the Hindu Kush. The wettest months are between June and August. December to February see warm, sunny days with cooler nights, then it's very hot until the rainy season starts. Can be very humid from May to September. The west is semi-desert. Monsoon rains are especially heavy in the northern mountains.

Contacts Embassy of Pakistan, 36 Lowndes Square, London SWIX 9JN (0171 235 2044).

Palau

Climate Tropical oceanic climate. Warm and humid year-round, with average daily temperatures around 30°C. The dry season is February to April, which is also the best time to visit. The wettest months are June to August, with lots of thunderstorms in June.

Contacts No tourist office or consulate in the UK. Visas are issued on arrival.

Panama

Climate There are two main seasons: the dry season runs from January to mid-April; the rainy season from May to December (the summer months) – but heavy rain is possible at any time of year. Rainfall is lightest on the Pacific coast. It is generally hot and humid in the lowlands (with temperatures fairly constant at around 32°C) and cooler in highland areas.

Contacts Panamanian Consulate, 40 Hertford Street, London WIY 7TG (0171 409 2255).

Papua New Guinea

Climate Tropical. Pretty hot and humid year-round in the coastal lowlands. Cooler in the highlands, which can have snow. The dry season runs from May to December. Lots of rain, especially between December and March.

Contacts Papua New Guinea High Commission, 14 Waterloo Place, London SWIY 4AR (0171 930 0922/4). Tourism Council of the South Pacific, 375 Upper Richmond Road West, London SWI4 7NX (0181 392 1838).

Paraguay

Climate Subtropical. Temperatures range from 22°C to 35°C. Rain is fairly constant throughout the year. Hot, rainy, humid summers from December to March. Mild winters. Hotter and drier in the northwest, where rainfall is more erratic. The best time to visit is between May and October, when it's relatively dry.

Contacts Paraguayan Embassy, Braemar Lodge, Cornwall Gardens, London SW7 4AQ (0171 937 1253/ 6629).

Peru

Climate Very dry along the coast but hot, humid and wet in the east. The wettest months are December to May, when travel can be difficult on mountain roads. The lower mountain slopes are temperate – but higher up they're covered in snow. Lima has hot summers, warm winters and very little rain. Coastal plains are cooled by the Humboldt current. Wide range of temperatures in the interior plateau.Equatorial situation, but altitude affects the climate. The Andes have a dry season from May to September – warm and sunny days, but it can be very cold at night. Their wet season is October to May, especially from the end of January.

The coastal areas have a dry season from January to March. Their coldest months are June to November, with little rain but high humidity and fog.

Contacts Peruvian Consulate General, 52 Sloane Street, London SWIX 9SP (0171 235 6867).

Philippines

Climate Tropical, but with a maritime tempering influence – warm and humid year-round. Hot, sunny and very humid in the rainy season (May to October), when the islands can also get torrential rains and typhoons, especially in the north. Southern islands are less affected by the monsoon and heavy rain-showers are interspersed with long sunny periods. The best time to visit is the dry season (November to March). March to May is usually dry and very hot.

Contacts Philippine Embassy, 9A Palace Green, London W8 4QE (0171 937 1600).
Department of Tourism, 17 Albemarle Street, London WIX 4LX (0171 499 5443/5652).

Poland

Climate Continental. Cold winters (December to March), especially in the mountains. There may be snow but the Carpathian mountains are sunny. Hot summers (June to August), especially on the coast. Summer/autumn is also when most of the rain

falls. In spring the days are warm but the nights can be cool.

Contacts Polish National Tourist Office, 1st Floor, Remo House, 310–12 Regent Street, London WIR 5AJ (0171 580 8811).
Polish Consulate General, 73 New Cavendish Street, London WIM 8LS (0171 580 0476).

Portugal

Climate Cool and moist in the north; warmer in the south, with mild, dry winters. Lisbon has a sunny, temperate climate, with hot, sunny summers and mild winters. Some rain, mainly in December, January and March.

Contacts Portuguese Tourist Office, 2nd Floor, 22–25A Sackville Street, London WIX 2LY (0171 494 1441).
Portuguese Embassy, 11 Belgrave Square, London SWIX 8PP (0171 235 5331).

Puerto Rico (Self-governing Commonwealth of USA)

Climate Warm, sunny winters. Hot, sunny summers. Rain throughout the year.

Contacts Puerto Rico Tourist Office, c/o Cerrano, 2-2 Izda, 28001 Madrid, Spain: 0800 898920 (toll-free number).
See USA.

Qatar

Climate Desert climate. Very hot summers (May to September), with average temperatures 37°C and sometimes as high as 50°C. Summers are also very humid. Winters are milder but still warm, and cool in the evening. Limited rainfall in winter but rain is generally low. Sandstorms can occur year-round, especially in spring. The best time to visit is November or late February/early March.

Contacts Qatar Embassy, 1 South Audley Street, London w1y 5dq (0171 493 2200).

Reunion
(Overseas Department of France)

Climate The hot, wet summer months (October to March) are prone to cyclones. Winter (April to September) is cool and dry. The east coast is wetter than the west. On the coast, average summer temperatures are 28°C. Mountain areas are cooler, and cold in winter.

Contacts See France.

Romania

Climate Continental, with hot, humid summers (though it can be cold in the mountains). The Black Sea coast has particularly warm summers, though temperatures are modified by breezes. The winters (December to March) are very cold

and snowy, especially in the mountains. Rainy in spring.

Contacts Romanian Tourist Office, 83A Marylebone High Street, London w1m 3de (0171 224 3692). Romanian Embassy, 4 Palace Green, London w8 4qd (0171 937 9666). Romanian Embassy Visa and General Information Service: 0891 880828.

Russian Federation (Russia)

Climate This huge country has big variations from sub-arctic in the north to Mediterranean to desert. Moscow has warm summers and very cold winters with snow and ice; coldest months are November to March; warmest, wettest months are July and August. St Petersburg is changeable with mild, sunny summers and icy cold winters, with snow and frost. The country has rain year-round, especially late summer and autumn. In Siberia, winter is very harsh (temperatures can fall to −25°C in January) but dry and sunny. Summers (July/August) can be warm, with temperatures going up to 30°C. Autumn (September/October) is changeable. Snow falls December/ January. East of Lake Baikal there is year-round permafrost.
The Black Sea coast has milder winters and warm, humid summers (June to September). November to May are the rainiest months.
The Volga region has a continental climate – temperatures can range from −10−−15°C in winter (January) to 20–25°C in summer (July). Low

humidity. May to September are the best months to visit.

Contacts Intourist House, 219 Marsh Wall, London E14 9PD (0171 538 8600).
Embassy of the Russian Federation, 5 Kensington Palace Gardens, London W8 4QS (0171 229 8027/3628). Russian Consular Information Service: 0891 171271.

Rwanda

Climate Tropical and warm year-round, with average temperatures ranging from 30–34°C, though highland regions are cooler. Dry seasons run from May to October and December to March. Rainy seasons run from March to May and October to December.

Contacts No embassy or tourist information office in the UK.

St Kitts and Nevis see Eastern Caribbean

St Lucia

Climate See Eastern Caribbean.

Contacts St Lucia Tourist Board, 421A Finchley Road, London NW3 6HJ (0171 431 3675).
Eastern Caribbean High Commission, 10 Kensington Court, London W8 5DL (0171 937 9522).

St Vincent and The Grenadines see Eastern Caribbean

Samoa

Climate Hot and humid year-round, but tempered from April to October by trade winds. Hottest months are December to April, which is also the cyclone season. The driest months are May to September, which is a good time to visit. Average temperatures are between 21°C and 32°C.

Contacts No embassy or tourist-information office in the UK.

Sao Tome and Principe

Climate Hot and humid, with lots of rain. The dry season is July to August. Consistent temperatures – up to 30°C year-round.

Contacts Sao Tome and Principe Consulate, 42 North Audley Street, London W1A 4PY (0171 499 1995).

Saudi Arabia

Climate Extremely hot in summer (April to October), when temperatures can reach 45°C. Winters are warm. Humidity is generally low but can be high in coastal regions in summer. The coast gets regular rain, but rainfall is generally low. The best time to visit is November to February.

Contacts Royal Embassy of Saudi Arabia, Consular Section, 30 Charles Street, London W1X 8LP (0171 917 3000).

Senegal

Climate Tropical, with temperatures generally ranging from 22–28°C. It is hot and humid in the rainy season. In the far south, this runs from May to October; in the rest of the country it is shorter, from July to September. From November to March the weather is cool and dry – this is a good time to visit. The coast gets cool winds. Dry, dusty winds blow from the Sahara from December.

Contacts Senegalese Embassy, 11 Phillimore Gardens, London w8 7QG (0171 937 0925).

Seychelles

Climate Tropical – hot, sunny and humid. Rains all year round but especially from November to April. January is the wettest month; Mahé is the rainiest island. The driest months are July and August. Temperatures are pretty constant year-round, between around 24°C and 30°C.

Contacts Seychelles Tourist Office, 2nd Floor, Eros House, 111 Baker St, London W1M 1FE (0171 224 1670). Seychelles High Commission, address as above (0171 224 1660).

Sierra Leone

Climate Hot and tropical year-round, with high rainfall. The rainy season runs from May to early November; it's especially wet and humid from July to September. The dry season runs from November to April but dry winds blow dust from the Sahara from December onwards. November, after the rains and before the dusty winds, is a good time to visit. The weather is cooler in December and January.

Contacts Sierra Leone High Commission, 33 Portland Place, London W1N 3AG (0171 636 6483).

Singapore

Climate Equatorial – hot, sunny and humid year-round. Temperatures range from 20°C to 30°C. Rain falls year-round: the wettest months are October/November to January; the driest months are May to July.

Contacts Singapore Tourist Board, 126–30 Regent Street, London W1R 5FE (0171 437 0033). Singapore Consulate, 9 Wilton Crescent, London SW1X 8RW (0171 235 5441).

Slovak Republic (Slovakia)

Climate Continental, with warm to hot summers; steady rain; and cold winters with snow. The Danube lowland has the most attractive climate. The high Tatra mountains have extremes of climate and are the rainiest part of the country.

Contacts Slovak Embassy, 25 Kensington Palace Gardens, London w8 4QY (0171 243 0803). Information service: 0891 600360.

Slovenia

Climate Continental, with warm summers and cold winters (with snow in the mountains). Mediterranean on the coast; more extreme in the mountains inland. The best time to visit is late spring to autumn (April to September).

Contacts Slovenian Tourist Office, 2 Kenfield Place, London NW6 3BT (0171 372 3767).
Slovenian Embassy, 11–15 Wigmore Street, London WIH 9LA (0171 495 7775).

Solomon Islands

Climate Tropical. The summer wet season (November to April) is hot, humid and wet, especially from January. This is also the cyclone season. The best time to go is in the winter months (May to December), when temperatures are in the mid-20s, with light rainfall, though there may sometimes be high winds bringing heavy rain at this time of year. The northern islands are hot and humid year-round.

Contacts Solomon Islands Consulate, 19 Springfield Road, London SW19 7AL (0181 296 0232/ 946 5552).
Solomon Islands Tourist Office, Hunter House, Biggin Hill Airport, Biggin Hill, Kent TN16 3BN (01959 540737).
Tourism Council of the South Pacific, 375 Upper Richmond Road West, London SW14 7NX (0181 392 1838).

Somalia

Climate Hot and humid on the north coast; otherwise very dry. The Indian coast gets moderate rainfall.

Contacts No embassy or tourist-information office in the UK. The Somali Community Information Centre, 490 Harrow Road, London W9 4QA (0181 964 4540) may be able to help.

South Africa

Climate The coast round Cape Town has a temperate Mediterranean climate – wet and cold in winter (May to August); hot, sunny and often windy in summer (October to March). January and February can be very hot; the coolest months are June and July. The flowers of the Cape are best in September. Jo'burg has dry, sunny, mild winters and warm, sunny summers, with most rain falling in the summer; humidity is low. Summers in the Transkei and Natal can be very hot and humid but highland areas are pleasant. On the east coast, the climate becomes more tropical the further north you go.

Contacts South African Tourist Board, 5–6 Alt Grove, Wimbledon, London SW19 4DZ (0181 944 8080). Brochure request service: 0181 944 6646.
South African High Commission, Trafalgar Square, London WC2N 5DP (0171 930 4488/451 7229).
South African Consulate General Information Service: 0891 441100.

South Korea

Climate Winters are dry, sunny and very cold. Summers are hot, wet and humid. The rainy season is June to September, when over half of the annual rain falls and it can be very hot and humid. Most snow falls from November to March. Can get typhoons in summer. The best times to visit are spring and summer. September to early November have warm, sunny days and cool evenings. It can be windy in spring.

Contacts South Korean Tourist Board, 20 St George Street, London WIR 9RE (0171 408 1591/409 2100). Korean Embassy, 4 Palace Gate, London W8 5NF (0171 581 0247).

South Pacific
(Cook Islands, Fiji, Kiribati, New Caledonia, Niue, Papua New Guinea, Solomon Islands, Tahiti, Tonga, Tuvalu, Western Samoa – see individual entries)

Contacts Tourism Council of the South Pacific, 375 Upper Richmond Road West, London SW14 7NX (0181 392 1838).

Spain

Climate Temperate maritime climate in the north; hotter and drier in the south. Extremes on the central plateau. Hot summers, cold winters, very little rain. Can get hot winds and dust.

Contacts Spanish Tourist Office, 57 St James's St, London SWIA ILD (0171 499 0901).
Brochure request and information line: 0891 669920.
Spanish Embassy, Consular Section, 20 Draycott Place, London SW3 2RZ (0171 589 8989).
Spanish Consulate Visa Information Service: 0891 600123.

Sri Lanka

Climate Tropical. Equatorial with hot summers, warm winters and rain year-round. High humidity. Breezes on the coast; cooler in the highlands. The north-east of the island is hotter and drier than the south and west. Very hot in the north (temperatures over 38°C); cooler in the south. The south-west monsoon brings rain from May to August in Colombo and the south-west. North-east monsoon affects the north-east from November to February. The best time to visit is our winter time.

Contacts Sri Lanka Tourist Board, 22 Regent Street, London SWIY 4QD (0171 930 2627).
Sri Lanka High Commission, 13 Hyde Park Gardens, London W2 2LU (0171 262 1841).

Sudan

Climate Much of the country, particularly the north and west, is hot, arid desert. The south is humid, tropical and equatorial, and usually has rain from April to November. The hottest months in the south are February and March, when temperatures can reach 40°C. Dust storms can occur in summer.

Contacts Sudan Embassy, 3 Cleveland Row, St James's, London SW1A 1DD (0171 839 8080).

Suriname

Climate Tropical, hot and humid with lots of rain (especially from April to July and December to January), especially inland.

Contacts No embassy or tourist-information office in the UK.

Swaziland

Climate Hot and dry in the east; cooler and wetter in the high veld. Warm, wet season from October to March; drier and cooler from May to December.

Contacts Swaziland High Commission, 20 Buckingham Gate, London SW1E 6LB (0171 630 6611).

Sweden

Climate Mild in the south. Stockholm has cold winters and warm summers. Plenty of rain year-round (though less in the east) and snow in winter. Long winters in the north and lots of snow.

Contacts Swedish Tourist Board, 11 Montagu Place, London W1H 2AL (0171 724 5868).
Brochure request: 01476 578811.

Embassy of Sweden, 11 Montagu Place, London W1H 2AL (0171 724 2101).

Switzerland

Climate Seasons are the same as in the UK, though slightly warmer most of the year. Mild, warm summers (average July temperatures of 18–19°C) and cold winters. Altitude means cold winters and snow. Rainy in the summer months (May to September), with snow on the mountains. The best months to visit are May to September (unless, of course, you plan to do some skiing), when most mountain passes are open. The alpine flowers are at their best in June and July. July and August can be crowded and expensive.

Contacts Switzerland Tourism, Swiss Centre, Swiss Court, London W1V 8EE (0171 734 1921).
Swiss Embassy, 16 Montagu Place, London W1H 2BQ (0171 723 0701).

Syria

Climate The coast has a Mediterranean climate, with average daily temperatures ranging from 29°C in summer to 10°C in winter. The steppe regions are warmer with less rain. In the mountains, there can be snow in winter. The south-east is arid desert with high temperatures (up to 46°C) and low rainfall.

Contacts Syrian Embassy, 8 Belgrave Square, London SW1X 8PH (0171 245 9012).

*Tahiti see French Polynesia
and South Pacific*

Taiwan

Climate Tropical monsoon climate.
Hot and humid in summer, with
typhoons likely from July to
September. In winter, the north-east
coast gets almost continuous rain and
there is snow on the mountains. The
south-west is warmer and drier.
Monsoon rains fall from June to
August, especially in mountainous
regions.

Contacts Taipei Representative
Office, 50 Grosvenor Gardens,
London SWIW OEB (0171 396 9152).

Tajikistan

Climate Continental to subtropical.
Lower western areas have warm
summers and cold winters. Very cold
winters in the mountains. Low
rainfall.

Contacts Embassy of the Russian
Federation, 5 Kensington Palace
Gardens, London W8 4QS
(0171 229 8027).
Russian Consulate Information
Service: 0891 171271.

Tanzania

Climate Tropical. Especially hot and
humid in the central lowlands, on the
coast and in Zanzibar, though
tempered by sea breezes. The central
plateau is semi-arid. The highlands
near the Kenyan border are
semi-temperate. The rainy season
runs from March to May. There is
another shorter rainy season in
November and December/January.
Inland temperatures average 25°C
year-round.

Contacts Tanzania Tourist Office,
80 Borough High St, London SE1
1LL (0171 407 0566).
Tanzania High Commission, 43
Hertford St, London W1Y 8DB
(0171 499 8951).

Thailand

Climate Hot, humid and tropical,
especially from March to May.
Monsoon rains from May to October;
cooler between November and
February (the best time to visit).
Wettest months are: in Bangkok, May,
September and October; in Chiang
Mai, July to September; on the east
coast, October to January; on the west
coast, May to September.
Temperatures rise to 36°C.

Contacts Tourism Authority of
Thailand, 49 Albemarle Street,
London W1X 3FE (0171 499 7679).
The Royal Thai Embassy, Consular
Section, 1–3 Yorkshire House,
Grosvenor Crescent, London SW1X
7EP (0171 259 5005).
Visa Information Service:
0891 600150.

Togo

Climate Tropical, with average
temperatures around 27°C.
Temperatures are highest from

mid-February to mid-April. Coastal regions are hot and humid; the interior is drier. The rainy season runs from May to October. The south has a dry season from July to September – a good time to visit.

Contacts No embassy or tourist-information office in the UK.

Tonga

Climate Tropical oceanic climate – warm and hot year-round. Heavy rains, especially from February to March. The best time to visit is January or February, when humidity is low and temperatures are in the mid-20s to low 30s. High temperatures year-round, average around 26°C.

Contacts Tonga High Commission, 36 Molyneux Street, London W1A 6AB (0171 724 5828).
Tourism Council of the South Pacific, 375 Upper Richmond Road West, London SW14 7NX (0181 392 1838).

Trinidad and Tobago

Climate Tropical and generally pleasant, with no real extremes of temperature. It is hot and humid much of the year, but trade winds relieve the humidity, especially from January to April. Rains throughout the year, especially between June and November, but the islands are far enough south to miss out on hurricanes.

Contacts Trinidad and Tobago Tourist Office, International House, 47

Chase Side, Enfield, Middlesex EN2 6NB (0500 892313).
Trinidad and Tobago High Commission, 42 Belgrave Square, London SW1X 8NT (0171 245 9351).

Tunisia

Climate Mediterranean – hot, dry summers and mild, warm winters (though winters in the north can be wet and windy). Not much rain; what there is falls mostly from October to March. Arid in the south.

Contacts Tunisia National Tourist Office, 77A Wigmore St, London W1H 9LJ (0171 224 5598).
Tunisian Embassy, 29 Prince's Gate, London SW7 1QG (0171 584 8117).

Turkey

Climate Mediterranean on the coast. More extreme inland – cold, snowy winters and hot, dry summers. The wettest months are December to February. Istanbul has hot, sunny summers and mild, wet winters. Most rain falls between November and January.

Contacts Turkish Tourism Office, 1st floor, Egyptian House, 170–73 Piccadilly, London W1V 9DD (0171 629 7771).
Turkish Consulate General, Rutland Lodge, Rutland Gardens, London SW7 1BW (0171 589 0360).
Visa enquiries: 0891 600130.

Turkmenistan

Climate Arid desert climate. Very hot in summer; below freezing in winter.

Contacts No embassy or tourist-information office in the UK.

Turks and Caicos Islands
(UK Dependent Territory)

Climate Best time to visit is February, when it's not too hot. There is no rainy season. Hurricane season is August to November, when it also gets uncomfortably hot. From December to July temparatures average 23°C.

Contacts Turks and Caicos Information Office, International House, 47 Chase Side, Enfield, Middlesex EN2 6NB (0181 364 5188). British Dependent Territories Office, Clive House, Petty France, London SW1H 9HD.

Tuvalu

Climate Hot year-round, with plenty of rain. Violent storms in the hurricane season.

Contacts Tourism Council of the South Pacific, 375 Upper Richmond Road West, London SW14 7NX (0181 392 1838).

UAE (United Arab Emirates)
(includes Abu Dhabi and Dubai)

Climate Hot, humid summers (May to September), when temperatures can be in the low 40s, but there is little rain. Winters are mild, but night-time temperatures in the desert can be very low. Dusty winds blow in winter and spring. The best time to visit is November to February.

Contacts UAE Embassy, 48 Prince's Gate, London SW7 1PT (0171 581 1281). Consular department: 0171 589 3434.

Uganda

Climate Generally tropical – warm year-round but modified by altitude. Average temperature 26°C but cooler at night. December to February are the hottest months. In the south, the rain falls from April to May and October to November. In the north, the rainy season runs from April to October, when it can be humid; the dry season is from November to March.

Contacts Uganda High Commission and Tourist Office, Uganda House, 58–9 Trafalgar Square, London WC2N 5DX (0171 839 5783/9).

Ukraine

Climate Continental. Temperatures in winter can go below freezing. The west is warmer than the east. On the coast, the climate is more Mediterranean, with warm summers and milder winters. June and July are the wettest months inland.

Contacts Ukrainian Embassy, 78 Kensington Park Road, London W11 2PL (0171 727 6312).
Visa information service: 0891 515919.

Uruguay

Climate Equable, mild, temperate, with warm, sunny summers and mild winters. Temperatures range from 15°C to 28°C (cooler at night). Coastal temperatures can be very hot in summer but cooler in higher inland regions. Moderate rainfall year-round.

Contacts Uruguayan Embassy, 2nd Floor, 140 Brompton Road, London SW3 1HY (0171 589 8835/8735).

USA

Climate Such a huge country has great variations in weather conditions. The south-east has hot, humid summers and mild winters (Florida and the Gulf states, like Hawaii, have a tropical climate). The south-west states have a desert climate, mostly hot and dry. The rest of the country is more temperate. Chicago has very cold winters and hot summers. LA has hot, dry summers and mild winters and can be affected by smog. San Francisco has mild summers with sea fogs and mild winters (November to March), which are also the wettest months; it rains throughout the year but mostly in July and August. Miami has hot, sunny summers and mild, sunny winters, with May to October the wettest months, when there can also be lots of thunderstorms and the odd hurricane. Winter temperatures in the north can drop to −40°C (Alaska), and even in the south they can be very low. Long winters in the north. Sunny summers, often extremely hot. East-coast seasons change gradually but the weather can be more extreme in the north – New York has humid heatwaves in summer and freezing winters (especially January and February) (NY can be hotter than SF though far further north). Cyclones can occur anywhere in the US.

Contacts Discover the Real America information line: 0891 136136.
US Embassy, Visa Branch, 5 Upper Grosvenor Street, London W1A 2JB (0171 499 6846/9000).
Visa information line: 0891 200290.

US Virgin Islands (St Thomas, St Croix, St John)

Climate See British Virgin Islands.

Contacts US Virgin Islands Tourist Office, 2 Cinnamon Row, Plantation Wharf, London SW11 3TW (0171 978 5262).
US Embassy: see USA.

Uzbekistan

Climate Dry and arid. Very hot summers; cold winters.

Contacts Embassy of Uzbekistan, 41 Holland Park, London W11 (0171 229 7679).

Vanuatu

Climate Tropical. The north is hotter and rainier than the south. The dry season, the best time to visit, runs from May to October. Between November and April it is wetter and hotter, and cyclones can occur.

Contacts No embassy or tourist-information office in the UK.

Venezuela

Climate Tropical, hot and humid but cooler in the highlands. Warm year-round, but hottest during the summer (May to August), which is also the wettest time of year.

Contacts No embassy or tourist-information office in the UK.

Vietnam

Climate Big climatic differences from north to south. In Saigon and the south, temperatures are fairly constant at around 25–35°C year-round. In Hanoi and the north, winter (December to February) is grey and cool but dry, and the summer months (May to September) are hot and humid. The wettest months are May to October, when typhoons are possible. The best time to visit is between January and April.

Contacts Vietnam Embassy, 12 Victoria Road, London W8 5RD (0171 937 1912).
Vietnam Tourist Office, address as above (0171 937 3174).

Virgin Islands, British see British Virgin Islands

Virgin Islands, US see US Virgin Islands

Western Samoa

Climate Tropical and hot year-round, with high humidity, but tempered from April to October by trade winds. The hottest months are December to April, which is also cyclone season. The driest months are May to September, which is a good time to visit. Average temperatures are between 21°C and 32°C.

Contacts Tourism Council of the South Pacific, 375 Upper Richmond Road West, London SW14 7NX (0181 392 1838).

Yemen

Climate Hot desert climate but moderated by altitude. The southern coast gets little rain (most of it usually between July and September) but flooding is possible in the rainy season. This region is hot and humid year-round, with dusty winds. The central highlands are mild and dry; any rain falls in March/April and August. Winter nights can be frosty.

In the western mountains rainfall is higher and falls steadily throughout the year, especially in July and August. The north and east are dry and the country arid desert.

Contacts Yemen Embassy, 57 Cromwell Road, London SW7 2ED (0171 584 6607).

Yugoslavia (Serbia and Montenegro)

Climate Mediterranean on the coast; continental inland (hot summers; cold winters, with snow), but varies with altitude and from north to south. Rain is even throughout the year.

Contacts Yugoslav Embassy, 7 Lexham Gardens, London W8 5JJ (0171 370 6105).

Zaire

Climate Tropical and humid. North of the equator rain falls year-round. The east of the country has a Mediterranean climate, with two rainy seasons (March to May and mid-September to mid-December). In the rest of the country, the rainy season is from February to May, with a dry season from June to September. Travel in the rainy season can be very difficult.

Contacts Zaire Embassy, 26 Chesham Place, London SW1X 8HG (0171 235 6137).

Zambia

Climate Tropical. Three seasons – cool and dry (May to August), hot and dry (September to October), wet (November to May). Droughts in the south-west.

Contacts Zambia National Tourist Board, 2 Palace Gate, London W8 5NG (0171 589 6343). Zambia High Commission: as above.

Zimbabwe

Climate Tropical but temperatures are moderated by altitude. Generally pleasant and warm. The winter months are May to October, when the weather is warm, dry and sunny during the day, with cool, clear nights (sometimes very cold). This is the best time to view wildlife as the animals cluster round the limited water holes. The wet season is November to March/April, which is also very humid.

Contacts Zimbabwe High Commission and Tourist Office, Zimbabwe House, 429 Strand, London WC2R 0QE (0171 836 7755).

Chapter 18 / **Any More Questions?**

Making up your mind to go is just the beginning. Now there are a dozen other things to think about, or questions people will be asking you when you tell them your plans. Here are some problems you might have to consider before buying your ticket.

What should I do with my flat if I go away for a year?
If you're planning to rent out your property, start thinking about this at least six months ahead. A company let is the safest (and probably most lucrative) option. Contact estate agents in your area and have two or three value your property for a letting.

Estate agents will find you a tenant, take up references, draw up a tenancy agreement and collect the first month's rent (for a fee, of course). For a larger fee, they'll collect the rent every month and take care of minor repairs, should any be required.

You can, of course, find tenants yourself. Ask your friends if any of them need somewhere to stay, or if they know anyone who does. You could also put a notice on the e-mail or a bulletin board at work. You'll need to vet prospective tenants carefully and ask them for personal and employment references, bank statements, and a month's deposit plus a month's rent in advance.

Your solicitor should draw up a shorthold tenancy agreement which should be signed by you and the tenants. Make any obligations clear – are the tenants responsible for maintaining the garden, for example? You should also draw up an inventory of contents, which both parties should sign. Anything valuable or sentimental should be locked away or given to friends to look after.

Always inform your building society, bank manager and insurers if you're letting out a property. Let your local council know, too. You won't be responsible for council tax if you're abroad, but the tenants will be.

Transfer all bills, including the telephone bill, into the tenants' names.

If you have family or close friends, you could ask them to keep in touch with the tenants to make sure there are no problems. It also lets the tenants know there's someone keeping an eye on the place.

I'm going to South America for a year as part of my degree course. My boyfriend can't come with me, so how can we keep our relationship alive?

It can be difficult for someone whose partner is going off to travel, for whatever reason, if they're being left behind. Try to make him feel part of your plans. Get the atlas out and show him exactly where you're going to. Suggest that he flies out to join you for two or three weeks halfway through your trip so you both have something to look forward to. Alternatively, he could fly out towards the end of your stay and you could travel around the area together.

Reassure him by writing on a regular basis. It doesn't have to be a twelve-page letter every week – funny postcards and quirky cuttings from the local newspapers are a good way of keeping in touch. Ring him on special occasions, such as his birthday or your anniversary.

My friend and I have booked to go on a nine-month working holiday to Australia. I'm looking forward to it, but I'm very close to my family and worried that I'll miss them.

Of course you'll miss your family! When you're watching the sun set behind Ayers Rock, you'll wish they could share it with you. As you pose in front of the Sydney Opera House, you'll think how much they'd love to be there. Homesickness hits most travellers at some point and nine months away from your family seems like a long time. But once you're on the road making new discoveries, meeting new people and enjoying new experiences every day, you won't believe how quickly the time will pass. Make sure you have a contact address where friends and family can write to you with all their news, plus what's happening on Brookside/the Street/whatever. If you feel the urge to talk to your family, treat yourself to a phone call home occasionally. Don't worry about it too much. You'll be so busy having a great time, you'll be home again before you know it.

Someone told me I should make a will before I go travelling. I'm only 27. Isn't this a bit morbid?

No one likes to think about it, but it is a good idea. You may not think you're worth much alive, but if you're insured, you could be worth quite a lot if you die. Also, you can stipulate in a will whether you wish to be buried or cremated, donate favourite items to favourite friends and generally relieve the burden on your family at a very emotional time. It's not difficult – W. H. Smith stock simply drawn-up wills you fill in yourself. All you have to do then is get a solicitor to sign it. You don't have to think about the subject again unless you marry/divorce/have a child.

Where will I stay while I'm away?

Don't worry about accommodation *en route*. You'll find a huge range of hotels, hostels, guest-houses, bungalows and dormitories on the travellers' trail – especially if you're following a well-worn route such as overland from Bangkok to Bali, or hostelling round Australia or New Zealand. The only time it might be wise to pre-book a room is for your first couple of nights away, especially if you'll be arriving late at night. Most travel agents will pre-book a room for you at a discounted rate when you book your ticket. It's useful, too, if you're arriving in a country when there's a public holiday or festival and accommodation is hard to find.

Once on the road, never accept a room without seeing it first – it's perfectly acceptable to check it out before you commit yourself. Some places may have smart receptions but dreadful rooms. Check that the light switches/fan/air-conditioning work and that the shower and toilet (if you have one) have water. If you don't like the first room you're shown, ask if they have anything better. Otherwise, look for somewhere else. Remember that the first price you're quoted is often negotiable.

This may sound trivial, but I have lots of plants I've lavished tender, loving care on for years. What can I do with them – and with my cat?

Friends or family should be happy to look after your plants for you – after all, it doesn't take too much effort. Cats are another matter. You'll have to find someone who's a cat-lover and who wants to take on the responsibility of your pet. You should also leave them money for cat food and possible vet bills. If someone volunteers, maybe you could take your cat there for a weekend to see how they get on. And don't forget to bring back some thank-you presents!

I've just returned from a round-the-world trip that I enjoyed hugely. So why do I feel so fed-up?

Coming home can be a huge anti-climax in the beginning. Friends and family are delighted to see you at first, but don't want to spend the next six weeks discussing every aspect of your trip. If you have any friends who have done something similar, get in touch with them. They'll understand your enthusiasm and will enjoy comparing notes and anecdotes. You have experienced so much while you've been away that it can be a surprise to find that nothing's changed at home – or that everything's changed. You've changed too – you'll probably find you're more independent, more confident, more adventurous. Family, friends or your partner may even have trouble coming to terms with the new you.

Give yourself time to get back into some kind of routine and allow time for people to get used to having you around again. If you find it hard being in one place all the time, after being used to being on the move constantly, perhaps you could go away for a few weekends. If all else fails, start planning your next trip!

I'm going to South-East Asia on my own. None of my friends share my desire to travel or seem interested in my plans. I'm worried we'll grow apart.

Perhaps you'll grow apart from some, but the rest will be proud that you're doing something you really want to do – and on your own, too! There's no law that says friends must do everything together. Some of our best friends are happily married mums who would no more want to travel round China than have all their teeth extracted. But they love hearing our stories and sharing our adventures second-hand. Your friends will, too, and just think of all the new friends you're about to make!

I have a job I enjoy, but can't resist the lure of taking a year off. Will future employers think I'm irresponsible?

Some people worry that employers will see the fact that you have taken time off as negative, but this isn't necessarily the case. How can it be negative to have displayed qualities such as independence, self-reliance, confidence, initiative, organizational ability and success? You will be seen as a 'doer' and as having achieved something positive and worthwhile. Look around your friends who are working. Have their jobs changed dramatically in the last year? Have they been promoted to a brilliant new position? Increased their salary by £5,000? Probably not. Things don't usually change that much in a year. Remember, it's not the things you do that you regret, it's the things you don't do. So what are you waiting for?

Travellers' Tales

You should think carefully about what time of year you come back. If you come back for summer, you can go to festivals, meet other travellers there, and have a good time. You're used to living on a budget and it's a good time to travel round the UK. If you come back in winter, everyone looks tired and ill – and it can be a big shock having to be inside so much when you've got used to being outdoors a lot.

I did find it hard to settle down when I came back. I thought of everything in terms of my trip – it was 'this time a month ago', 'this time a year ago', etc. When you're travelling you get used to travellers' camaraderie – then you're back here on the tube or bus and no one's speaking to each other. And the cost of going out to drink or eat is a shock – it's so much more affordable abroad.

Luckily I managed to get a job that involved a lot of travelling and going to new places, so that helped. I couldn't have come back and gone straight back to a routine. And I liked having other travellers coming to stay because friends back home can't relate to how you're feeling unless they've done a similar trip. We were out of sync for a while.

Lots of people said 'so you've got it out of your system now then' – but it's not something to get out of your system. I came back thinking I wanted to plan my life so I could continue to do more of this, have more of this kind of experience – and I have. I've had no problem getting a job – a lot of employers saw it as a positive attribute. The time we had away made me think about life. I came back with a list of things I wanted to do – and I have done some of them. My friend and I both wished we had more practical skills – lots of people travelling could play the guitar, cut hair, etc. and we liked the idea of swapping skills, so when I came back I did an aromatherapy course. I also decided while I was away that I wanted to do voluntary work for Amnesty International and I have done. It's true to say that the trip completely changed my life – the ramifications have gone on and on.

Emily Lindsay, 38

Chapter 19 / **The Final Countdown**

Six Months to Go

- Start reading up on your destinations. Find out what the climate's like in each country and work out your route accordingly, if possible.
- Visit several travel agents with your rough itinerary and dates. Ask them for estimates and compare prices.

Three Months to Go

- Book your ticket and pay a deposit. Take out travel insurance at the same time so you're covered if you have to cancel.
- If you need to rent your flat, you should be thinking about it now (see chapter 18 for details). Visit a couple of estate agents and ask for a valuation for rental purposes. Ask your friends if anyone needs somewhere to stay, and put up notices at work.
- Make an appointment with your doctor to discuss vaccinations, malaria medication and contraceptive precautions.
- Start looking for someone to look after any pets or plants while you're away.
- Check that your passport has enough time to run and plenty of blank pages for all your visas and stamps. If it has expired, apply now for a new one.
- Check your financial situation. Have you arranged for bills to be paid by standing order? If not, set them up now.
- If you're going to be trekking or hiking, buy new boots now so that they're well broken in by the time you leave. You can't go anywhere with blisters.

Two Months to Go

• Check if you need any visas and, if so, apply now.

One Month to Go

• Go to the dentist/optician for a check-up.
• Check the date on your credit card. If it's due to expire during your trip, order a new one now.
• Check that things like camera/torch/Walkman are working properly. Do they need repairing/cleaning?
• Set aside a Saturday for shopping. Make a list (see chapter 14) and tick off everything as you go. Doing it now gives you time to buy anything you might forget.
• Organize any discount cards (see chapter 6).
• Start recording tapes of your favourite music to take with you.

Two Weeks to Go

• Order travellers' cheques and foreign currency.
• If parents/friends are paying bills for you while you're away, give them blank cheques and make sure there's enough money in the bank to cover them.
• If you've bought a new rucksack, make sure it's properly fitted to your frame.

One Week to Go

• Deliver your pets and plants to whoever's looking after them. Leave enough money to cover food, cat litter, any injections, etc.

- Get your hair cut – who knows when you'll get the chance again!
- Get some passport photographs taken for visas *en route*.
- If necessary, arrange for the Post Office to redirect your mail.
- Prepare an itinerary with any forwarding addresses and copy it to your friends and family.
- Photocopy your ticket/insurance details/passport and visas/credit cards, etc.
- Arrange a *bon voyage* drink with your mates (don't fix it up for the night before you leave – long-haul flights with a hangover are *no* fun!).
- Start taking your malaria tablets.
- Start making a pile of everything you're planning to take with you.

Three Days to Go

- Reconfirm your flight and check that any vegetarian meals etc. have been requested.
- Go through the checklists in chapter 14 to make absolutely sure you've got everything.

The Day Before

- Pre-book a cab to take you to the airport or ask a friend to give you a lift. Allow plenty of time – try to arrive two hours before your flight leaves.
- If your flight's an early one and you're worried you'll sleep in, get the operator to give you an alarm call, as well as setting your own alarm.
- Go to bed early and get a good night's sleep.

The Big Day

Don't leave home without: passport with visas, tickets, money, insurance documents.

Last, but by no means least, have the time of your life! And while you're out there, if you have any great travel tips, wonderful anecdotes or general words of wisdom, we'd love to hear from you. Write to Suzanne King and Elaine Robertson at Brand Extensions, National Magazine Co., 72 Broadwick Street, London WIV 2BP.

READ MORE IN PENGUIN

In every corner of the world, on every subject under the sun, Penguin represents quality and variety – the very best in publishing today.

For complete information about books available from Penguin – including Puffins, Penguin Classics and Arkana – and how to order them, write to us at the appropriate address below. Please note that for copyright reasons the selection of books varies from country to country.

In the United Kingdom: Please write to *Dept. EP, Penguin Books Ltd, Bath Road, Harmondsworth, West Drayton, Middlesex UB7 ODA*

In the United States: Please write to *Consumer Sales, Penguin USA, P.O. Box 999, Dept. 17109, Bergenfield, New Jersey 07621-0120.* VISA and MasterCard holders call 1-800-253-6476 to order Penguin titles

In Canada: Please write to *Penguin Books Canada Ltd, 10 Alcorn Avenue, Suite 300, Toronto, Ontario M4V 3B2*

In Australia: Please write to *Penguin Books Australia Ltd, P.O. Box 257, Ringwood, Victoria 3134*

In New Zealand: Please write to *Penguin Books (NZ) Ltd, Private Bag 102902, North Shore Mail Centre, Auckland 10*

In India: Please write to *Penguin Books India Pvt Ltd, 706 Eros Apartments, 56 Nehru Place, New Delhi 110 019*

In the Netherlands: Please write to *Penguin Books Netherlands bv, Postbus 3507, NL-1001 AH Amsterdam*

In Germany: Please write to *Penguin Books Deutschland GmbH, Metzlerstrasse 26, 60594 Frankfurt am Main*

In Spain: Please write to *Penguin Books S. A., Bravo Murillo 19, 1° B, 28015 Madrid*

In Italy: Please write to *Penguin Italia s.r.l., Via Felice Casati 20, 1–20124 Milano*

In France: Please write to *Penguin France S. A., 17 rue Lejeune, F–31000 Toulouse*

In Japan: Please write to *Penguin Books Japan, Ishikiribashi Building, 2–5–4, Suido, Bunkyo-ku, Tokyo 112*

In South Africa: Please write to *Longman Penguin Southern Africa (Pty) Ltd, Private Bag X08, Bertsham 2013*

READ MORE IN PENGUIN

A CHOICE OF NON-FICTION

Mornings in the Dark   Edited by David Parkinson
The Graham Greene Film Reader

Prompted by 'a sense of fun' and 'that dangerous third Martini' at a party in June 1935, Graham Greene volunteered himself as the *Spectator* film critic. 'His film reviews are among the most trenchant, witty and memorable one is ever likely to read' – *Sunday Times*

Real Lives, Half Lives   Jeremy Hall

The world has been 'radioactive' for a hundred years – providing countless benefits to medicine and science – but there is a downside to the human mastery of nuclear physics. *Real Lives, Half Lives* uncovers the bizarre and secret stories of people who have been exposed, in one way or another, to radioactivity across the world.

Hidden Lives   Margaret Forster

'A memoir of Forster's grandmother and mother which reflects on the changes in women's lives – about sex, family, work – across three generations. It is a moving, evocative account, passionate in its belief in progress, punchy as a detective novel in its story of Forster's search for her grandmother's illegitimate daughter. It also shows how biography can challenge our basic assumptions about which lives have been significant and why' – *Financial Times*

Eating Children   Jill Tweedie

'Jill Tweedie re-creates in fascinating detail the scenes and conditions that shaped her, scarred her, broke her up or put her back together ... a remarkable story' – *Vogue*. 'A beautiful and courageous book' – Maya Angelou

The Lost Heart of Asia   Colin Thubron

'Thubron's journey takes him through a spectacular, talismanic geography of desert and mountain ... a whole glittering, terrible and romantic history lies abandoned along with thoughts of more prosperous times' – *The Times*

READ MORE IN PENGUIN

A CHOICE OF NON-FICTION

African Nights Kuki Gallmann

Through a tapestry of interwoven true episodes, Kuki Gallmann here evokes the magic that touches all African life. The adventure of a moonlit picnic on a vanishing island; her son's entrancement with chameleons and the mystical visit of a king cobra to his grave; the mysterious compassion of an elephant herd – each event conveys her delight and wonder at the whole fabric of creation.

Far Flung Floyd Keith Floyd

Keith Floyd's culinary odyssey takes him to the far-flung East and the exotic flavours of Malaysia, Hong Kong, Vietnam and Thailand. The irrepressible Floyd as usual spices his recipes with witty stories, wry observation and a generous pinch of gastronomic wisdom.

The Reading Solution Paul Kropp with Wendy Cooling

The Reading Solution makes excellent suggestions for books – both fiction and non-fiction – for readers of all ages that will stimulate a love of reading. Listing hugely enjoyable books from history and humour to thrillers and poetry selections, *The Reading Solution* provides all the help you need to ensure that your child becomes – and stays – a willing, enthusiastic reader.

Lucie Duff Gordon Katherine Frank
A Passage to Egypt

'Lucie Duff Gordon's life is a rich field for a biographer, and Katherine Frank does her justice ... what stays in the mind is a portrait of an exceptional woman, funny, wry, occasionally flamboyant, always generous-spirited, and firmly rooted in the social history of her day' – *The Times Literary Supplement*

The Missing of the Somme Geoff Dyer

'A gentle, patient, loving book. It is about mourning and memory, about how the Great War has been represented – and our sense of it shaped and defined – by different artistic media ... its textures are the very rhythms of memory and consciousness' – *Guardian*

READ MORE IN PENGUIN

A CHOICE OF NON-FICTION

The Pillars of Hercules Paul Theroux

At the gateway to the Mediterranean lie the two Pillars of Hercules. Beginning his journey in Gibraltar, Paul Theroux travels the long way round – through the ravaged developments of the Costa del Sol, into Corsica and Sicily and beyond – to Morocco's southern pillar. 'A terrific book, full of fun as well as anxiety, of vivid characters and curious experiences' – *The Times*

Where the Girls Are Susan J. Douglas

In this brilliantly researched and hugely entertaining examination of women and popular culture, Susan J. Douglas demonstrates the ways in which music, TV, books, advertising, news and film have affected women of her generation. Essential reading for cultural critics, feminists and everyone else who has ever ironed their hair or worn a miniskirt.

Journals: 1954–1958 Allen Ginsberg

These pages open with Ginsberg at the age of twenty-eight, penniless, travelling alone and unknown in California. Yet, by July 1958 he was returning from Paris to New York as the poet who, with Jack Kerouac, led and inspired the Beats . . .

The New Spaniards John Hooper

Spain has become a land of extraordinary paradoxes in which traditional attitudes and contemporary preoccupations exist side by side. The country attracts millions of visitors – yet few see beyond the hotels and resorts of its coastline. John Hooper's fascinating study brings to life the many faces of Spain in the 1990s.

A Tuscan Childhood Kinta Beevor

Kinta Beevor was five when she fell in love with her parents' castle facing the Carrara mountains. 'The descriptions of the harvesting and preparation of food and wine by the locals could not be bettered . . . alive with vivid characters' – *Observer*

READ MORE IN PENGUIN

A CHOICE OF NON-FICTION

Fisher's Face   Jan Morris

Admiral of the Fleet Lord 'Jacky' Fisher (1841–1920) was one of the greatest naval reformers in history. 'An intimate recreation of the man in all his extraordinary complexity, his mercurial humours, his ferocious energy and bloodthirstiness, his childlike innocence, his Machiavellian charm' – *Daily Mail*

Mrs Jordan's Profession   Claire Tomalin

The story of Dora Jordan and her relationship with the Duke of Clarence, later King William IV. 'Meticulous biography at its creative best' – *Observer*. 'A fascinating and affecting story, one in which the mutually attractive, mutually suspicious, equally glittering worlds of court and theatre meet, and one which vividly illustrates the social codes of pre-Victorian Britain' – *Sunday Times*

John Major: From Brixton to Downing Street   Penny Junor

Within a year of a record-breaking general election victory, John Major became the most unpopular Prime Minister ever. With his party deeply divided and his government lurching from crisis to crisis, few thought he could survive. This absorbing biography uses interviews with family, friends, foes, Cabinet colleagues and the Prime Minister himself to uncover the real John Major.

The Bondage of Fear   Fergal Keane

'An important source for anyone trying to understand how South Africa achieved its transfer of power' – *Independent*. 'A first-class journalistic account ... likely to be the most memorable account of this terrible, uplifting time' – *Literary Review*

The Oxbridge Conspiracy   Walter Ellis

'A brave book that needed to be written ... Oxbridge imparts to our élite values which, in their anti-commerce, anti-technology, anti-market snobbery, make them unfit to run a modern economy. It is the Oxbridge élite which has presided over the decline of this nation' – *Financial Times*

READ MORE IN PENGUIN

A CHOICE OF NON-FICTION

Thesiger Michael Asher

'Compiled from lengthy interviews with the man himself, meticulous pilgrimages over the same ground, and conversations with his surviving travelling companions, the book both celebrates Thesiger and incorporates what you might call the case against' – *Guardian*

Nelson: A Personal History Christopher Hibbert

'Impeccably researched and written with Christopher Hibbert's habitual elegance of style, this is a fine biography of a figure genuinely larger than life' – *Sunday Telegraph*

The History of the Ginger Man J. P. Donleavy

Combining literary history with autobiography, this is the dramatic story of J. P. Donleavy's struggle to create and publish his contemporary classic *The Ginger Man*. 'An endearingly revealing book ... vintage Donleavy' – *Observer*

Ireland and the Irish John Ardagh

'He has conducted dozens of interviews in all the provinces of the island, with schoolmasters, poets, nuns, bishops, businessmen, farmers large and small, and anyone else, it seems, in any walk of life, who might have anything to say' – *The Times*. 'This scholarly, balanced and compassionate book ought to be read by every British politician – every British citizen, for that matter' – Jan Morris

South of Haunted Dreams Eddy L. Harris

In the southern United States, there is an imaginary line – the Mason-Dixon line – that once marked the boundary of the almost unimaginable institution of slavery. Lost behind it is the history of almost every black American. 'Harris went out looking for the face and mind of white racism. What he found wasn't what he expected – at least, not exactly. Harris finds his own very real, and contradictory, history on the highways of the American South' – *Washington Post Book World*

READ MORE IN PENGUIN

A SELECTION OF TRAVEL BOOKS

Hindoo Holiday	J. R. Ackerley
The Innocent Anthropologist	Nigel Barley
South from Granada	Gerald Brenan
The Road to Oxiana	Robert Byron
An Indian Summer	James Cameron
Granite Island	Dorothy Carrington
The Hill of Devi	E. M. Forster
Journey to Kars	Philip Glazebrook
Journey Without Maps	Graham Greene
South of Haunted Dreams	Eddy L. Harris
Mornings in Mexico	D. H. Lawrence
Between the Woods and the Water	Patrick Leigh Fermor
Mani	Patrick Leigh Fermor
A Time of Gifts	Patrick Leigh Fermor
The Stones of Florence *and* Venice Observed	Mary McCarthy
Calcutta	Geoffrey Moorhouse
Among the Cities	Jan Morris
Spain	Jan Morris
Sydney	Jan Morris
Travels in Nepal	Charlie Pye-Smith
The Kindgom by the Sea	Paul Theroux
The Pillars of Hercules	Paul Theroux
The Marsh Arabs	Wilfred Thesiger
Behind the Wall	Colin Thubron
Journey into Cyprus	Colin Thubron
The Lost Heart of Asia	Colin Thubron
Ninety-Two Days	Evelyn Waugh
Third-Class Ticket	Heather Wood
The Smile of Murugan	Michael Wood
From Sea to Shining Sea	Gavin Young